ADVANCE PRAISE

When We Disappeared is phenomenal, and kept me on the edge of my seat with every turn of the page. I felt like I was standing right beside Elsa through her courageous journey. The strength and resilience demonstrated by the brave women and men is inspiring.

　—Katherine Agard, LMSW, author of *The Adventures of Albert the Not-so-Ordinary Elephant Series*

In this final book in the Resilient Women of WWII trilogy, Elaine Stock introduces her readers to two very different women who become friends while hiding in plain sight in war torn Germany. *When We Disappeared* is a book about friendship, family and love and two brave and resilient women who take dangerous chances to help their families.

　—Susan Roberts, girl-who-reads.com

From the first page, the female characters in *When We Disappeared* have made me wonder how they will conquer their next endeavor. It was exciting to see how Elsa and Adela's friendship strengthened during this horrible time in our history. It was a privilege to read this story.

—Marcia Rossetti, Library Clerk, Upper Hudson Library Systems

---

Chilling. Terrifying. Hopeful. Elaine Stock takes readers on a journey that reveals how far parents will go to protect their family. *When We Disappeared* is a story of survival and risk for the Jews and Roma hiding in plain sight and for those providing shelter. It's a death sentence for both if discovered. Danger lurks and the threat of betrayal is real at every point of the final book of the Resilient Women of WWII Trilogy.

—Eileen Harrison Sanchez, Author of *Freedom Lessons - A Novel*

WHEN WE DISAPPEARED

A WWII STORY OF WOMEN OF DIFFERENT
FAITHS WHO RISK THEIR LIVES TO SAVE FAMILY
AND FRIENDS

ELAINE STOCK

ISBN 9789493276598 (ebook)

ISBN 9789493276574 (paperback)

ISBN 9789493276581 (hardcover)

Publisher: Amsterdam Publishers, The Netherlands

info@amsterdampublishers.com

Author Website: https://elainestock.com

When We Disappeared e is Book 3 of the Trilogy **Resilient Women of WWII**

CONTENTS

AUTHOR'S NOTE

Colorful, gypsy, smile, kids, 1940 Photographer unknown,
Wikimedia Commons

When We Disappeared, Book 3 of the trilogy Resilient Women of
WWII, was both a challenge and a pleasure to write. As I've discussed
with my publisher, the brilliant and insightful Liesbeth Heenk of
Amsterdam Publishers, to set a story in Nazi Germany not only in
1943 but to have the central characters escape from a country that was
hermetically sealed with its closed and heavily guarded borders,

proved a challenge. Yet, it was essential for both Edith and Vonni, who were brought to Germany from other countries, to leave Germany for several reasons. Carefully, I researched how and when this could be done, both before or after massive bombings to certain areas of the country. I believe I have the timing right for such a journey during the month of January 1943. From the starting point when Edith left Nijmegen (bombed 22 February 1944) then to Monschau, Germany through Koblenz, Nuremberg, Mühldorf, Salzburg (Austria), the Salzkammergut Region, Hallstatt, and finally Vienna, before fleeing into the Tatra Mountains, the characters, fueled with the desire of finding loved ones and standing on the right side of fairness to all, did escape fatal disasters. Although, along this road trip, they most definitely encountered tribulations that put them to the test. Any inaccuracies are fully my own and are unintentional. As for the pleasure part of the writing equation, after receiving notes and reviews from devoted fans of the first two books of this trilogy, it was fun to write the conclusion of this series, with them in mind.

For further reading about this time, you may appreciate some of the books I've used in my research:

- *Flowers in the Gutter* by K. R. Gaddy
- *Holocaust Memories: Annihilation and Survival in Slovakia* by Paul Davidovits
- *Signs of Survival: A Memoir of the Holocaust* by Renee Hartman with Joshua M. Greene
- *The Nazi Persecution of the Gypsies* by Guenter Lewy
- *We Are the Romani People* by Ian Hancock

When We Disappeared is a story about the Holocaust, friendship, and the role of mothers and daughters. With that in mind, I would like to dedicate this novel in the memory of my mother, Sandra Berger Pakula. There's not a day that goes by when I don't think of you.

I also want to dedicate this conclusion of the trilogy Resilient Women of WWII to my faithful readers who have enjoyed We Shall Not Shatter and Our Daughters' Last Hope. I hope When We Disappeared brings a smile to your face.

PROLOGUE

We are all wanderers on this earth.
Our hearts are full of wonder,
and our souls are deep with dreams.
—Roma Proverb

Unusual bright December morning sunshine swept into the bedroom that Edith shared with her younger sister, Krista. Typical of the winter month, it brought no warmth. But that was the only speck of normalcy that frosty day. Soon the calendar would begin a new year —1943—and it was already failing to offer promises of goodness.

They stood face-to-face with each other, neither one wanting to look away. In a sprinkling of awful minutes, this room was about to become her bedroom alone to claim—and not for long, either. This wasn't how life was supposed to happen for either of them. In the past, they might have had their share of bickering, complaining about the lack of privacy, and teasing the other about how potential suitors would one day run away from them because they were inseparable. If pressed, they'd both admit that was part of sisterly love. But, this? Edith never dreamed of a forced separation from Krista.

Krista's eyes were dry; no worry lines crinkled her forehead. How could this be? Krista was the one leaving her, leaving Mama... leaving home. Edith swiped her teary eyes and looked once more at her sister to see if she was mistaken, but her eyesight hadn't failed her. "You're about to leave us..." She couldn't bear her sister's absence, and the words wedged halfway in her throat in a stubborn protest.

"Be honest, Edith." Krista grasped Edith's hand. "Finish your sentence."

How could she? To do so, she'd have to admit that her sister, her one constant, faithful companion, was seconds away from walking into a different life. And then in a few weeks, it would be her turn to disappear. Their mother would tell her in the guise of cheerful words that despite the necessity of going into hiding, all would be fine. One day, and soon, the war and their troubles would end. Life would return to normal. They'd be reunited and happy. But the odds were stacked against them. Tales of happily ever after were nonsense.

"Edith? You look awful. You're holding your belly like you're going to be sick." Krista took her hand. "Let me help you to the bed. Sit for a minute."

"No, there's no time."

"We both know there is no other choice." Krista glanced over her shoulder at the bedroom door that was cracked open. "Let's lower our voices so we don't upset Mama."

Edith nodded.

"Good," Krista continued after a pause. "You must stop crying, must tend to Mama. Most of all, you must be brave."

Edith cringed. More tears and dry hiccups followed until she saw her sister's grin. "What?"

"You always have the silliest hiccups. And I'm going to miss them!"

"Are you trying to get me to stop crying or to cry more?" Edith pulled Krista into a hug, a tender moment she didn't want to end. "How am I going to live without you?"

"You will. Just like I'm going to live through this mess, you will too. Think about our friends and schoolmates that went into hiding

—their parents wouldn't have put them there to make life worse. We won't stay away forever from Mama or from each other."

Her little sister's bravery couldn't be real. Edith pulled away and stared into Krista's eyes. "You aren't afraid?"

"Are you looking for me to promise you a storybook ending? That I'll wave a magic wand, and the people we'll soon be living with will be the kindest people, that there will be lots of food, and the other children that might be hiding there will be our new friends? Or better yet, the Nazis will never find us?"

Edith shrugged, perplexed yet aware she was no longer young enough to pretend to live in a world of make-believe. She sniffled. "I think you're the older sister. At least, the wisest."

"I'm just trying to be brave. But here's the truth. Of course, I'm nervous about what will happen. At the same time, I'm not paying attention to my fears. It's like the bad boy or girl in school—the more you look at them, the more trouble they cause."

"I never thought of it that way."

"It's my turn to leave home and go into hiding, but next it will be yours. Will you be brave, Edith? You're the oldest sister. If I can be brave, you can be brave too."

Unexpected joy fluttered in Edith's heart. One day, even if she didn't know when or how, she'd again see her sister, her mother, and hopefully, her father if he'd managed to live through his arrest and false charges. She had to believe that as a family, they'd come out of this horrid time alive, well, and happy. "Yes, for you, I will be brave."

1

Nijmegen, the Netherlands, January 1, 1943. From within the attic room, Elsa Hoffmann—once Edith Weber a long time ago—pressed her ear against the old, warped door that had proven useless keeping out people from entering the small space she'd called a bedroom for the past four days. She breathed a little easier upon hearing silence from the stairwell.

"No one?" Maud asked. Unlike Elsa, who had the attic to herself, her new friend—another Jewish girl-in-hiding—shared an overcrowded sleeping area on the second floor of the safe house. When Elsa faced Maud, her friend winced. "You poor dear—that shiner the worthless brute gave you must be killing you."

"In more ways than one." Elsa lifted her hand to rub her swollen left eye but caught herself in time before worsening the tender bruise. "By my own hand, he would have had it far worse if his old lady didn't arrive home and he ran downstairs to greet her—the miserable beast. Believe me, I'm holding back other vile words about him—I no longer want to say his name aloud." She studied Maud sitting on the cot. "How do you put up with him? That was his first and only time with me."

"That's what I thought after he had his way with me the first time."

"There will be no next time with me."

"What are you going to do? Leave and take a stroll down the city streets patrolled by the Nazis? Don't you think that shiner of yours will have heads spinning your way—and not necessarily from the people you want?"

Within a few short strides, Elsa knelt beside the only one she could trust in this godforsaken house that was far from safe. At age 16, Maud might have been only a year younger than her, but she was terribly naïve about how people worked. "Maud, he... the slimy creep... won't stop using you or me. He'll take all he wants." She leaned closer to her friend to whisper. "He can easily abandon the younger children hiding here—and us if we stay—tell the Nazis he never operated a safe house, and bring us to the SS headquarters in Utrecht as random Jewish-prizes he found walking along the streets. Now tell me, would the SS likely believe him or us? We must leave. Now."

"I can't. I promised my mother to stay put."

Not again with this nonsense! The heat of anger and disgust twisted Elsa's insides. "You didn't promise your mother to be taken advantage by a man bored with his wife."

Maud stared at her feet, bare like old Dirk preferred. "It's safer here than facing the Nazis."

"Let's leave right now. I'll be with you—you don't have to be afraid of him ever again." At Maud's wide-eyed look of panic, Elsa grabbed her friend's hand and yanked her toward the window, combing her mind to think of a stronger tactic since, obviously, no other line of reasoning was working. "It's the first day of a new year, and I, for one, am not going to let the remaining 364 days be the ruin of me. Is that what you want for yourself—to let Dirk control you and have his way with you whenever he desires? Don't you see that is exactly what Nazis are doing to Jews and whoever they want? They're the ultimate authority deciding how best to use a person for their own pleasure.

Or if that doesn't suit their needs, then snuff, say goodbye to your life."

"Dirk isn't about to kill me."

"Is that what you believe?" Elsa crossed her arms. "If you don't hop into bed with the beast, then there's no stopping him from tossing you into the company of Nazis, is there?"

"Stop. You haven't thought out this notion of escaping thoroughly." Maud paused, breathed in deeply then exhaled slowly. "I'm more terrified of the Nazis and what they'd do to me than I am of Dirk. There is a difference between the two—Dirk wants to keep me alive and well, at least for that reason alone."

Elsa wanted to sigh heavily in her friend's face. She wanted to lecture her about the risk of pregnancy and diseases—God help them if either was already in the family way. She also wanted to remind Maud that ratting on Dirk to his wife only made them vulnerable to her nasty temper and physical blows. While she dreamed about disappearing into the proverbial thin air until this war, persecution, and victimization ended, she was painfully aware of the impossibility. The clock ticked away. With his wife absent from the house, Dirk was due for a visit. It was now or never to take action. She opened her mouth to speak and hopefully shake sense into her friend, but Maud shushed her by pressing a firm hand against her mouth. The century-old stairs leading up to the attic jostled and squeaked in both complaint and warning. Fortunately, the old man's gout-stiffened legs slowed him down a bit; unfortunately, it didn't interfere with his bedroom pleasures when his wife was away and he was home with *de arme kinderen* in his safe house. Although the *poor children* whose lives were already ripped apart suffered more calamity from his activities.

"He's on his way," Elsa said as loud as she dared. "We must take our chances and leave. Can't you see that?"

"No." Maud pulled away and stepped back a few paces. "You go. You're braver than I am. I'll keep Dirk busy at the door while you leave."

While they'd known each other for less than a week, Elsa

considered Maud a friend and believed Maud felt the same way. And, friends stayed together. They helped each other. About to tell her this, Maud stopped her cold. "You're out of time—he'll be back for the next round, and you know that. He likes his girls. Go now. I'll keep him busy."

"I won't let him touch you or me again." Elsa rubbed at her churning stomach. Dirk's house was the second safe house she'd been relocated to since she went into hiding the day after Christmas, barely a week ago. If she had to hide from the Nazis like other Jewish children—though as a teen, she was no child—the first safe house in Den Helder was somewhat bearable. The single mistress of the household, along with her mother, was at least kind and most pleasant. The two women had offered food they had, not holding back despite the country's severe rations. The children housed there spoke affectionately about past safe houses where they had experienced decent and kind treatment from both the host family and by the other children in hiding. At least it was as good as one might have in a home that wasn't one's own, separated from one's family, and during a war. Yet, with the arrival of a younger child, Elsa was relocated to Dirk's Nijmegen house. Now, with her life radically changed, first, from being a beloved daughter in a family that always stood by each other no matter what to losing a father to the Nazis to the separation from her dearest sister, and then the final hurt: her mother's betrayal and abandonment. The one week that Elsa had been hidden away like a commodity rather than a person had also ticked by like an eternity. No matter. She might not have choices where she was relocated to and who she was housed by, but no way would she become a slave for Dirk's physical needs or another safe house "uncle." "I'm not giving Dirk another chance."

"That's why I gave up trying to stop him. As long as you live in his house, he'll have his way. Why? Because we are Jewish. He knows we have to hide here, under his mercy, and can't do a thing about it." Maud pointed to the window. "Go now." She proceeded toward the door that they'd blocked with a chair.

Elsa whipped her attention back and forth between her friend and the window. If it would make a difference, she'd again grab

Maud's hand, drag her back to the window and shove her out—anything to keep her away from that grimy Dirk. Maud groaned from beside the door, pulling Elsa from her thoughts. She glanced at Maud, aware that it was likely the last time they'd ever see each other.

"Your papers?" Maud asked. When Elsa stared blankly at her, Maud sighed heavily. "Do you have your identity papers? You know you'll be stopped sooner or later. And for goodness sake it's winter! At least grab your sweater."

"What would I do without you?"

"You, my friend, are stronger than you realize. You'll do just fine."

Strength? Since her childhood days in Berlin when antisemitism escalated to the horror of *Kristallnacht* and forced her family to flee the country, she'd believed each daily action she'd undertaken, whether making a small decision or carrying out a larger task, was out of a primeval need to survive. Might her strength be summoned from a deeper, more human level of wanting to live a more fulfilling life rather than mere existence? She didn't know whether this desire was ignited by selfishness or a fiery resiliency to make the most of life.

Elsa bounded to her bed, stuffed her hand under the lumpy mattress, and withdrew the papers stating her newest identity: Elsa Hoffmann. She then slipped into her gray woolen sweater she'd managed to keep since arriving in the Netherlands with her family in 1939. When she'd originally gone into hiding, she had worn a coat, but the garment had been stolen from her and she'd never gotten a replacement to keep her warm again.

A pounding came at the door. "Elsa? Maud? You blocked the door? Open up!"

"One moment," Maud replied. She faced Elsa and mouthed, "Go. Now."

Elsa had no other choice but to leave. If she snitched on Dirk to his wife, the woman who acted like she and her husband were the only ones who mattered in the world would do what she'd done with Maud—slap her face, call her a vile name, and threaten to alert the SS. She and her husband needed the income promised to them for hiding Jewish children from the Nazis, and she complained little to Dirk. Truth be told, Dirk's wife cared more about the money than her husband and was probably relieved her husband was occasionally occupied with Maud. She probably assumed Elsa would be his next target, if she wasn't already.

Aware that Maud wouldn't change her mind, and with Dirk on the other side of the door, Elsa yanked open the window, slipped out, and hoped the two-story drop to the ground wouldn't hurt her, or worse.

A split second after the leafy green leaves of Dirk's prized rhododendron broke her fall, twigs sliced through her clothes and scratched her arms and legs. At least the thicker branches didn't impale her. If she could survive the fall, one way or the other, she'd manage other obstacles to come. Now it was time for her to disappear. Fast.

Ignoring her head-to-toe aches, Elsa rolled and dropped out of the bush. She disregarded the tingling cold that crept under her skirt and slipped under her sleeves, wrapping around her like a threadbare scarf. Where should she go? What should she do? Minutes ago, the only notion she'd entertained as reasonable was escaping, not the afterward part. Impulsive? No. She wished Maud the best, but unlike the younger girl, she wasn't ever going to give Dirk—or any man—the right to have his uninvited way with her.

On her feet, yet unfamiliar with the city, she thought of her mother, the one person she'd wanted to keep at the back of her mind. Yet now, Herta Weber's advice rang sharp and clear in Elsa's mind.

"Mama, what do I do if I encounter danger?"

"You hold your head up as if you've done no harm, refuse to look petrified, and carry on as if not confused." Not expecting that complicated response, but remembering the trouble her family had encountered because of their Jewish faith—Elsa understood that her mother, a woman who never spoke unnecessary words, advised her from experience. She'd give her mother that little credit.

Now, Elsa walked in the direction of what promised to be a busier area of Nijmegen, despite *Nieuwjaarsdag,* New Year's Day. With luck, she'd blend into a crowd rather than stand out. Though she stood tall and strived to walk with little concern etched across her face, she glanced away each time she approached a passerby. She didn't need strangers, or worse, the police, staring at her, curious as to why her clothing was spotted with blood and her eyelid sported purplish black and green colors. It was early morning, and the few people left, who either maintained a job or were busy running errands, rushed by her as if she were invisible. She was willing to wager that during this time of people squealing on each other for the tiniest reason, these strangers were likely more concerned about her pointing an accusing finger and calling for the attention of the Gestapo or the Dutch police—if they weren't one and the same these days—and have them hauled away.

When she'd arrived at Dirk's safe house, it was after midnight, a time deemed secure enough to relocate children from house to house. A middle-aged woman had collected her from the previous location, pressed into her palm her newest forged identity papers. At first, she'd ridden in the back of a delivery truck, hidden under empty flour sacks. Then she'd walked the remaining kilometers to Nijmegen and was deposited by the woman transporter whose name was withheld from her for both of their sakes. As they'd entered the city limits, streetlights spotlighted horrid sights. She couldn't help shaking her head at the German-worded slurs painted on boarded-up storefronts. One slur in particular, painted in black lettering with a bright red gun under the message *When filthy Jews are dead, Germany will again flourish* made her groan. But it was the sound of rattling garbage cans—by the hands of children—that would forever haunt her. "Orphans," the transporter had murmured. The sight of these hungry children made her gasp at the new reality she faced.

The transporter, likely a Jew herself and probably working in a resistance group, patted Elsa's shoulder, the first and only human touch she'd received by her. "Much has changed in a short time. That's why we're moving you. You will be in safe hands."

"I see that." Elsa understood she should remain silent but

couldn't. "They're children—younger than me. I'm sure they're homeless."

"The innocent have always paid the price of suffering. I can only pray that one day, if the ones who survive, these boys and girls will rise from the pits of despair they've been thrown into and help spread goodness."

Elsa wanted to say more, but the woman remained silent, only glancing around to see if anyone approached or followed them. That was when Elsa understood that yet again, to hide from the enemy was to become invisible to the world. To disappear. If she lived through this, she would step forward and become that person this transporter prayed for—someone who would overcome the circumstances of hatred that she and her family had been thrust into. Someone who helped to spread the goodness that might possibly wipe away evil. She didn't know how or when. She'd have to see what the immediate future would bring. Ironically though, she knew that it meant she needed to refuse to live in silence.

Now, on the run from the not-safe house, she came to a major intersection and waited for a few cars, a truck, and one tired-looking horse pulling a ragged cart packed with household goods that looked too heavy. Its exhausted driver was hunched over on his seat, apparently without concern over the animal. When it was safe to cross, she stepped down from the frosty curb, stumbled and landed on her left hip. *Stand up*, she ordered herself. *Keep moving. Don't stop now.* She rolled onto her knees and using her hands to push off the curbside, she managed to stand. Her left foot throbbed and burned; pain shot up her calf and knee. She eyed the other side of the road, hoped she could at least make it there, and hobbled on. Halfway across the road, the pain worsened. She wished a stranger could at least offer a helping hand until she was out of traffic's way. Not one of the passersby looked her way, let alone approach her to help her back on her feet. She didn't know which was worse, her suffering or that no one was coming to her aid. Had this war that threatened her family succeeded in wiping away the last threads of humanity by stripping people of their compassion? They couldn't even stop to help an injured young woman?

Someone firmly gripped her arm. She looked up to see a man in a crisp Gestapo gray-green uniform. Without saying a word, and disregarding her injury, he yanked her back to the curb. "Identity papers," he demanded in German.

She leaned against the lamppost and fished her papers from her skirt pocket. She hoped that her ready compliance—and understanding of German—indicated she wasn't suspected of wrongdoing, or worse, Jewish.

"Elsa Hoffmann?"

"Ja." He searched the back of the document for a stamped *J* that would have indicated her to be Jewish and condemned her to a fate she didn't wish to discover. Fortunately, like the original false documentation that Walter Süskind had arranged for her departure from Amsterdam, her newest paperwork stating she was Elsa was also as solid as a lie could get.

"Where are you going?"

"Shopping. *Für meine Mutter.*" She held her breath while he determined whether she was telling the truth about an errand that didn't exist, for a mother who didn't live in this city.

The officer shoved the papers at her and then pointed in the direction she'd come from. "Hurry home."

She smiled, though she wanted to snarl at him like a dog baring its teeth. "May I catch my breath for a moment longer?" The uniformed man eyed her injured foot and gave a curt nod. He crossed the road, the gray of his unform blending in with the dreary day.

"That was alarming," came a male voice from behind her, spoken in Dutch. "I'm relieved for you that he apparently found your papers in order and left you alone."

Fearing another officer, she didn't want to look the stranger's way.

"I can tell you're injured—may I help?" When she didn't reply or turn around, he repeated himself, but this time in German.

Embarrassed, and as defenseless and vulnerable as an ant crawling on the ground, she couldn't reply with a speck of truth. So that he wouldn't be too suspicious, she decided to speak in German, not Dutch. Likely, if he'd witnessed the whole Gestapo officer's interrogation, he would have heard her speak German, and it would be best not to play the fool. She kept her back toward him. "I was about to shop when I twisted my ankle, and now..." The pain kept her from thinking straight. She fixed her attention on a store sign across the street and tried to concentrate on the conversation. If luck was on her side and she could keep it short, he'd go one way and she the other.

"Your mother? Yes, I heard." He paused. When she failed to reply, he continued. "What's your name?"

"Elsa," dry-mouthed, she croaked her name. Had the stranger heard her or cared enough to listen?

"A lovely name. My name is Erich. Why won't you look at me? You can trust me."

She didn't know one iota about him. Lately, as far as trust went, she also understood less and less about that belief. Slowly, using the lamppost to ease her weight off her smarting foot, she turned around and observed a tall, clean-shaven young man; he wore his tartan brown-beige coat quite smartly. Likely only a few years her senior, he was of slim build, with sandy-colored hair and green eyes. His sudden whistle pierced her ears.

"I know, between my bruises, black eye, and now swelling foot, I must be one sorry sight."

"Let me help you. It must hurt to walk." Erich stepped up to her.

She pulled back.

"I'm no Nazi. I won't hurt you."

She didn't care to experiment with how Erich defined Nazi and decided to remain cautious. "I'm grateful for your offer to help. *Danke*. Mutter is expecting me, and I must go."

"Well then, the least I can do is escort you home."

She looked away.

"There's no mother, is there?" he said. "At least not here in Nijmegen. Nor, I suspect, do you have a home here in this city."

His sudden aloof tone shook sense into her. Rather than wait for him to announce that he'd personally escort her to the nearest police headquarters, she'd leave now and get away from him as quickly as she could. Her ankle protested and caved in. She collapsed to the ground.

He dropped to his knees before her. "Who blackened your eye? A husband? A boyfriend?"

Had he thought she was older than her 17 years? She'd been told by others in the past that her womanly figure and maturity made her appear older. Older she'd be, then. Since she was turning 18 in November, she'd push it a bit and reinvent herself as a 19-year-old young woman—if he should ask. For now, she'd act as distant and cool as he'd come across a second ago. "An acquaintance. Doesn't matter."

"These days, we all have mere acquaintances. It's safer that way, I agree."

She hadn't asked for his opinion nor cared to hear it. "I'm fine. I tripped over my own clumsy feet. After a rest, I'll be as good as ever."

"Two stories explaining your condition? First by the hand of an acquaintance, but now by your own doing?" He lifted a brow, whether out of concern or disbelief, she couldn't tell. "Do you have a place to stay? Don't go telling me your mother's house."

What a fool she was. She'd gotten confused—the result of telling untruths. A second ago, she'd fabricated an acquaintance who had given her a shiner, but then she jumbled it, thinking he'd referred to her hurting foot. She needed to get back on track. "My identity papers checked out fine with the Gestapo officer. There's no reason that if he believed me, you should have your doubts."

"If you like, Elsa, I can get you to a doctor."

"No," she said too fast, failing to hear the conviction in her own tone.

Erich stood and extended a hand to help her up. "Fine. If you want to refuse my offer of help and go your own lost way, then stand up now and get going before another officer stops you and has a different opinion about you and your papers."

A gust of wind whipped between them. She tensed from the cold.

He had a point; she couldn't remain on the ground. She accepted his hand and stood, a wave of anxiety roiling about within her, threatening to swell like a storm. Could her foot bear her weight? Would this stranger take advantage of her situation and cause harm? She'd called it quits on trusting others the second she left Dirk's establishment.

"Why are you without a coat?" When she remained silent, he mumbled what she believed was *probably best if you don't tell me*. He let go of her and started to peel off his coat. Down she went, her left side smacking the sidewalk. Fire scorched her. A black void approached with promises of relief. As she reached out to grab the darkness, she heard the words *my parents' home... our doctor... you rest.* Yet, she couldn't tell who had spoken, or why.

———

She wanted to keep her eyes shut and never see the real world again. The sadness and agony were unbearable. But when she heard what sounded like a door slam, she snapped her eyes open, expecting to find that she'd been tossed onto a transport vehicle en route to one of the dreaded work camps. Talk about those awful places had become the norm ever since the Nazis had stepped up their hostilities against the Jews in the Netherlands when they first occupied the country in 1940. The emotional contagion of fear extended beyond her family and friends. One only had to walk the streets to see worry lines etched across strangers' faces. Children stopped playing on the streets. Grownups dropped out of corner gatherings for social chitter-chatter. It was as if they knew a monster would one day strike and preemptively, like a toddler crawling under a table believing he couldn't be seen, hiding in plain sight but wishing away the danger. Until wishes became useless and actions, like in her situation going into hiding, became the new standard in a country surrounded by the North Sea and landlocked by Germany and German-occupied countries.

"Ah, Elsa, you're awake."

Elsa? She lifted onto an elbow and searched for the mysterious person speaking to her. She caught a pair of eyes watching her in a rearview mirror.

The man's brows wrinkled. "How's your foot?" The stranger spoke perfect German and sounded concerned, if not kind. Yet, she couldn't place him. She glanced about—she was in the back seat of a luxurious sedan, its splendor she'd never encountered before. A Mercedes-Benz? The driver was about her age, give or take. She couldn't imagine how he could afford a fine car during wartime. She recalled her father speaking of Hitler and his specially chosen elite, as the only ones with access to these cars and how they were used for parades during the late '30s. Since then, might Mercedes have become more affordable for the common person? Although a nice thought, she doubted it. She stiffened as memory flashed before her eyes. She was Elsa... and the driver was Erich, the man who, after witnessing the Gestapo officer's interrogation, had offered his help to her.

"Where am I?" she asked as she slid further under a thick layer of blankets placed over her. Like a young child, she'd sought protection from the blankets, but as the adult she was trying to portray, she was aware too that there was no comfort to be found. "Have you abducted me? Where are you taking me?"

A throaty chuckle had her returning her attention to the mirror. "When you passed out, I made the unilateral decision to take you home to be seen by my family physician. Back to my question: how's your foot? For that matter, how's the rest of you? Is the pain better or worse?"

The scene of herself with a black eye and on the run from the safe house with an injured foot, played out before her eyes. She winced.

"Still smarting, I see," Erich said.

She moved her foot, and pain rippled through her, though slightly less than she remembered when she first landed on the paved road earlier. "Yes, it hurts." She brushed her right foot against her left and felt a soft object under her injured foot. "You've propped my foot up?"

"Yes, using the limited first aid I know, I elevated your bad foot on top of my coat. And I fished a couple of blankets out of the trunk— hopefully they don't smell musty."

"They're fine. And warm. *Danke*. Is this a private car or an ambulance?" She caught a grin on his face.

"Good. You have a sense of humor. That will come in handy."

"Come in handy? That sounds quite like warning bells."

"Relax. It will work out for the best. I'll see to it. By the way, this is definitely a private car. Mine, to be exact. I try my best to avoid lifts from strangers these days."

"Since I can't manage to push my way out of this vehicle and expect to flee on foot, I don't have a choice except to stay put. However, relaxing is a whole different matter. Now, tell me Erich. Where are we? And exactly where are we going?"

"We're in Germany."

Elsa whipped the blankets off and sat up. Dizziness swept her into a tailspin. She fought against herself as her head swiveled left, confused if it was from her lightheadedness or a raging panic. She gripped the car seat to steady her balance. "Take me back. Right now. I never agreed to cross the border."

"Sorry, can't do. We've already traveled an hour's distance, and I'm not turning around."

Can't do or won't do? "How did we cross the border, and apparently easily, considering you have me in your back seat?" She patted her skirt pocket where she kept her identity papers. Good. They were in place. Blazing-hot panic spread within her as if she'd been violated again by Dirk. Had Erich searched her while she was out... touched her... invaded not only her privacy but intruded where he wasn't welcome?

"No worries," he said as if he'd read her mind. "No one searched you while you were asleep. Elsa, do you have a concern about your papers that I should know about?"

"No," she said without delay. She was in the backseat, injured, traveling through Nazi-infested Germany, and with a man she only knew by his first name. If Erich was his true name. Like hers, his identity documents could have been illegitimate. "As I've already pointed out, my papers—as determined by that Gestapo officer—are in perfect order. I just... I can't... Germany is the last place I want to be."

"It's a bit war-torn, but it's a lovely country."

"Stop playing with me."

"Stop dodging my questions."

She sank back into the cushiony seat and gathered the blankets around her again. "Fine. I'll tell you. But it's not pretty."

"Most of us don't have pretty life stories," he said. His tone had been soft, reflective. Whether he spoke from experience wasn't her concern, not if she was his captive. He could say what he wanted, disguise and gloss over his story, but she had to take control. Or, at least, make an earnest attempt.

And if she was going to put on an act, then she'd have to do it convincingly. "Before the war, I lived in Berlin. My parents—who have since died—sent me to live with my aunt in Amsterdam. When she too passed and I had no other family, I moved in with a friend. One day, not long ago, when Greta was at work, her boyfriend visited." Elsa pictured Dirk's face, his seedy appearance. His smell of stale tobacco and unwashed body. His touch of grimy, filthy fingers. "He made advances on me... That's where the black eye is from— lousy hands of a lousy person. He threatened that if I squealed on him to Greta or dared to leave, he'd come after me."

"But you left."

"Oh, yes. I've been wandering the streets, considering the state of the Netherlands—of this stinking world—until I fell and hurt my foot. And that's when you found me." She met his gaze in the mirror. "Greta's boyfriend was from Germany and knows I'm from Germany. Saying I'm uncomfortable here in this country is not saying enough."

"I understand where you're coming from. I'm sorry that what you just shared happened to you."

Elsa quietly exhaled. "So, tell me, Erich, how did we cross the border that I imagine is swarmed with Nazis on their diligent guard?"

"Let's just say that through my father, my connections are quite excellent. I'm never questioned. And if that means I have a gal passed out in the back seat of my car, it's a matter of no consequences. *Verstehst du*?"

No, she didn't understand but nodded. If Erich could pass through the Dutch-German border without gathering a concern or two, he most likely was a Nazi. And most likely, his father was of higher Nazi influence. She had to be careful in how she acted and what she said. "Erich, what's your last name?"

He glanced over his shoulder, and smirked. "It's not Hitler."

She glared at him.

He returned his attention to the road ahead. "Sorry, I couldn't resist that one."

"Your last name, please."

"Friedrich. And if you're curious, my *Vater* is Maxwell Friedrich, a judge."

Elsa relaxed a little, though she couldn't quite imagine how a judge could be influential to a government, she remained guarded. She tried for a conversational tone. "Were you returning home to Germany when we met?"

"Yes. I left home last evening to run an errand, stayed overnight, and was heading to my car after a bite to eat. Speaking of, you must be hungry. I apologize I'm unable to offer a snack. I'll remedy that once we arrive home."

"I'm fine." She hoped she didn't sound cotton mouthed. She also hoped her stomach didn't growl in betrayal.

"What's your last name, Elsa?"

"Hoffmann. Elsa Hoffmann."

"A good German name."

"It is." She rushed to elaborate, hoping she didn't sound defensive. "My family goes back a long way in Germany. Centuries." A truth, but one she was uncertain whether to be proud of these days. Or, more aptly put, a truth her instincts shouted not to boast about. *Truth can backfire*. She needed to switch the subject off herself. "So, we're going to your home? With your wife and little ones?"

"My parents' place. I'm not married, nor have children. These days, the way the home front is operating, I have mixed thoughts of ever wanting a wife, let alone a family of my own."

That was an odd way of describing his situation, hinting at his share of private battles. With her own family rich in love, she couldn't imagine parents and children not sharing close ties. Then again, not too long ago, she couldn't have imagined the cohesiveness that held her family together would ever break. She would have never dreamed that the destructive hand of evil would come between the four of them, sending them in separate directions.

She didn't want to think about her parents and sister. It hurt. Besides, her heavy eyelids won, and she again rested them. "Where in Germany is home?"

"Monschau. It's a town by the Belgium border."

"Sounds quaint."

"Quaint, it's not," he uttered.

Had he replied regarding his home or the town? More and more, bewilderment had become her automatic reaction, but that, too, was becoming less of a shock. Day by day, as the war raged on, and families were ripped apart, and people were persecuted and considered subhuman—*Untermenschen*—for observing a different faith, she understood very little. She doubted she would ever make sense of it all.

When the car veered an abrupt right, Elsa blinked awake, surprised she'd fallen asleep again. She gasped at the unexpected beautiful view. Woods and mountains appeared to roll endlessly for kilometers, its evergreens thick with green and meeting the sky with blue and gray misty fingers reaching downward to greet the land. As beautiful as it was now, it must have been spectacular in the springtime and summer. She could hear the birds singing. See the roe deer grazing on fresh grass. People enjoying a picnic... well, at least during the prewar years. War. Germany. Erich. She glanced toward the front of the car. Erich stared at her with his green eyes in the rearview mirror.

"The North Eifel region is breathtaking, don't you think?" he said. "Not only in winter-white beauty, but you should see it during all four seasons—spring-green, summer-gold, and autumn-red."

Poetic, was he? Or was that an attempt at charm? Not that it mattered to her. "I'm unfamiliar with this area. It is pretty, though. Pity I've slept most of this trip."

"You're injured. You need to rest. As I've said, we'll soon arrive home."

Absent from his usage of *home* was a happy tone. She could not blame him since the term had become an elusive one these days. Lately, Elsa found it difficult to recall her old family home in Berlin before the Nazis corrupted the meaning of life. Had she once sat around a supper table, exchanging jokes and tales with her little sister, recounting school lessons to her mother, asking her father for advice? Had she once been Edith, not Elsa, and not separated from her family? While she didn't have the answers, it occurred to her that home wasn't simply the structure of the house or its age or location, but rather its occupants tucked cozily under its roof, and the memories connected to them.

Erich made a right turn, and they started to pass a few modest houses and two shops. The dirt road turned to cobblestone and narrowed as they crossed a river.

"The Rur." Erich looked into the rearview mirror, his grin wide. "Don't worry. I can't read your mind."

"Good. I value my privacy." After driving through a short, narrow alley between two buildings, Elsa's mouth dropped open at the rows of half-timbered houses and shops, all with slate roofs, a storybook come alive. "Did we just travel back in time to the medieval ages?"

"This is Monschau." Erich chuckled. "Much of its historic structures are in original shape. My parents live just another few kilometers away."

When he made another turn and they began to exit the enchanting town, Elsa cried out. "No... let's stay." She detested the youthful whine that had escaped her lips but was convinced if they remained there, she could forget her worries and fears, at least long enough to give her a sense of a haven that she so desperately needed.

"Trust me, as far as charm goes, this town isn't what it used to be."

More riddles. She had no knowledge of Monschau's history or its present state, but one particular factor caught her curiosity. "Erich, I saw adults, but where were the children?

Monschau is a perfect winter wonderland. I'd expect little ones to be outdoors, enjoying sledding or a good snowball fight."

Silence crept between them. His flexing his fists around the steering wheel did not escape her attention. She accepted his choosing not to reply and settled back into her seat. A glance at his eyes in the mirror at his eyes, suddenly heavy with anguish, jolted her upright. The fiery spasms of pain in her leg competed with the grating of her emotional nerves. Apparently, he too was unnerved.

"Children once were plentiful in this town," he said softly. "Germany has become a place where children aren't seen, for one reason or another. Mainly, it's a safety concern. Monschau is a good example—good explanation..."

When he trailed off, Elsa raced to comfort him, a surprise reaction. "If it's about keeping children safe, I can understand."

"Yes and no. We now keep our own children in mostly private schools or, like my little brothers, home-tutored."

"What do you mean by *our own children*? Aren't all children in this town children in need of education?"

"There used to be a fair number of Jewish children. At the end of 1938 until 1940, a Jewish organization got them into a *Kindertransport* to England, and now the town is free of them."

So, when Erich had said *our own children*, he'd meant Aryan German children. Was it that the children were finally free of the town—of Germany—or, as Erich expressed, did the town consider themselves free of the Jewish children, as if ridding themselves of lice? Elsa tamped back a groan. Instead, she asked, "What became of these children's parents?"

"Several changes have occurred in Germany when it comes to education, particularly since 1934... I was only 11 then."

That year, she was eight. She recalled general changes in schooling in her home city of Berlin, though she couldn't remember the exact changes. "My memory's foggy—what changes do you recall?"

"For starters, teachers were required to join the National Socialist Teachers League."

"That sounds like a mandated oath of obedience to Hitler."

He nodded. "And if the teachers didn't correlate their lessons to the party ideals, students and fellow teachers were encouraged to report them. They faced dismissal."

"Or worse, I imagine."

"The whole curriculum became slanted toward racial biology and population policy."

Images flashed through her mind. She was about to use the word propaganda regarding the onslaught of Nazi indoctrination, share how her own parents pulled her and her sister out of the Berlin public schools, and relay how her mother began to teach them at home. She stopped herself before she could reveal too much information that he might use against her. Showing her passions against Nazi Germany to Erich wouldn't be in her best interest.

"We're only minutes away from home, now."

"Will I be meeting your family?"

"Honestly, when it comes to my father, I never know these days. As for my older brother, he lives a distance away and seldom visits. My mother and the twins—Fritz and Wil—will be home."

"Twins?"

Erich grinned. "Twin five-year-old terrors, but I confess to adoring them."

"But you're—"

"You're the curious one! I'm 20. It's Mutter's second marriage—I was five, Richard ten when she remarried. The twins came along as a surprise, 15 years later." He made a left turn, driving off into the countryside.

"I thought you said you lived a minimum of kilometers from Monschau. Are we going elsewhere?"

"Vater appreciates his privacy. Wearing the shoes that he does, I can't blame him."

Her throbbing ankle robbed her of asking for clarification. Yet, she couldn't hold back an *ooh* when they drove through a large yellow brick archway and continued on a single-lane road with alternating gray and gold paving blocks. They passed a row of tall hedges that she suspected were burning bushes. In a few more months, they would have vibrant, fiery red leaves. They came to an off-white stucco cottage with reddish-brown wooden shutters and gabled windows. Surrounding the building were the tallest pines she'd ever seen. "What a charming house and what I'm sure are lovely grounds come warmer weather."

"Thank you. I'll inform Herr Weber, the gardener, of your appreciation. After losing his own home decades ago, he'd gladly accepted the work appointment from my grandfather and has been happily living here, putting up with us all."

Weber? "What a fine house for only a gardener." Although she didn't want to sound biased—certainly not over a man she'd never met before—right or wrong, she'd hoped to remove Erich's attention away from her surprise at the gardener's name Weber—her true family name. Was the gardener Jewish too? Her inkling told her no, that wouldn't be acceptable at the Friedrich estate. Unwilling to disclose the similarity of names and frazzled from Erich's coded way of talking, she shifted and pressed her cheek against the window. After more burning bushes and pine trees, Erich slowed as they approached a looming structure. "You live in a castle?"

"Not quite. It's more a combination of an Italian villa and German gothic. Suits the family..." His words trailed off, at least failing to reach her ears as she took in the estate before her. Like the archway entrance, the monstrous structure had been built with yellow bricks. A Victorian tower—shingled by crisscrossed slate with smaller matching turret-topped dormers—stood on each front corner like sentries on patrol. Iron ornamental trim lined the walks along the varying levels of the roof. Softer, mauve house trim showcased a grand main entrance with double glassed doors framed nicely in a fancy arch, adding to the villa atmosphere that Erich had downplayed.

They circled around a large round plot ringed by red brick, full of holly bushes with red berries that the birds and squirrels hadn't ransacked. She imagined Herr Weber using a trick or two up his gardener's sleeve to combat the critters.

"Josef—Herr Weber—does magnificent work," Erich said. Although he'd playfully said earlier that he couldn't read her mind, she'd wondered about his uncanny timing. Actually, she also wondered why he seemed to always glance at her in the mirror before speaking. Or, for that matter, why she was drawn to looking at his reflection in the mirror?

"In the spring you will see the gardens flowering with red, purple, and pink azaleas," he continued. "We have the most stunning rose garden... Why the frown?"

He'd assumed she'd be with him in the springtime, without asking about her plans or thoughts. She averted her eyes back to the view outside of the car and released a little groan. She'd banked on her condition as an efficient cover-up to cease his further questions.

Erich stopped the car at the front entrance she'd admired seconds ago. A silver-haired man dressed in a black uniform dashed out of the house and toward the driver's door. Erich leapt out. "Nein, Werner. Please help me with Fräulein Hoffmann. She's injured her ankle."

"I'll fetch your father's chair."

"Excellent." Erich watched the servant hurry off back into the house. He then stooped into the vehicle, his cheek nearly brushing hers. "Nowadays, you wouldn't know unless it was a stinking rainy day and the dampness aggravated him that Vater broke both legs in a skiing accident five years ago and was forced to use a wheelchair for a while." He glanced toward the house. "Werner Schulze is always one step ahead of us. He's the best butler we've had yet."

Before she could come up with a suitable reply that didn't involve more questions than a guest should be asking, Werner returned, pushing a wheelchair. With the wheel locks secured, Elsa thought the servant would be the one helping her transition from the car to the chair. Instead, Erich lifted her effortlessly and placed her onto the seat, mindful of her injury. He also surprised her by pushing the wheelchair while Werner walked ahead and opened the double doors.

The entrance hall looked like the grand lobby of a Berlin museum she once visited with her family before the trouble began. Artwork hung on the walls. Potted ferns graced each of the two large and narrow stained-glass windows and added a touch of coziness to blot out the lingering cold hand of a winter that appeared not in a hurry to go away. A large round table—whose graining matched the smaller rosewood table that once belonged to her oma before she sold it for needed cash—centered the interior. It was bare but grand enough that it needed no decorative enhancement. All this was tucked under an ornate wooden ceiling.

Appearing at the far end of the hall, on ruddy marble flooring, a woman stood so still that Elsa rocked back in shock when the woman narrowed her eyes. Despite her conservative two-piece black skirt outfit with a touch of a white silk neck scarf with tiny black polka dots and the dull black flats on her feet, she was so striking that Elsa could imagine she was a model fresh from a Paris runway. Elsa also visualized her dressed in the brighter, flashier outfits before Hitler had his say in what fashions *good* German women should wear. However, her bright blue eyes lacked a sparkle with warmth or a hint of hospitality, as well as a smile failed to lift the corners of her mouth, definitely accommodated the no-nonsense look the German leader idealized for a proper woman.

"Erich, I'm glad you're home." The woman patted the black beret on her head. "My, it looks like you're competing against your older brother. What trophy have you brought home this time, son?"

2

Trophy? Elsa had never met Erich's mother before, and already this woman had to categorized her with the insult of an insignificant prize —an object—that her son had won. Why couldn't she see her as a human being? If her leg wasn't throbbing, if she hadn't been on the run, and if she hadn't regrettably accepted Erich's help, she'd waste not a second before turning her back and scrambling faraway from this house. A petty part of her wanted to slink back into her childhood days and hurl a verbal barb at her, but she had better manners than that. Her mother had taught her to be considerate of others, unlike this woman. "*Now, now,*" her mama would have said. "*Don't stoop to the stranger's level. That's how wars begin—over the ridiculous.*" Although Erich's mother avoided looking at her, Elsa smiled the most pleasant smile she could muster.

"Where's Vater?" Erich asked.

"No 'Hello, mother dearest,' for me?" As Erich remained silent, the woman stood taller and gestured outward. "The least you can do is introduce me to your... acquaintance."

Erich strode toward his mother and kissed her on the cheek. "It's nice to see you, Mutter. This is Elsa Hoffmann." He smiled at Elsa.

"Elsa, this is my mother, Frau Friedrich." Elsa waited for a first name to be added, but none came. Neither did an acknowledgment come from the mother.

"After I made the delivery for Vater," Erich continued, speaking exclusively to his mother, "I stopped in Nijmegen for breakfast and found Elsa with an injured foot. She's originally from Germany—her papers are in order if you're curious."

Elsa held her breath. The last concern she needed was Erich's mother suspicious of her and demanding to see her documentation, despite what her son had just verified.

Frau Friedrich searched her son's eyes. "Why is she alone, like a stray mutt without a home?"

"It's a long, sad story. I thought we could help with medical attention." He crossed his arms against his chest and grinned. "We must have a wee bit of Friedrich hospitality to spare."

"Pleased to meet you, Frau Friedrich," Elsa said.

Frau Friedrich's eyes turned icy. "We're at war, Elsa. What's the true story of why you're by yourself?"

Other than the fib she had told Erich about a fictional friend's boyfriend making advances on her and propelling her to roam the streets, Elsa had been living in the moment and hadn't formulated any other explanation for why she was alone. Just eyeing this unfriendly woman unnerved her, and she glanced away. There was no way she would even hint about an untoward situation with a man. Still, feeling more like an intruder than a guest, she needed to justify her predicament, considering, as the Frau had said, it was wartime, and she was unescorted, let alone not engaged at a workplace.

"Where is Vater?" Erich jumped in before Elsa could rattle off a foolish answer. He stared hard into his mother's eyes. "Is he in court or attending another meeting?"

"You know your father—important work keeps him busy these days."

"I call his work a different name, but as he always reminds me—what do I know?"

Despite her downturned lips, Frau Friedrich appeared unfazed by her son's reply. "Little, unlike Richard."

Erich covered his heart and groaned, though with a hint of affection. "Insults—and this I came home to?"

With three strides, his mother rushed to her son. She lifted her hand as if to strike a blow across Erich's face, but instead pulled him into a tight hug. "You might have been gone for only a couple of days, but I've missed you, even your silly sense of humor."

"I've missed you too." Erich leaned back from his mother. "As always, you look sharp. Are you stepping out for a while?"

"*Danke schön*, darling. Yes, I have plans I cannot get out of too easily—your father isn't the only one who contributes to a good cause. Right now, the twins are with Adela. Richard was smart for bringing her home with him. She's certainly earned her keep as an efficient hodgepodge of a servant, filling in whenever there's a staff absence." A little grin played with her lips. "But you're deflecting... you know I'm right about Richard."

"The brother who can do no wrong? And to think he's the university dropout and I'm the scholar."

"Again, this competition between you and Richard? He's serving our country and that alone deserves your respect. There's a few lessons to learn from your smart brother."

"Serving Germany? For the past five years he's been acting more like a lone wolf, doing what he sees fit and when he sees fit. And you know the only way that's plausible is through—"

"Let's get back to your question, Erich," Frau Friedrich said through tight lips as she gave Elsa a sideways look. "As for your father, he plans to return this evening. Your brother is in Austria, slowly making his way back home."

"Richard has an infatuation with Austria. Hopefully, neither he nor Vater will be bringing their Nazi pals home."

Gray fuzzy dots exploded before Elsa's eyes. She swayed to keep up with the odd swirl of these tiny specks as if they were a bunch of... of... Nazis marching at a Hitler rally. A curse in German that she hadn't heard in years whipped over her head. A sturdy hand on her shoulder stopped her from toppling from the chair and landing on the floor.

"Phone for the doctor, Mutter."

"But I have a meeting."

"They can wait, not Elsa."

In an attempt to halt the spinning, Elsa closed her eyes to the world and drifted off into an abyss that promised quiet, not quite peace or calmness, but she latched onto it and escaped, which she'd wanted to do from the start of her journey.

"Thank you, Adela," Erich said. "Leave us alone, now."

Elsa opened her eyes in time to see a woman with a shock of shoulder-length blonde hair, dressed in a white uniform and holding an empty tray, open the door and leave. Erich had not offered a helping hand. Curious of her surroundings, she tried to prop herself on an elbow. A fresh wave of pain washed over her, and she groaned.

"Easy, *meine kleine Freundin*." Sitting on a chair beside the bed where she'd apparently been moved to, Erich leaned forward. "You don't need to hurt yourself again."

She opened her eyes and blinked at the sight of Erich. "I'm not your little friend."

"Oh, I think you are. At least, I'd like to be your friend."

He was bold! She was prepared to put him in his proper place. But his drawn mouth, as if he'd forgotten how to smile, stopped her argument. "Sorry I snapped. I'm accustomed to people my age competing against me—always trying to knock me down and make me less mature. I'd like to be your friend. With a war raging, one needs a friend one can count on. Yet, you don't know me. I might be an awful person."

"I know you well enough compared to others of various ages and backgrounds. You aren't a simple schoolgirl but quite intelligent and perceptive."

"But how? Aren't you taking a chance by bringing me here to your family's house?"

"And aren't you taking a chance by trusting me?"

She peered down at her leg propped on two pillows. "I don't have a choice, do I?" She looked about the room. "Whose bedroom is this? Does it belong to the woman who was just here?"

He rocked back. "Adela? No, of course not. She's a servant here. You're in a guestroom for now. Since you won't be going anywhere else for a while, I hope you'll find it comfortable."

She was about to question him, but he continued. "Anyway, I'm relieved to see you're awake—I was beginning to think that I needed to chase down the doctor and bring him back to re-examine you."

"The doctor's been here already? What did he say? I slept through the visit?"

"Not quite." Erich's forehead furrowed. "You don't remember? You held strong while he asked you a few questions, like whether you'd heard a popping sound when you'd fallen, or which hurt the most when he touched your foot above your ankle or in the ankle's soft spot—"

"I'm ashamed to say that I never had a high tolerance for pain."

Erich's left eyebrow quirked up. "Pain endurance does not define one's character."

"Did I mumble an oddity or two?"

"No. Are you worrying again?"

Change the topic, she commanded herself. "So, at what point did I fall asleep?"

He leaned further toward her, his mouth a breath from her ear. "The good doctor has a long-time friendship with my father. You didn't pass out from the pain when the doctor rotated your foot, though you did moan a bit on the high side, bringing my mother running in to see what was happening. And believe me, if you think she's dispassionate—or as others see her, cold and not one to mess with—you aren't far off. So, her barging in was certainly a surprise."

"I'm sure she wanted to see the situation with her own eyes," Elsa mumbled, instantly wishing she hadn't. "I mean... sorry. I misspoke."

Erich lifted a hand to pause her. "Mother can be straightforward. And she'll never admit it or apologize. It's just her way. But to answer your question—when the good doctor mentioned an SS meeting slated for tomorrow evening and inquired whether my father had plans to be there, you passed out cold."

She again tried to sit up, but Erich stopped her with a shake of his head. "Can you at least tell me the verdict?"

"Which one? Your ankle or my father's meeting?"

She rolled her bottom lip. "Both are a mystery."

"Doctor Prentiss believes you've sprained your ankle moderately, which is better than a break. He recommends plenty of rest, ice, and elevation." Erich jutted his chin toward her foot. "That's why your foot is lifted on the stack of pillows. Looks like you'll be staying here with us for a while to recuperate."

"How can I stay here in this house? It's obvious I'm not welcomed here by your mother. What exactly did she mean by you claiming me as your trophy?"

Erich's serious look stretched to a full smirk. "Ah, you do remember that."

"Of course. You would too if you were in my shoes."

"Well, Freundin, in a way, I am in your shoes. See, my older brother is notorious for bringing home trophies, whether animals or people. The last trinket he brought home was Adela."

"Oh, the woman who was just here when I awoke."

"Yes. Adela's story is vague—Richard is the evasive type when it comes to answering questions since he knows he can get away with it —he found her in Vienna during *Kristallnacht* and brought her home with him."

"Is she Jewish?" Elsa asked before she could think twice.

"You won't find a Jew in this house," he said with no hesitation. "Let's leave this as is—no more questions."

Yes, indeed, Elsa thought. No more questions about Jews taking residence in the Friedrich household. "I understand."

"As for my mother, she enjoys fostering a playful rivalry between us brothers. Richard loves the attention, the sport, the gloating over how wonderful Mutter claims he is. Probably because he'd never get that from our father." Erich leaned closer to her as if to keep their words away from listening ears. "Right now, I've persuaded my mother that you will remain here to recover." He swept his hands to indicate the room. "This guestroom, complete with its own private bath, will be yours during your convalescence. The doctor estimates it will be around six or so weeks."

"I can't stay here that long!"

"Might be less than six weeks—depends on whether you listen to the doctor's advice these first few weeks by staying off of your foot and how fast your body naturally recovers."

"And afterward?"

"There are a few possibilities, but we shall see what and where fate brings us."

Erich would have a rude awakening when he to discovered that she wasn't one who allowed fate to determine her days. That's why she'd fled the supposed safe house she'd been cast into. She might have been relegated to the role of a forgotten daughter, but she wasn't about to permit others to shape and mold her into an individual less than who she truly wanted to be. And, if by chance Erich didn't see that in her, then she certainly couldn't pity him.

"I have a few tasks to do now," Erich said. "Is there more I can do for you?"

Perhaps to help her tolerate what was beginning to feel like a prison sentence here in the house, and in this country, an impulsive idea stormed her mind. She cast Erich a sly smile. "Yes. May I have a few sheets of writing paper?"

"Easy enough." He strode to the desk before the window, slid open the sole drawer tucked under the writing surface, withdrew a notebook and fountain pen, and handed it to her. "Here you go. Write away. If you need more, or paper of finer quality, let me know."

Surprised for the immediate gratification, as well as nervous and intimidated to begin what she'd dreamed about doing for weeks, she took the paper and pen from him. His touch to her hand was both warm and startling. She struggled to annunciate her words in more than a murmur. "Thank you. It's as if too many thoughts are bottled up inside me."

"Putting them in inked words might help."

Confused that Erich understood her situation, as if he'd experienced similar emotions, she chewed on how to address this. But he slipped out of the door, leaving her alone in her room, to her thoughts and blank paper. As soon as the bedroom door clicked shut, she opened the notebook, picked up the pen that she'd let fall to her lap and hovered it over the paper as if it was a bird deciding where to land. Where should she begin?

Her hand shook. The pen dropped back onto her lap. A little voice from within nudged her: *Write anything. One word—a beginning. It's not as if these thoughts will be graded... it's for my eyes only.* Again, she lifted the pen.

Dear Mama,

Do I tell you I hate you, or that I love you? I'm terribly confused. Here's what I do know: you're my mother and I suspect that you know the answer to this question, though it might take me a while to decipher. I know it shouldn't be that way and believe me, deep shame fills me as I write this note.

I don't understand what is happening in this world that slants more upside down by the second. I don't understand why I'm away from you, from Papa, from sweet Krista, hiding... running for my life when there's no certainty that I'd be alive tomorrow, and reunited with all of you.

Mama, where are you? Are you well? Are you...

Alive? Elsa—once upon a time, Edith—couldn't dare finish the thought. Here she was, angry and confused at her mother while not knowing if she was alive. Elsa set the pen down; swept the notebook to her side. Resting her eyes shut, she thought the tears she'd harbored since she stepped away from her mother and into the first safe house would brim and overflow from her eyes. None came. Instead, a jumble of images clouded her mind, then faded. She rested her eyes shut, hoping blackness would take over as sleep swept her away. The relief of drifting off to a place of tranquility, a place where peace could restore her spirit failed to claim her and transport her to that sweet existence. Instead, wide-eyed, she stared at the ceiling, trying her best to shove away each new horrific worry that came in the substitution of slumber.

3

Bratislava, Czechoslovak Republic, February 15, 1938. A rare blue sky and golden sunshine teased the day with a touch of spring. It was the warmest February day that Ivona Kazik could remember, though a trace of a chill still hung in the air. Vonni, as she preferred to be called, shed her bulky winter coat to soak up the sun's rays, placing it as a cushion on the low stone wall before sitting down. Her thin red and violet skirt failed to provide warmth. Too bad. She would not slip back into the coat, no matter what. She'd turned 18 a week ago and secretly hoped a young man might look her way. She wanted to show her womanly curves and not to appear as a stuffed sack. Although, she had her doubts because she was a Roma. For centuries, her people had not had it easy. Yet, here in Bratislava, if they kept quiet and mostly unseen, they weren't given too much trouble by outsiders —the *Gorgios*. After turning 18, all she wanted was to meet a nice and kind man, fall in love with him, and have a family of her own. Wasn't that normal? Lately, however, it was becoming nearly impossible for the Roma to obtain work, let alone love. Life wasn't fair.

Vonni desired to push aside the grief in the world. Today she'd choose to be as cheerful as the sun. And if that meant placing the daydream of falling in love to the back of her mind, then so be it. She peered across the Danube River at the ruins of Bratislava Castle. The historic structure had sat like a proud old, crinkled, wise woman. Uncle Emil, her father's brother, had explained that the castle had burned in 1811. Uncle Emil always warned that further harm was also in the Roma's destiny, though no one ever asked him to elaborate. The less said, and therefore the less learned, the better. Like her family and the rest of her *vista*—the encampment of her beloved people—Vonni pushed her uncle's version of the truth aside. She needed to believe in goodness, an easier life, even if it was a mere fantasy.

"Vonni, there you are. Come quickly." That nasal, squeaky-when-stressed tone could only belong to her 25-year-old sister, Antonina. Vonni didn't have to turn around to know that Antonina would remain rooted in place unless she slid from the wall, planted her feet on the ground, and faced her. Her lungs were tight with the questions she wanted to ask of her sister but didn't dare. She grabbed her coat and began to follow her sister like one of the obedient camp dogs following its master.

They were complete opposites. Although Antonina was unmarried and without children, she was normal, unlike Vonni who appeared different from her Roma family and friends. When she was younger, Vonni had convinced herself that she'd been kidnapped. But what kind of prize was she? Her blonde hair had never darkened since birth. Her blue irises didn't resemble the dark brown-black of the countless pairs of eyes that stared curiously at her back home. Her pale flesh didn't match the others' olive skin. All these differences set an invisible word on her forehead: *Błąd*. Mistake. Additionally, her name was wrong—stemming from yew, a tree that offered poisonous berries. Antonina was raven-haired, dark-complexioned and beautiful. She appeared to sparkle even on the dimmest of days or the blackest of nights—no wonder why her name meant "priceless." Despite her parents telling her how much they loved her, at times, it was easier on Vonni's heart to believe she'd been abducted as an infant than to think she was born a mistake.

"Ouch," Vonni cried as her sister pinched her.

"Don't stop now and look about foolishly." Antonina dug her nails further into Vonni's arm. "Come with me immediately. Matka's worried."

At the mention of their mother, Vonni's belly turned to sludge. She rubbed at the churning to calm the disturbance. "What's wrong? Is she sick again?"

"She has news to tell us both."

This summons wasn't good. The men, women, and children of their *vista* always looked out for each other. Their mother hadn't sent her sister to find her and demand her to come home since they were little girls; there had to be an unfortunate reason now.

Vonni searched her mind for plausible explanations. "Have I forgotten a chore? Have I not made enough good luck charm bracelets—does Matka want me to string more?" Trying to match her sister's large strides, sweat rolled down the back of her neck and spread across her arms. A burning itch ignited her right forearm. She scratched as if her life depended on it.

Antonina stopped so abruptly that it took Vonni an extra few steps to realize that her sister was now behind her. Holding her sore arm in her hand like a limp animal, Vonni turned around. "What now? And why the sour face?"

"You."

Typical Antonina—never mincing words. Another proof of how they were complete opposites. "You have a fine, independent mind, my sister. You wouldn't have broken away from your boyfriend just to drag me home unless there was an emergency." Vonni willed her attention away from her fiery arm. She made herself cross both arms and spread her feet as she'd seen her father do in defiance of another's scorn. "I can stay here all day if that's what you want."

That's when Antonina did what Vonni wouldn't have thought her sister capable of—she started to sob. Not a mere dramatic tear or two, enough to irritate Vonni but not cause alarm. No, this was an out-and-out stream of tears that gushed down the usually stoic Antonina's face.

Vonni closed the gap between them and touched her sister's shoulder softly. "What's wrong? Tell me why you're so upset."

Antonina shook her head.

"Please." Vonni tried to sound her gentlest and most caring while her insides heated with impatience. She glanced about, then jutted her chin to the right. "Would you like to sit and talk? We can take advantage of this unusual warmth."

"No time."

Obviously, Antonina wasn't about to divulge what troubled her. Vonni would have to find out for herself and like in the past, she'd probably have to resolve the difficulties herself. "All right, then." She clipped her thumb and index fingers around her sister's slim wrist like a bracelet. "Let's continue home."

As they made their way toward the Starý Most bridge, Vonni fought the temptation to wiggle her sweaty hand into her sister's grip. The most harm Antonina could inflict was to either roll her eyes or chide her behavior. What would it take to soften the ways between them? An earth-shattering miracle? Like Roma boys who were encouraged to be tough and to grow into men not to be underestimated, Antonina stood her ground. Unlike when she sobbed minutes ago, she kept back her emotions and never cared what others thought of her. From one end of the camp to the other, Vonni would never hear the end of it if she begged her sister to hold her hand.

They crossed the Danube, the largest river winding its way through Slovakia as well as other countries on its way to the Black Sea. Seagulls squawked huoh-huoh. As they passed the square of Old Town, life appeared as usual. Children chased each other in play but stopped and stared with wide eyes or fear-lined foreheads at Vonni and Antonina's colorful skirts and blouses, the gold coins embedded in their hair, and the bangles on their wrists and ankles. Grown women, who scurried from one shop to another, hurried away from them with a livelier step. Men lifted their chins and averted their eyes, behavior fueled by jealousy over the fine horses that her father, his brothers, and the other men in their camp owned. This attitude from the others in town, this making of Vonni's people as dirty people who shouldn't be acknowledged, was one of those prejudices she'd tried to block from her mind moments ago. The unfairness of how people treated others always saddened her heart. Weren't they all people wanting the same essentials necessary to live, like food, water, and shelter? It was only manmade definitions that made life ridiculous. She wanted to talk about this with her sister, but Antonina continued to clamp her lips shut, physically blocking further communication between them.

Finally, when they were crossing over the stone road by Saint Michael's Gate, Antonina again made Vonni falter in her steps, this time with news about a bird. She grabbed Vonni by the elbow to steady her. "Clumsy. Watch your feet."

"Never mind scolding me like a mother. What did you say about a bird? I can't believe my ears."

Antonina steered Vonni against a patch of wall between two shops, where they leaned against the bricks that scratched their backs. "That's because you don't want to."

At the most, they'd have a handful of minutes before a patron or shopkeeper ordered them to move on. Vonni thought her usually clipped-speaking sister would hurry through her thoughts, but the way this whole bizarre afternoon was playing out, her doubts doubled in size as the silent seconds dragged by.

Antonina stared aimlessly at the shop window across the road. "It's Tata. He's missing."

Wringing information from Antonina was the equivalent of digging deeper and deeper into a well with a given history of producing little water. Vonni released a slow breath. If she spoke in a quiet, calm tone, her sister would likely respond more favorably. "Yes, with Tata's fancy for disappearing, I can see why Matka's upset. Tell me, again, about the bird. I'm not doubting you—just want to check my own ears. It is odd about a bird flying about this time of the year."

Antonina grunted as if shoving out the truth was not only reliving the nightmare but also making the horror of the situation bigger than a simple superstition. "It was a raven. It flew indoors this morning and sang Tata's name, while you relaxed, staring at your once-upon-a-time dream castle." She pointed to the side of her head. "All you ever do is play fairy princess in your mind. You need to grow up."

"Grow up?" Vonni wanted to shriek. To remind her sister, for the millionth time, that in addition to turning 18—an adult in their parents' eyes—there was no shame in longing for an easier life on earth. To tell precious, delicate Antonina, that she too, would enjoy life better if she'd fill herself with hope and cheer. Vonni glanced at her sister once more. Antonina stood rigid against the wall, her hands crisscrossed over her mouth. Mentally, Vonni shook her head. Unable to tell whether her sister was truly upset or regretted her nasty words, Vonni tried a different approach.

When Antonina slipped her hands down to her sides, Vonni locked fingers with her sister. She jolted from the icy cold touch of her hand. Different too were her sister's eyes, displaying unquestionable dread and fear. All because of foolish superstitions? Contrary to what outsiders to the Roma liked to imagine, Vonni's people didn't believe in magic or curses. But they did have an array of good luck signs and omens indicating bad luck was on its way. To see a raven, and indoors, did not bode well.

"Poor Matka. Poor you." Vonni squeezed Antonina's hand. "A bird in the house during the winter is strange, let alone frightening with it flapping its wings and knocking over bottles or lights or swooping up a necklace. Worse is the raven's message that a death is near. No wonder you and Matka are upset, especially with Tata away."

Antonina wiggled her fingers free from Vonni's grip and cupped her throat. "Who do you think will die? Please don't say Tata."

According to their mother, Tata, their father—Lash, as he was commonly known—and his brothers came from the Polska Roma, outside of Wroclaw on the Oder River. They settled in Bratislava where Lash met Queenie and declared her the most beautiful woman on the planet. Lash was tall, lanky, and street-smart with a penchant to roam, very unlike Queenie's desire to remain home with her family. They fell in love, hard and fast. Queenie couldn't resist the dark-haired man with the boyish grin and loving heart; like a magnet,

Lash couldn't—didn't want to—step away from the petite woman with a ready smile and kindness in her words.

Lash was a hard worker and a decent provider for his family. That was, when he was able to overcome the prejudices against Gypsies—as *gorgios* referred to them. The belief was that they did not want to work, with the consequential attitude that it was useless to offer them a job. When he wasn't busy as a horse trader or used-automobile-parts dealer or knife sharpener, he spent his days—and often nights—defending the meaning of his name: renowned warrior. Her father differed from his five brothers by not bunching his fists; with a stubborn determination he wanted to wear his opponent down by his hard-headed actions and way with words. No one wanted to argue with him.

Queenie was practically a child bride at the age of 16, forced to leave her family and move in with her new husband and his extended family. Her attempts at getting her husband to do the things he didn't want to do were a waste of her energy. A contradictory woman, she lived more in fear of how to carry on if death came for her husband first, despite others seeing her as strong and courageous.

Across from where Vonni and Antonina stood, a beet-faced bald man stepped out of his shop clapping two pots together. "Move on, you two. Go away, beggars."

As if one, Vonni and Antonina sighed together. They'd heard the insults before. No arguments would be good enough to convince this man that the Roma weren't beggars, or thieves, or the source of disease and other contagions. As it were, the *gorgios* relished in labeling them as Gypsy tramps, as if branded livestock. Rumors had spread through the years that like livestock, these Gypsies were also expendable. They served no purpose other than the occasional cheap deal. Certainly, there were also non-Roma who resorted to scrounging, stealing, or begging. But to speak this truth was useless and usually got a Roma locked up behind bars.

"Let's continue home," Antonina said and hurriedly strode away with those dainty feet of hers.

"Wait up," Vonni called as she raced after her sister. "I've thought more about the raven. Where was Tata at the time the bird visited?"

"I don't have patience for you," Antonina said over her shoulder.

"Where Tata was may make a difference."

"Matka said Tata was the only camp man out of sight when the bird visited. I wasn't about to upset her with more questions than she could handle."

Vonni understood her sister's absent words: I don't know, I was too nervous to ask, too anxious to find out. As they left Bratislava proper, Vonni swallowed back the last bit of conversation itching to bubble out. They wove their way over the narrow sandy paths and as they heard voices of women and children coming from the other direction, ducked behind bushes, waiting for them to pass. Vonni breathed easier. Soon enough they'd arrive home, back to their own *vista*. Her people had beautiful dark eyes, gleaming hearts, and a love of family so large and fierce that others should weep with jealousy. That was, if these outsiders would take the time to get to know the Roma rather than paint pictures of hackneyed and false people.

The number of people standing outside her family's house alerted Vonni that her world had tilted far from the daydream life of princesses and castles she'd enjoyed. Outsiders to the Roma believed an untruth: Vonni's people were travelers, moving constantly from one place to another. It was as if "home" was a dirty word. For years, governments throughout Europe had ordered the Roma to become sedentary. Stay put. Settle. Couldn't be simpler. Or more complex, considering employment opportunities were withheld. This *why don't you work but let's take away your rights to hold jobs like the rest of society* was a constant battle of contradiction and headache. Lately, the tensions between the Roma and *gorgios* had thickened. Where it would lead was a subject often talked about by their father, his brothers, and their friends.

Home consisted of a two-bedroom wooden house with a small kitchen, and a detached barn for the goats, chickens, and their father's two horses. Roma life may have evolved around fostering close family ties, but Vonni detested sharing a room with her sister.

As if she were allergic to the confines of the house, Vonni spent much of her time in the open air.

Now, their uncles, aunts, and cousins blocked the entranceway and stood at solemn attention. In control of who entered the house, Old Mina—the oldest woman of their clan, possibly of the whole of earth—sat in the sole chair beside the door, a quilt of kaleidoscope colors draped over her knees. Of course, that meant her extended family of four daughters, their husbands, and grandchildren with their parents also waited. Matka's wails cut through the air.

Vonni gulped and faced Antonina. "What should we do? Never mind that we live here—we can't move through this crowd."

"Let us in," Antonina shouted.

Her sister's sudden and uncharacteristic demand jolted not only Vonni but the crowd. One by one, they stepped aside. Hand in hand, Vonni and Antonina made their way to the door. To catch Old Mina's attention, Vonni bent down to the woman's eye level. In another universe, she might have felt a fool for asking permission to enter her own home, but respect was a foremost expectation between *vista* members. Without hesitation, Old Mina lifted her blue-purple veiny hands and gestured for them to go indoors. They darted to their parents' bedroom.

"Oh, Matka." The words nearly caught in Vonni's dry mouth as she reached her mother, who was bunched up tight on the side of the bed that she shared with their father. His untouched side, with a fluffed-up pillow, looked so empty, as if it could swallow their mother in its void. Vonni sat on the bed and weaved her fingers gently through her mother's shiny black hair. "Tell me what's upsetting you."

Her mother turned enough that Vonni could glimpse her red eyes. Vonni had never seen either parent cry, and though her mother's tears made her want to cry as well, she concentrated on helping to lift her mother's spirits. "Antonina told me about the bird. You must be nervous since Tata is away. Do you know where he is? Would you like me to find him and bring him home?"

Matka propped herself up on an elbow. A grimace wrinkled her face.

Vonni reached for her mother's shoulder. "Let me help you sit more comfortably." She glanced at her sister, narrowing her eyes in the way sisters had shared secret messages since the beginning of time. *Don't stand around like a ninny.* It worked. Antonina fluffed Matka's pillow, propped it back against the headboard, and asked if she'd like a drink of water.

Matka shook off the offer. "Bring Tata home before death claims him."

Vonni silently cursed their controlling superstitious ways. "It was just a bird."

Both her mother and Antonina's eyes shot open. Their brows lifted in angular peaks.

"Don't say nonsense," Matka hissed. "Do you want to curse us more?"

"No." Vonni wrapped her arms around her middle, searching her mind for a way to gain control of this awful conversation. "Where did Tata say he's going?"

"To a *grunter's* house in the next village. He doesn't tell me the names or places of the people he works for. That's why I worry."

"Did he take one of his horses?"

"No." A lone sob escaped her thin lips. "I'm to become a widow. We'll be beggars before the week's end. A bird, particularly a raven, is never wrong."

"Now look what you've done," Antonina murmured into Vonni's ear. "You've made her think about Tata dying."

"She didn't need coaxing," Vonni said through gritted teeth.

"Hush up," Matka said. "My ears are working fine."

Vonni turned away from the other two and thought about the *grunters*, older *gorgios* that lived outside of Roma encampments. Like several other men, Vonni's father supplemented their income by performing small tasks for these old folks such as helping in their garden, tending to cows or horses, or home repairs. Demanding his privacy and the trust of his family, her father never left any contact information. With the complication of the stupid bird flying into the house during his absence, this left Vonni and her family in turmoil.

Vonni tried to wrap her thoughts around the different possibilities. With several of their men, she could lead a search for her father. She had a photograph of him stashed under her mattress and could circulate it around Bratislava to see whether anyone might recognize him. She could also try to talk sense into her mother by reassuring her that Lash would soon arrive home. Once again, they would be Lash and Queenie, the happiest Roma couple ever.

"Matka," Antonina said, her tone strong enough to power over the hysteric cries. "I'll look for Tata. It's my fault."

What revelation was this?

Her sister reached for one of Matka's ribbons from the bedside table, twisted her hair in a quick braid, and tied it in a bun with the ribbon. "If I had remained home like you asked—and not visited with Stephan as you forbade—I would have seen the bird fly in and would have batted the horrible creature outdoors before he had a chance to do us harm."

"Stay here." Matka seized Antonina's wrist. "It's not your fault—it's no one's. It's only normal to want to spend time with your charming suitor. It was time for death to visit, and your poor Tata is the only one of us unaccounted for. You can't leave me. I won't have you and him go in death's presence."

"Your words won't hold me back." Antonina spun and ran outdoors, not once looking Vonni's way.

"Vonni, you too must search."

Her mother's request set Vonni shaking. "Of course, I will. I'll find both Tata and Antonina. I won't come home until I find them and bring them back. I promise on my life." A torrent of her mother's wails accompanied her as she ran from the room.

4

Once out the door and past the crowd of family and friends, Vonni flew with not one glance over her shoulder. She ignored Uncle Emil's shouts and she stopped her ears to five-year-old Adora, who was more like a baby sister to her than her friend's daughter, when she cried, "Wait, Vonni. I want to go, too." She continued on, daring herself to take one step after the other. Like a determined soldier on an assignment, she marched on. The voices of her loved ones finally faded.

For her mother's sake, she'd be the bravest she'd ever been and would think of her family rather than her own comfort. She'd find her father, and when she located him, she'd find her sister beside him. It would be that simple. Those two were more like old friends than father and daughter. She'd convince them to return home with her and never leave again. The strength of their people rested in remaining together. A short while ago she'd filled her head with thoughts of meeting the love of her life. Now, after seeing her mother upset, all she cared about was reuniting them.

She never counted on the wind picking up. By the time she reached the town square, the temperature was dropping considerably, and she regretted not taking her winter coat. After pausing a few seconds to button her blouse all the way up, she checked each alleyway and peered through the windows of the shops to see whether her father and Antonina were inside talking with the shopkeeper. They were nowhere. The sky darkened with heavy storm clouds, but she convinced herself they were full of rain, not snow, and hurried on.

Following a hunch that her father might have gone to visit his last customers in Petržalka, she scurried down the lanes that past churches, shops, and schools and out the gate. A few minutes later, she arrived at *Hviezdoslavovo námestie*, the Square of Hviezdoslav, previously part of Hungary for a thousand years. She'd heard stories that the square was named after a late 19th-century poet, lawyer, and politician, Pavol Országh-Hviezdoslav. Upon learning of this writer, she'd fancied herself as taking up pen and paper and creating tales and poems about faraway places or set right here in Bratislava and about the Roma, but her mother had discouraged her. Women were made with bodies to bear children and hearts to take care of them, she'd said. Men were made to work with their hands, they had the imagination and foresight to carry out their dreams. Vonni thought her mother, imprisoned by her fears, lacked inspiration. Yet, the other Roma women also thought this way. Out of respect for her dear mother, she wouldn't argue. Besides, with missing family members and trouble brewing with none-too-faraway Germany, her dreams were inconsequential in society's eyes. However, she refused to surrender to the silly notion that she couldn't choose the path of her own life. Once, she'd shared these thoughts with Antonina, but her sister had retorted with a nasty laugh followed by cutting words. "See, Vonni. You're a dreamy, starry-eyed little girl. Adults see the truth for what it is, and they don't bother changing their ways. Children, on the other hand, always play pretend." Vonni refused to listen to her sister, or anyone for that matter, that dashed her hopes and dreams.

She arrived in Petržalka, the largest borough of Bratislava. On the right bank of the Danube, it shared a land border with Austria. The Nagy brothers were three unmarried *gorgios* with a reputation for secreting their personal lives, including what they did for work. They weren't the nicest of folks, but owed her father a handsome amount of pay for servicing their stable of horses. Those three had lots of money yet didn't want to hand it over to her father. Eerily, their houses neighbored each other, an encampment of sorts. No one gave them grief over this, but the Roma were ridiculed and mistrusted because they too often chose to live peacefully within their own clusters of family groups.

Once, when Vonni asked why one group of people was against another, she received mixed reactions. Papo—the old man her family affectionately called grandfather—covered his mouth and laughed. As an attempt to teach her the way of people rather than a rebuke, the women chided her that she'd find out on her own about this never-ending friction. But her father? He cupped her cheeks, peered adoringly into her eyes, and murmured that he hoped she would never have to learn about that awful truth. And that was why she had to find her father: he always kept her best interest close to his heart. Without question, she knew he loved her for whom she was as he'd expressed on her latest birthday: "You were a fine, bright child and now you're a brilliant, capable young woman."

A barking dog announced her arrival at the Nagy complex. When it bolted toward her, Vonni dropped her arms to her side and willed herself to relax, the extreme opposite of what she wanted to do. Familiar with both the friendly and always-on-guard dogs at her own *vista*, she was aware that dogs were smart and had keen senses. A dog could absorb one's composure—or lack of—at first encounter. Not wanting the approaching animal to pick up on her pounding heart, she inhaled deeply and slowly let her breath out. Calm down. If I want the dog to relax, then I must relax. She pivoted sideways and averted her eyes from the dog standing beside her, relieved but uncertain why the dog had stopped its fussing. Then she heard a commanding voice: "Andil!"

The dog's name was Angel? Not the best name for this mongrel at all. She peered up, thankful to see a gray-bearded, tall man. He'd pulled the dog to his side and ordered him to sit and to be quiet. "He won't hurt you," he said.

"His teeth bite hard, I'm sure."

"You're the intruder, not my dog. What do you want?" The man crossed his arms. "You look familiar. I can't place you, though."

Vonni stood straight and lifted her head in pride. She peered into the stranger's eyes, though she refused to glance at the dog. "I'm Lash Kazik's daughter, Vonni. I'm looking for my father and sister."

"Lash's daughter?" These judgments always twisted Vonni in knots. She steeled against his following words. "But you're blonde and white like the moon. Did he adopt you or what?"

Vonni understood what he meant because goodness, wild Gypsies went about stealing children day after day and selling them for desperately needed money because Gypsies had no morals. Just for once, she'd like to live one day without falling into the pigeonhole of how her beloved people were assumed to look and act. "I'm my parents' youngest," she replied. Although acting out of spite wasn't her natural tendency, Vonni chose to make the most of his fixation on her blonde hair. She fluffed her hair dramatically; her locks flipped over her shoulders. When he grimaced, she imagined he pictured her father kidnapping a blonde baby girl in Scandinavia. "My father's missing—as well as my sister—and I thought to look here."

"Look elsewhere. They're not here, nor at my brothers' homes. Believe me, with Lash's last shoddy work here, he's not welcome back. Do relay my words to your father, if you should ever see the Great Kazik again." He spat on the ground then waved her away. With the dog bounding off in the direction of the house, the Nagy brother took a step away, then stopped and faced her with glaring eyes.

She had no problem understanding his nonverbal command to get off his property. And to keep off of his land forever. He—who hadn't deemed it necessary to share his first name—was waiting for her to leave. Scramble she did, before she told him exactly what she thought of him and his worthless dog.

Back on the dirt road, she faced two options. Go back to her *vista* and confess to her mother that after she'd met up with a Nagy brother, she wanted to call it quits. She couldn't do that. She was Vonni Kazik; surrendering was an unfamiliar concept that she had no desire to embrace. Instead, believing her father was no longer in Bratislava or elsewhere in the country, she chose the other direction: the unknown. She'd find her father and sister. And, like she'd promised her mother, she wouldn't return home without them both. Surely, she'd meet a man or woman who would have seen them. Two people simply couldn't disappear. But in which direction should she head? Directly north lay Poland. She would have to cross the Tatra Mountains to reach this generational homeland. Memories washed over her of uncles telling of the family's daring crossing of these mountains and the harsh conditions they encountered. She remembered that as a young child she'd thought they were merely scary campfire stories, told to frighten the little ones. At the time, she imagined a trip of this extent to be an exciting voyage, on the level of how the ancient Roma had left their native India to seek a better life. Now, without the proper gear, food, and wilderness survival skills, it seemed much too dangerous.

To the west of Bratislava, Austria called her. Her father had worked for several Austrian *gorgios* through the years and with work documentation, had never encountered trouble crossing the border. The country was practically their country as well, considering how commonplace it was for people to visit. A person might remember seeing him if Vonni showed his photograph and added a little description. Then again, rumors had darkened the air lately of the changing political climate. Talk had already traveled down to Bratislava of the difficulties the German ruler was inflicting upon the Roma in his country. Was it unsafe to leave Bratislava? She'd never had complications before—her family were travelers, called that for a reason. The urge to roam flowed in her father's blood. Although no one was around to see her, Vonni shrugged her shoulders. It made sense that her dear father, the fearless Lash, would follow-up on either a work lead or to collect pay—he always did his best to care for his family—and it wouldn't have surprised her if he'd entered Austria without thinking twice to share his plans with others. Austria it would be for her as well.

She needed to think like Lash—a grown man, proud husband,

and father, one of the Kazik brothers with excellent standing within his community—and choose the path he would most likely travel. At the same time, she had to put herself in her sister Antonina's shoes: a loving and obedient daughter, but not necessarily daring or persistent, and with little endurance to see a task to its end.

Then, it came to her. Honza Pasek, the tinsmith. He always traveled back and forth between Austria and the Czechoslovak Republic. For a *gorgio*, he had taken a liking to her father, and upon learning that Lash was missing, would likely offer to help her. Honza would figure out how to transport her across the border. It wasn't as if a war had just broken out and the borders were closed.

When Vonni knocked on Honza's door with the news of her father and sister's disappearance, deep grooves wrinkled the man's forehead. With a promise to help Vonni to get through the Austrian border, Honza hitched up his two horses to his weathered old buggy and told her to hop on the seat beside him. As for the authorities at the border, he doubted they'd question him, but if a concern rose, Vonni would claim she was his daughter accompanying him to help him with his work. With his wife ill, he couldn't travel long, but he was more than happy to assist her in this time of need.

"Will the border guards believe I'm your daughter?"

"What? Is there a sudden war that no one has told me about?" His words nearly matched her own thoughts of minutes ago. However, the always cautious man shoved his oldest daughter's identity papers into Vonni's hands. Sadly, Adela had passed two years earlier from an illness she'd struggled with since birth.

"But I'm not your daughter. I'm Roma—won't they know that? Won't they care?"

Honza reached for her hair, unfastened her gold and violet ribbons and gold coins. He then asked for her to take off the bangles from her wrists. He stuffed them in his pocket. "You may be Roma, but with your blonde hair, you won't be easily labeled as the beautiful

Gypsy you are. Just don't wear these colorful ribbons and bracelets. I'll keep them for you—when you come back to Bratislava, see me, and I'll return them." His fatherly kindness touched her heart. "If Adela was with us now, I know she'd be pleased. Besides, it's just for an emergency—if someone should stop us and ask. I often go back and forth into Austria, and no one bothers to ask me for proof of who I am. That may be the way in Germany, but that's a world away from our homes."

"Hopefully, that won't ever change," she replied. Although she wouldn't be surprised if identity verification was mandated throughout all countries, consistently and with no exceptions.

Honza took Vonni to Kittsee, a good enough place to start her search since it was only 13 kilometers from Bratislava—a tolerable walking distance for a man like Lash, with his robust constitution. As she was about to leave the buggy, he reached for her shoulder and told her to wait a moment. When she turned around, he pressed a few korunas into the palm of her hand. "Take this. If you don't find Lash, though I'm confident you will, you can use this money to purchase a train ticket."

"I've never been on a train. Is it safe? Do I need special papers? Where would I go?"

"Do not worry—Adela's papers will work fine, and you will be safe." He paused, pulling his chin. "As for direction, my friend Lash has repeatedly told me about his work dealings in Vienna—not far by train."

Vienna? Her father had never mentioned traveling to Vienna, let alone working in that distant city. Then again, the way Honza was talking, her father—who worked hard to provide for his family, despite what the *gorgios* thought—would have visited for either owed payment or to obtain a new job.

"I feel foolish."

"Why?" Honza asked gently.

"I worry about my father rather than trusting all will be fine. If it weren't for the bird, we probably would have waited a few days to see if he'd come home." Honza's brows lifted. "It's a superstition we have

—that birds flying into a house means death is on the way to a family member."

He patted her shoulder. "If your mother was sick with worry, and told you to search for your father, then you did the right thing. Now, go make the most of this day before night falls. If you don't go to Vienna, you can easily find a ride home. You watch. Soon enough you'll be reunited with your father. I have a hunch that once you find Lash, you'll find your sister too." With a wave of goodbye, he urged the horses forward.

Fortunately, Vonni spoke and understood German well enough that she easily spent the next few hours stopping random people she passed on the street, showing her father's photograph and asking if they'd seen him. Many shook their heads, several ignored her, and a few smiled compassionately. Just when dusk crept up, she nearly stumbled into a man who righted her before she fell to the ground.

"Yes, I've seen this man," the stranger replied with a toothless smile when Vonni showed her father's photograph. "He was heading in the direction of Vienna."

Ah, Vienna. So, Honza's insights about her father stood correct. She started walking toward the Kittsee train station. With luck, the next train for Vienna would soon arrive. She rubbed at the chill numbing her arms, glancing warily at the thickening clouds, signaling a storm she was ill-prepared for was fast on its way. A black Volkswagen slowed to a halt next to her. Her father, who always dreamed of one day owning a car, had told her that Volkswagen— which means the "people's car"—was founded by the German Labor Front. Hitler then quickly grabbed the company and operated it as a state-owned manufacturer, enabling the common man to afford a car. That was, if he saved up his money.

The middle-aged driver of the Volkswagen cranked down the passenger window. "*Ahoj!*" he said in greeting, surprising her with the Slovak word for hello. His cheerful tone relaxed her. "You look lost. May I help?"

"I'm going to the train station."

"You're heading in the wrong direction. I can offer you a ride."

Vonni grew nervous but scolded herself. He may be a stranger, but he offered to help her, and though she was a stranger to him, he evidently trusted her. No one else was coming forward with an offer of assistance. If he could trust her, she should trust him. With the weather uncooperative and night quickly descending, her options were few. "If you're offering to give me a ride to the station, then yes, that would be nice."

He grinned and again the tension eased in her tight muscles. "I'm heading toward Vienna. Is that where you're traveling to?"

This couldn't have been coincidental. The stars had to be behind this good fortune.

"Yes." She patted her skirt pocket that contained the money her father's friend had given her. With this offer of a ride to Vienna, she wouldn't have to spend any cash, so when she found her father, she could purchase two train tickets to Bratislava to return home sooner than later. She flashed a smile. "That's exactly where I'm going. Ďakujem."

He pushed open the passenger door in invitation. "Get in."

Vonni wanted to ask his name, but since he hadn't shared it, she kept back her curiosity and remained quiet. She slipped into the vehicle. A smell of fried onions and sour cheese reached her nostrils, and she tried her best not to react. Her parents had brought her up with good manners. However, in addition to his stench, she didn't like his looks. She hated to think this way. Most of her own people didn't own a plentiful supply of clothing or the means to easily wash them. While his shabby shirt and stained pants made her nervous, it was the crumbs in his silver and white mustache that she found most unsettling. She pushed aside these disagreeable aspects that she'd failed to take notice of before she got into his car. He might have seen her father. Might have offered a ride to him earlier that day. Because her parents had also taught her not to be demanding, she waited until ten or so kilometers had whipped by before waving her father's photograph before the nameless man.

"Have you seen my father? He's gone missing. If you have information—"

The man slammed on the brakes; the tires squealed. "Time for you to go." His gray beady eyes grew narrower, and she shoved open the door. He grabbed her arm and pushed her against the seat, pressing his forearm against her throat. "I give you a ride. You give me money."

"But I—"

He pushed harder. She couldn't speak. Within seconds, she wouldn't be able to breathe.

"My car. My rules. I won't ask you again. Understand?" His last word flew from his mouth with spittle hitting her face.

Ask? They weren't at a party, and he wasn't asking whether she preferred meat or chicken. She could try stamping on his foot and jumping out of the car, but he had her where he wanted—and money wasn't worth holding onto when it came to choosing life or death. This stranger was certainly no Roma. Once home, she'd never leave her people again. She stared at the stranger and managed to give the slightest of nods.

"Good. I'll let you go, but if you make a move to run without turning over your money, I'll make it worse for you."

As he slid his arm from her throat, he leaned closer. His breath reeked worse than the fried onions she'd smelled earlier. She'd never eat that vile bulbous vegetable again, even if her life depended on it. Without another word, she reached into her skirt for the few coins given to her. Not wanting to touch him, she dropped them one by one into his waiting, dirty hand.

"Go!" he ordered.

She jumped out the door. No questions asked. She was once again on her own, and that was fine with her.

Unfamiliar with the roads in Austria, Vonni had only plodded a few short steps when the clouds broke open and a heavy cold rain began to fall. It was only a matter of minutes before it would turn into sleet and she'd be forced to take shelter. Ill-prepared for surviving the rough outdoors, she took stock of her surroundings. Trees. Pastures. And one glorious barn about a ten-minute walk away. She reached the tattered farm and found a horse and a donkey standing in the center of a paddock. The white house with battered black shutters was unlit; no smoke billowed from the central chimney. Whether the occupants were home or not was a guess. At least, unlike in the Nagy household, no barking dog was chasing after her for sport. She sloshed through a muddy path toward the barn, not caring if she'd find hogs, cows, or a goat or two. She hoped to find a pile of hay to burrow under and fall asleep. She'd deal with tomorrow when it arrived.

Vonni opened her eyes and blinked at the gray-blue daylight. Someone was shaking her shoulder.

"Hello," an older woman greeted her, her white hair just short of reaching her shoulders. "*Sprichst du Deutsch?*"

Her best option was to deny her native Romany language. "*Ja*, a little German."

"Where you from, *Kind*?" The woman narrowed her eyes when Vonni flinched. "Yes, compared to my eighty years, you're a child. Don't act like I've insulted you. You're the one hunkering down in my barn."

Considering her ill luck with the strangers she'd encountered since leaving home, Vonni thought to twist her story a bit. "I'm from Bratislava. I'm on my way to Vienna to search for my sister, who has run away to taste city life."

"Vienna? You're heading in the wrong direction." The old woman's voice creaked like a door slowly shutting. She pointed over her shoulder. "Vienna's that way, northwest from here. You're in Bruck an der Leitha."

That was the second time within two days that she had been told that she was going in the wrong direction. In hope this woman was a more caring soul than the man she'd encountered, Vonni repeated the town's name, tripping over the syllables. She looked down when the woman laughed.

"Pshaw." The stranger swatted the air with a hand. "You better get used to me laughing since it's better than crying. Now tell me, when did you arrive here?"

Vonni rubbed at her sleep-crusted eyes, trying to wake up. "Last night, when it began to snow."

"That was the time I settled down under the bedcovers." The woman glanced to her right. "You must have been exhausted—from what I can see, my girls didn't disturb your slumber."

Vonni followed the woman's gaze to an entirely white cow in the far barn stall. Closer, two black chickens strutted about. A sly grin lifted her lips. "I guess I was tired."

"I suspect after a hike from Bratislava you would be. My name is Clara Gruber. Clara is fine."

Vonni wasn't about to correct the woman and explain how she hadn't walked from Bratislava but had been given two rides. Let her believe what she wanted—perhaps, in this case, the old woman would pity her and show a modicum of kindness. They'd reached the point in polite conversation where she needed to share her name. The only documentation she had was the one that Honza had given her, stating falsely that she was Adela Pasek. Yet, on a mission to find both her father and sister, she needed to inquire about them—at least, her sister in order to maintain the fabricated part of her story.

"I'm Vonni."

"Pretty name, Vonni. What's your last name?"

The woman's stern tone caught Vonni off guard. She instinctively clammed up.

"Fine, then. Vonni will do nicely. Come keep me company over breakfast." Clara scrutinized her from head to toe. "I have a change of clothing to lend you as well."

"I'm ashamed to say, but I have no means to pay you back."

"My hospitality has no cost. With the way it's snowing out, you won't be going anywhere, probably for days. These late winter snowstorms can be relentless. A change into dry, warm clothes will do you good." Clara walked on ahead, never once looking to see if Vonni followed. That she did, scrambling like a child after her grandmother, not that she'd ever admit she was needy and dependent on a stranger's mercy. The wise women of her *vista* always told her to never question a slice of good fate.

Clara hadn't exaggerated the snow falling steadily, the white blanket a good twelve or more centimeters deep. Her heavy boots made nice impressions for Vonni to step into as they headed toward the house; the wind's shove against her back encouraged a lively step. A glance to her left to the now empty paddock had her questioning where the horse and donkey had vanished until she saw the gray outline of a run-in shed against the blowing snow. She stopped short of plowing into Clara at the doorway to the house.

The woman crossed her arms and looked over her glasses and down her nose. "Don't concern yourself with my old nags. Together, we've survived plenty of long winters." She pushed open the door and told Vonni to step in quickly so they could keep the warmth in and the cold out.

The house stood humbly unadorned, cool though warmer and dryer than outdoors. Wind rattled the heavy-curtained windows. As Vonni entered the kitchen, a cat's loud purr served as a greeting. The animal was seated contently in the center of the table, its tan and white tail wrapped snuggly around its body. Vonni scratched under his chin and was rewarded with a head bump against her fingers. "He's cute."

"It's a she."

"What's her name?"

Clara winked. "Cat. I'll gather those warm clothes and shoes for you to change into and will leave them on the bed. Stay put." Seconds later, she appeared and pointed down the hallway. "Go change in the first room on the right, my bedroom. The only bedroom. You'll be sleeping on the sofa." Vonni opened her mouth, but Clara hushed her. "Use your common sense, girl. It's an awful storm—can't see but a bit ahead. You can't carry on like it's a spring day, family or no family to find." Without shooing Cat off the table, Clara poured milk from a glass bottle into a saucer and offered it to the animal. "You're smiling again," Clara said. "Good. Apparently, you also like cats—we'll get along."

Without further hesitation, Vonni left the kitchen and entered Clara's bedroom. A plain room, it had a single bed shoved against the wall and piled high with three knitted afghans of different colors. An old dresser painted multiple times judging by the chipped areas of paint showing the previous colors of brown, white, and a dingy red sat in the corner topped by a dust-covered stack of books. A gray jumper, two white blouses, a green sweater, two pairs of woolen socks, and undergarments were strewn across the bed. Thankfully, a pair of slip-on shoes that looked like they'd fit were beside the bed, inviting her to wear them. She peeled off her soggy clothes and slipped into the fresh dry ones. She then made her way back into the kitchen.

Clara stood by a pot on the stove. "Drape those wet clothes on the stand in the corner there, and I'll take care of them after we eat."

Vonni nodded and sat down, but then jumped to her feet. "Shall I help?"

"Not necessary, at least not today." Clara ladled porridge from a pot into two bowls and set them on the table. The cat ignored them in favor of washing her paws now that she'd finished lapping her milk. "It's room temperature. I can heat it if you prefer."

"This is fine."

Clara sat down opposite Vonni and stroked the cat. "Would you like hot tea to chase the chill away?"

"Yes, please."

Clara didn't move. Instead, she leaned over the table. "Now, tell me your full name. I'm most curious to know who I'm putting up as a guest under my roof."

"You live alone, then?" As soon as the nosy question flew from her mouth, Vonni slapped a hand over her mouth. "Sorry for not minding my business," she mumbled around her fingers.

"I've lived alone for several years now." Clara's gaze strayed momentarily to the sole window over a sink with a hand pump that reminded Vonni of her family's kitchen. A pang of homesickness streaked through her chest. "My husband," Clara continued, "died five years after we married; two months after our son was born."

Clara didn't look like a person who needed another to define, protect, or to keep her company, but Vonni was relieved for Clara's sake that she at least had someone to love and who loved her back. And a little baby to love and to cherish? Vonni glanced about for a framed portrait.

"You won't find a trace of my husband, Franz, here. A young man when the Great War began, he was conscripted into the Austro-Hungarian army."

"He was killed?"

"Not in combat—one of the lucky ones, supposedly. Franz was killed on his journey home after the war when a fellow soldier jumped him for his wallet. That worthless soldier that took my husband's life must have been a Jew."

Vonni held back questions and retorts. Just because one person was a bad apple didn't make the whole bucket of them rotten. That was what her mother always said upon encountering a *gorgio* barking his prejudice against the Roma. Jews, Roma. What was the difference when it came to being on the receiving end of hatred? At this point, though, it would be best not to address the prejudice spewing from her host's lips. Her mother's words rang in her ears. *Politeness is essential, my sweet daughter*. "That's sad. Is that why you don't have mementos around, because it's too much to bear?"

"Goodness, girl. That's a lot to judge me by. Never got around to professional photographs. It's my biggest regret."

"Vonni Kazik." She'd shared her full and true name without worrying—as she did now—that it didn't match the identity papers she carried. Then, she remembered Clara hadn't asked for her papers upon first meeting her. She breathed a little easier until the older woman leaned back into her chair, her brows lifting in question. Vonni's arms pricked with gooseflesh. "Kazik's my family name. Do you recognize it?" She was about to ask if Clara had seen her father, but remembered she'd only mentioned her sister. "Have you seen my sister? Her name is Antonina."

5

Germany, January 10, 1943. Elsa could not hold still a minute longer. With the pain in her ankle subsiding and the snow finally ceasing, it was time for her to leave her room for a little stroll. If she could tolerate it, she'd find her way downstairs and step outdoors for a breath of fresh air, the cool against her cheek a welcome balm. Although the guest room was pleasant enough with its cheerful yellow and red pansy-print wallpaper, she hadn't been outside its four walls since she'd been carried upstairs by Erich when she passed out. He was the only one who visited her, bringing her trays of steaming hot food and tea, the likes she hadn't enjoyed in years—ironically not since she and her family had fled Berlin back in 1939.

As she swung her feet off the bed, her thoughts strayed to Erich. Along with meals, he brought little surprises. A slim volume of poetry. A short-story collection by Thomas Mann. Five scrumptious chocolates on a fine blue china dish; he made her vow to keep both the candies and the dish secret from his mother. Once, he'd pushed the bedroom door open and carried a portable Victor phonograph player. At first, she'd mistaken the machine for a small suitcase, but then she had seen that he also held a few paper sleeves of records in his other hand.

"With my family away for the afternoon, I wanted to surprise you with cheerful music." He'd cranked up the machine, and the lively tune of Fritz Kreisler's "Gypsy Caprice" filled the room with an atmosphere of holiday cheer that instantly brightened up her day. She shared with him that she'd never heard Kreisler's music and declared the composer her new favorite. Then Erich did the one thing she least expected—warned her to never tell his parents about the recording she'd just heard. The jubilant mood between them sobered. Gone was the warmth within her that had provided for an easy smile. Gone was the joyful spark in Erich's eyes. He said that his parents liked Wagner, though he didn't elaborate about his own preferences. "Best not to discuss it," he murmured, as if others might be listening.

"When will I meet your father? He must have arrived home by now."

Erich remained silent for a long stretch, and she believed he wouldn't reply. He then mumbled something as he packed up the phonograph.

"Can you repeat that?"

"I'm not sure whether you would want me to."

She grinned, hoping to keep the light mood they'd both enjoyed together until then. "Silly, Erich. Of course, I want to understand what you have to say."

"You don't recall what my mother or I mentioned about my father?"

She shook her head. "I must have blocked it when I passed out right before the doctor was summoned." She fingered the mahogany Victor sitting on the bedside stand. "Should I? I find it peculiar that your parents haven't visited me. Am I that unwelcomed here?"

Without a trace of a smile, he replied, "If you were that unwelcome, believe me, you wouldn't be here right now, no matter what state of health you were in."

Unsure how to take that, she tried again from a different perspective. "Sure, this is a huge house, but it's odd that I haven't heard one peep from your family."

"This room is on the third floor of a back wing, one my family has no use for. It's perfect for privacy."

The word "privacy" hadn't been misspoken or exaggerated. Elsa wondered what troubled her more: the fact that Erich's folks had avoided her, or the mysterious comment about his father.

Enough thoughts of Erich and his odd family! In wanting to embrace the day as best as her bum ankle would permit, relieved from verifying just that morning that she was not pregnant from Dirk, she hobbled to the dresser and withdrew the clothes supplied by Erich's mother. Not that Elsa was fussy, but she suspected the plain clothes did not belong to Frau Friedrich. Although the woman might have been close-lipped to the extreme and did her best to avoid her, she'd been gracious enough to provide a few outfits and sleepwear to use during her stay, and Elsa was thankful. Whose clothes they were originally was a different matter, a concern Elsa pushed away. She couldn't afford to be nosy. Dressed and ready to go, she moved as fast as she dared, happy not to experience much pain. She was healing faster than the good doctor had estimated. Just when she was about to slip on her shoes, she heard a knock at the door. The door pushed open.

"Oh, pardon," came a quick utterance from a woman carrying a stack of folded towels in her arms. She was about Elsa's age. Although Elsa didn't plan on remaining here past her convalescence, she could certainly use a friend in this odd house. She recalled seeing this woman when she'd first regained consciousness. "Are you Adela?"

The woman nodded, her blonde hair flipping behind one shoulder. Good, she apparently understood German. They wouldn't have a problem communicating. Elsa gestured to the chair beside the bed. "I'd love some company—another woman to talk to. Stay for a few minutes, why don't you?"

"Oh, no. I'm a servant." Adela pointed to Elsa, then herself, and back to Elsa. "Verboten."

"I won't tell," Elsa said, smiling. She watched Adela place the towels on the chair she'd been invited to sit on, then starting to back out of the room. "Wait. I have a question."

"Yes? What may I do for you?"

Elsa made herself overcome the awkwardness of asking about personal hygiene matters—she certainly wasn't a little girl any longer. Dirk had seen to that. "I'm in need of feminine hygiene products." A small lift of Adela's right brow indicated the woman understood her reference. "How may I obtain them?"

"I'll get them for you right away. If you should leave the room, I'll set them on your bed. No other staff member is permitted to enter the room but myself."

"Thank you, that's a relief." It certainly was—she didn't want to ask Erich about those personal necessities. "So, you won't keep me company?"

Adela, without explanation, slipped out the door.

How unfortunate. Elsa wanted—needed—another woman close to her own age to talk with. She imagined asking Adela if she'd like to accompany her on a walk—just long enough to exchange pleasantries and stretch her sore legs. Not long enough to keep her from her work and to get her into trouble. What kind of place was this if a servant couldn't be permitted to enjoy a few minutes of leisure? With endless questions riddling her mind, she reached for her notebook and pen.

Dear Mama,

My life has taken unexpected twists and turns. Forced to leave my last residence, a young man, Erich, found me alone on the street, in need of medical attention for a hurt ankle. He brought me to his parents' grand house in Germany. Yes, Germany! They're seeing to my physical recovery and personal needs. I have lots of good food— food I haven't enjoyed in a long time. His family is aloof, to say the least. I have yet to meet Erich's father. Although I'm thankful I didn't wind up someplace worse, my circumstances leave me lonely, frightened, and wanting to see you, Papa, and Krista.

Speaking of Papa... Forgive me. My eyes are again watering with tears as my mind is twisting in emotion faster than I can write. I thought of Papa last night, remembering the last time when he told Krista and me the tale of Hansel and Gretel. Although we were certainly too old for bedtime stories, this was the first night after the German occupation. I must admit I was scared. Who wasn't? But Papa, the kind person and protector he is (was? I pray not!), asked me to set an example of bravery for Krista, though before I could say yes or no, I had voiced my fears of what might happen to us by the hands of the enemy. What he told me I took to heart: that he—and you—would always watch out for Krista and me. And I believed him. I guess that's why I was shocked that he disappeared on us and then terrified when you sent Krista and me away from you. My place was with my family. And here, with this family in their elegant home and intact as a family, there is an atmosphere of sterility and desolation that is quite haunting.

Mama, in the name of honesty, I want you to know that though we are not together, you always keep me company.

Until next time...

She wanted to write the I-love-you words, but awkwardness fluttered within her. With trembling hands, she shut the notebook and slipped it into the drawer. Tomorrow, she'd try to write more.

Gingerly, she hobbled over to the door and opened it to find two adorable identical little boys.

She smiled widely. "Hello, there. And who is visiting me?"

The blond boy on the right pointed to the other child. "He's Wilhelm. But you can call him Wil."

Wil pointed to his mirror image. "He's Fritz." He held up a hand, wiggling his fingers. "We're both five."

"I'm Elsa. You two look alike—how am I supposed to know if you are telling me the truth about who is Wil and who is Fritz?"

Wil pushed the pair of round tortoiseshell glasses further onto the bridge of his nose. "I always wear my glasses."

"And I don't have to wear glasses." Giggling, Fritz playfully gave Wil a shove.

"Ah! I'm glad you've taught me the trick of how to tell you apart."

"What happens if I let Fritz wear my glasses to fool you?" Wil asked.

With a squint of her eyes and a furrow of the brow, Elsa feigned worry. "Erich warned me about you two."

"But he always says we're good," Fritz said.

Wil stood on his toes in an attempt to peer inside the room. "We know who you are. Mutter said to keep away from you."

"She doesn't like visitors," Fritz added.

Elsa decided to change the topic. "I was about to go downstairs and get a breath of fresh air. I'll tell you what—if you both want to accompany me, I won't tattle on you to your parents."

"Can you tell us about nature?"

"Yes. I know lots about the outdoors. My mother taught me well." She mentally cringed, regretting that she'd mentioned her mother. She didn't want to reply to questions about her mother: where she was, or why Elsa wasn't home with her. She also reminded herself that she'd told Erich that her parents had died.

"Good." Fritz frowned. "Our teacher said goodbye yesterday. She said that this time she's not coming back."

"Oh, dear. That's a shame. Your mother will find a new teacher, and fast."

Both boys shook their heads as if they were one.

"No? Guess you boys will enjoy a holiday today. I'll tell you what. If you help me to get downstairs safely, we'll have ourselves a grand time. Would you like that?"

In agreement and with smiles, they proceeded downstairs. She grasped the handrail with her left hand while Fritz held her right hand. Wil followed behind, holding onto a belt loop in her slacks. There was no way those boys could help steady her if she became wobbly, so she navigated the stairs slowly, thankful she didn't feel dizzy. Once downstairs and out of the door, she looked for a place to go.

"Though we shan't go far, which direction would you boys like to go?"

Wil shrugged. Fritz suggested indoors because it was cold outside and they didn't have their coats on. She regrettably agreed. The first few minutes of fresh air were divine, but the January temperature soon sneaked up on her. As they turned around, Fritz let out a shout.

"Mutter! Look. We're outside. Elsa is teaching us about nature."

Frau Friedrich scrunched her forehead. "You are a teacher, Elsa?"

Elsa startled at the usage of her first name coming casually from the austere woman's lips. Aware she was healing faster than the doctor had originally stated, but in need of additional time of rest, Elsa thought fast. This wasn't the time to carefully weigh up the consequences. "Yes, I am." She smiled at the twins. "I love to teach young children."

6

Austria, March 5, 1938. Vonni didn't know what to make of Clara ignoring her question a few days ago. She'd asked about whether she recognized her family name of Kazik or Antonina's name. Now several days had passed, and she sensed she shouldn't bring it up again. Despite wanting help in finding her father and sister, and her growing curiosity about Clara's husband and son, she avoided the topic of families. The winter storm over eastern Austria made for a lot of work and kept her occupied. In addition to shoveling paths, she helped Clara take care of the animals, chop wood, tend to the wood stove, cook, and clean the house. Clara hadn't pressured Vonni, but the older woman didn't refuse her offer to help, and this made Vonni feel as if she wasn't such a burden after all. When they were finished with the day's chores, they listened to the radio or read aloud to each other from one of Clara's mystery novels.

"Clara?" Vonni set aside the novel she'd just read a chapter from, though she'd omitted the ending of the passage. She rubbed her arms. "It's chilly—would you like me to make us a pot of tea?"

"That would be nice." Clara eyed the book. "It's been a while since I've read that book, but I don't recall the author trailing off at the end of chapters, leaving one guessing. Tell me. Did you stop reading for a reason?"

"Well, it is a mystery novel." Vonni tapped her lips which sported a playful grin. "Should I be delighted that you were listening to me or nervous that I can't keep much from you?"

"Both." Clara's eyes dimmed. "If you share with me what you left out from tonight's reading, then I can give you a fair answer."

Images of the novel's plot and characters chugged through Vonni's mind. The story's two central characters were adult sisters traveling on a train. In the particular section Vonni had just read, they were chitchatting about what they'd like to accomplish upon arrival at their aunt's house. Since other passengers could overhear their conversation, what they refused to talk about was that they were on the run from the police after killing a neighbor, though out of self-defense. Far worse—in their perspective—was that they were willing to stand up for themselves but their mother had ordered them to leave: *Whether or not you've committed the murder, you must run as if you're escaping for your lives. Darlings, it's not what you might have done, but how others will perceive you. If they declare you are a criminal and undeserving to live a day more, believe me, you will be treated as an unfit human and lose rights those around you enjoy.*

Clara inched to the edge of her seat. "Does the story match your own life? Has it spooked you? It's only fiction, child."

Vonni was the only one that read in her family, a skill she'd picked up from a young woman who had stayed with their *vista* for a couple of years before moving on. During those months the woman had observed Vonni enjoying the elders sharing stories over campfires and had tutored her.

Vonni glanced at Clara and anchored back to the present. "Yes and no. I confess to leaving out the part about whether or not the sisters killed their neighbor, because I found it quite disturbing. But have no fear. I never engaged in murder, and never will."

"Well, it's obvious you're troubled—don't tell me I'm wrong. Has the story stirred up past memories—possibly around why you're here in Austria rather than safe and sound with your family in Slovakia?"

How had she known this?

Clara smiled softly. "Why the look of surprise? I can understand why you miss your family. I imagine this is your first time away from your parents, yes?"

Vonni gave a small nod.

"I'll tell you what." Clara stood. "I'll fix us that tea you suggested while you fetch the photograph of your father you mentioned when we first met. With the weather clearing, tomorrow I'll visit a few friends and show them the picture in the hope they recognize your father or your family name."

"You mean my sister. I never—"

"Yes, you did mention your father and that he is missing, as well as your sister. The first night you spent in this house, you spoke about finding them both as you were drifting off to sleep." Clara winked. "I can see you're a good girl, and I want to help you. If I wandered away from home, I could hope and believe my own child would search for me."

A wave of anxiety filled Vonni. Would the old woman now recall the other omission? Not to trust a soul. She was beginning to despise her constant suspicion of others. Before her own eyes, she was turning into the exact person she detested—one who harbored bad views of others, inevitably leading to unfounded judgments, rivalry, and hatred. This was the rudest awakening she'd had since turning 18. To think that not too long ago, she had told Antonina she wanted to contribute goodness to the world—to help stop people from hurling doubts, replacing them with confidence and respect of others. Antonina had laughed so hard that her eyes watered. When she simmered down, she wagged a finger at Vonni. "You, little sister, are a dreamer. One day, all that nonsense will get you into trouble because you will trust the wrong person."

Now, staring in the direction of the kitchen where Clara was fixing the tea, Vonni's thoughts drifted toward her host. Clara could be the wrong person her sister had warned her about. Yet, here she was, in a country that was not her own, caught in the middle of bad weather, and at the mercy of a stranger. Clara had taken her in, given her shelter and food, certainly more than others would have done. That one Nagy brother—a man in her own country—certainly hadn't been helpful or hospitable to her. In all probability, even if his dog had bitten her, he would have turned his back and walked away.

"Have you fetched that photograph I asked you about?"

Vonni jumped at Clara's voice. "No, I was lost in my thoughts." She took the tray carrying a steaming red teapot and two teacups without saucers from Clara and set it on the table beside the sofa. "I'll get it now." She rushed to the set of wooden hooks by the front door where she kept the coat that she'd borrowed from Clara and withdrew from the right pocket the photograph of her father. She wished she also had one of her sister, but considering her family's lack of cash, it was amazing she even had one of her father. His brown eyes stared up at her from the photograph. As if her father had slid free of the paper and appeared in his glorious self before her, unexpected tears streamed from her eyes and down her cheeks. "I miss you, Tata."

"He must miss you as well."

Lost in her thoughts, Vonni hadn't heard Clara approach. She jumped and covered her pounding heart.

"Didn't mean to scare you," Clara said. She wiggled the photograph free from Vonni's grip but kept silent. Even so, her unspoken words rang out loud and clear.

Vonni peered into the woman's rheumy deep-set eyes that often made her nervous. "Yes, despite the differences you see between us, we are father and daughter. And yes, he is of darker skin and hair. My whole family is. I'm the one who is different. I've been called a freak, like I belong in a gruesome circus where people pay to see human oddities, like a bearded lady or a two-headed man. I probably can fetch a better price than a chained, dancing bear."

"I would never think of you as a freak."

"That's what I am, a freak." Why was she trying to explain who and what she was to Clara? No one ever understood or accepted her. They only stared, cold-heartedness darkening their eyes before they took a step backwards, away from her. "It's been suggested to my parents that they stand a chance of making decent money if they'd sell me to a freak show. They've also attempted to force my parents to admit that they snatched me from another family."

Clara's brows furrowed in deep lines that showed her age. "One is considered a freak—and wrongly so—because of an unusual appearance or abnormality. You're a beautiful and pleasant young woman. Just because you might not resemble your parents doesn't make you a freak of nature." A soft grin tugged at her lips. "Then again, if you had odd behavior to accompany their nasty accusations, then they'd be justified in calling you a freak." She rattled the photograph. "When I look at your father, I not only see a handsome man, but with his set jaw, I see a smart man. With the sparkle in his eyes, I see a man who is kind and able to live life to the fullest."

As if a young child once again, excitable in joy, Vonni bobbed her head several times. "You've just described Lash Kazik so well it's as if you've met him."

"Lash, is it?" Clara pulled at her chin. "What's that odd look for? You can trust me, girl."

Trust? Vonni shouldn't have said one word about her father and shouldn't have confided in this odd woman, who one second made her feel welcomed and the next made her wonder if she'd met an evil witch straight out of a fairytale.

"Although," Clara continued before Vonni could reply, "your father is of darker skin, no mistaking that." She peered at Vonni. "And you say the rest of your family is darker as well. Are you from a Palestinian Jewish tribe?"

Vonni didn't know which she hated the most—the unspoken accusation, as if a Jew from that area or elsewhere was criminal, or that someone's origin would matter to this particular woman. She returned the scrutinizing look at Clara and replied with the truth, which tore at her heart because her heritage and religious beliefs should not matter. "No, my family is not Jewish."

"That's good."

Vonni kept back a sigh, uncertain how she should reply to a statement like that.

Clara pulled her lips back, but not necessarily in a smile. "In this country, it's quite fortunate that you aren't Jewish." Clara gave Vonni a once-over, her eyes lingering on her hair. "Nor a dark, heathen Gypsy. You don't have to worry."

———

Upon hearing an unfamiliar voice, Vonni shot up from a deep sleep on the sofa, tucked under two blankets and an old afghan that Clara had crocheted. She swung her legs off the sofa and strained to make out what this new person was saying. She shuffled toward the kitchen and entered without a second thought.

A stranger—a woman about ten years younger than Clara—sat where Vonni had taken to eating her meals or keeping Clara company while listening to the radio.

Clara lifted her gaze toward Vonni. She nodded at a vacant chair. "You slept late. Have a seat and I'll fetch you a cup of tea."

The other woman chuckled. "I'm Adelaide, from down the road—Clara's closest neighbor and only friend."

"Don't fill that girl's head with nonsense." Clara stood tall and squared her shoulders as if reporting for duty. "I have plenty of friends."

"Like I have a handful or two of lovers."

"Nice to meet you, Adelaide." Vonni, thinking it was best not to comment on the talk of these two apparent friends, slid onto Clara's chair. "What did I miss?"

"Gibberish," Clara said. "Germany has banned Bock beer due to a lack of barley—the way they carried on about it, you'd think that beer is more important than what Hitler is up to these days."

Adelaide's lips twisted like she'd just sucked on a lemon slice. "Don't let my friend fool you. Startling was the announcement that Gottfried von Cramm—a German tennis star—has been arrested by the Nazis."

"I'm sorry, but I don't recognize that name." Vonni waited for Adelaide to elaborate on this athlete, but the woman remained silent. "What kind of trouble could a tennis player get into with the Nazis?"

Adelaide crossed her arms and looked at Clara. "I see what you mean."

"She's an innocent one, all right," Clara said while staring at Vonni. Vonni might have been far younger than both of these women, but at least she had the manners not to be condescending. She stared equally hard at Clara, waiting for her to continue. "Von Cramm has been built up by the German government as a stellar symbol of Aryan supremacy, but has yet to state his identification with Nazism. That's his trouble, if you ask me."

"Clara," Vonni began. Uncertain about how to continue with Adelaide in their presence, she decided to be straightforward. "Are you Aryan? Do you follow Hitler?"

If Vonni hadn't been looking intently at Clara, she probably would have missed the slight lift of the corners of the old woman's mouth.

Clara glanced at her friend, then focused sternly on Vonni, as if she was a schoolteacher who had just finished a lecture and Vonni the only student who had failed to understand its implications. "Do you think it is best *not* to follow the German leader?"

"But you live in Austria—"

"We think lots of good things here in Austria," Adelaide snapped. She paused as if waiting for a reaction from Vonni. Ready to pounce in disagreement, or worse? "Getting back to the tennis star, he was arrested for homosexual activity. You know, when a man likes another man."

"Yes," Vonni said, unable to keep back the exasperation within her. "I'm familiar with the word homosexual. Where I come from, what others do under their roof is their business. Apparently, it's different here."

Adelaide leaned over the table. "Your way is certainly different from the Nazi viewpoint. Hitler's views are for the best of mankind, and it's best if you remember that and keep your contrary, wrong thoughts to yourself."

So as not to wrap her hands around this woman's throat and throttle her, Vonni purposely fixed her attention on a crack in the wall across the room. Still, she rocked back when Clara thumped a dish with two biscuits before her.

"Jumpy, are you?" Before Vonni could speak up for herself, Clara continued. "You can relax. No one is threatening you here."

Here? Vonni tried to swallow, but her throat was parched. She stood, prepared to spew out the first excuse she could think of to get outdoors, away from these women.

Clara grasped her upper arm and ordered her to sit. "If anyone in Bruck an der Leitha can help—whether it's locating a pair of reading spectacles or a missing loved one—it's Adelaide."

"You've shown her my father's photograph?"

"She has," Adelaide answered for Clara and withdrew Vonni's photograph of her father from her sweater pocket. "I'd be a bit more appreciative sounding if I were you."

"You've seen him?" Vonni sat up straight from her slouched position. "Where?"

"This encounter was before the last snowstorm. I have no idea where he was heading."

"Did he seem well? Did he stop and talk with—"

"That's enough questions," Clara said. "Adelaide doesn't need an interrogation."

"But what about me? I need to find my father and bring him home." Both women eyed her as if she'd just accused them of murdering Lash. "What do you know that you aren't telling me about?"

"It's not us with a problem," mumbled Adelaide. "It's his darker skin color and what others think about him." Then, she clammed up and looked at Cat who had just jumped onto the table, brushing her chin against Clara's hand, and meowing.

Vonni sprang to her feet and stepped away from the old woman's reach. "Explain what I'm convinced my ears just heard— that because Lash Kazik is not as pearly white as the two of you, you and the majority of others in this town see him as a problem rather than a member of the human race? Please tell me I misunderstood."

"You're putting words into our mouths." Adelaide stood and bracketed her hips with her hands. "We live peacefully and respectfully in this town."

Vonni stepped forward.

"Then again," Adelaide said, stopping Vonni short, "we want to know if you and your family are Gypsies. The ones we're familiar with don't carry on respectfully."

Vonni turned just enough to catch both women with brows arched in suspicion. "It should make no difference where my people came from. We breathe air, consume food, need shelter. We laugh. We cry. We're just like you." She looked at Clara, then her friend, and back at Clara. "Is Lash hurt?"

"As far as we know, no one has gone after your father yet," Clara said. Her tone should have been edged with regret or concern—if she'd been the caring woman that Vonni had hoped she was rather than the shocking version that Adelaide had brought out in her.

"Yet? Tell me exactly what you mean."

One solitary twitch of Clara's right cheek lifted her brow. "Can't say if anyone else with suspicions is keeping an eye on him. No one here likes trouble."

"Lash Kazik doesn't like trouble either." Vonni took two steps backward and was about to turn again, this time planning to forget about gathering her few belongings and flee from this wretched house. Once again, Adelaide's words froze Vonni in place.

"It's not the two of us you need to fear."

"What do you mean?"

"Austria is seeing drastic changes by the second. If you leave now to search for your father, you'll also be in dire trouble."

"From whom? And why—just for searching for my lost father?" Vonni, beyond vexed, would give these women one more minute to explain. "Will the people in this miserable town come after me? Are you going to club me and my father because we're not like you?"

"Vonni," Clara said, surprising her with a gentle tone she'd never heard the woman use. "There are Nazis all around us. None of us know what will happen or who we can trust. It's best if you remain here and stay safe. My friend may be crusty, but you can trust her. As well as myself."

There was that awful, meaningless word again—trust.

She breathed in deeply. "Thank you, Clara, for sheltering me in your lovely home during the winter storm. I must leave now." She didn't pause this time but marched to the door, not bothering to grab the little she had.

"Take my coat, then. At least you can keep warm."

Although tempting, she wouldn't dare take the old woman's coat, lest she be accused of thievery. As much as she'd love to scoop up Cat and give the friendly animal one last hug, she dodged out the front door without looking back. It wasn't until she reached the road that she glanced down at her attire. Dressed in a borrowed set of double sweaters and woolen pants from Clara, she'd *stolen* from the old woman, though not intentionally. Another excuse for a Nazi to cart her off. Vonni Kazik was no more, at least not until she returned home. In her place, Adela Pasek marched forward to see what the future would present.

7

Germany, January 10, 1943. Elsa became Fritz and Wil's teacher that afternoon. She didn't ask one question about the boys' prior teachers or what they had been taught. Why the other instructors had been dismissed or left on their own accord was none of her concern. She thought it odd that their mother didn't lay out a host of lessons that her sons must learn and decided it was best to teach them the basics of reading, mathematics, nature, and exercise. The Frau's only concern was that their lessons conclude by three in the afternoon so they could attend the local Jungvolk. Elsa wanted to ask about this Jungvolk but didn't dare. Speaking German fluently, she, of course, could put together *jung*, meaning young, and *volk*, meaning people. When the timing was right, and she had Erich alone, she'd ask him.

With Wil holding her right hand and Fritz her left, mindful of her bad leg, they slowly navigated the spacious hallways until they reached a closed door. Fritz bounced on his toes. "This is Vater's special room. But we also have our lessons here."

"You do?" Despite a wave of trepidation stirring within her, Elsa fixed a smile on her face. This emotional reaction was foolishness. The boy's father wasn't home. She reminded herself that she had no reason to be nervous. She summoned a hefty dose of enthusiasm and faced the twins. "Does this room have giraffes, lions, and ostriches roaming about?"

With surprise sparkling in his eyes, Fritz looked at his brother and then back at Elsa. "What are ostriches?"

"Well then, that will be our first lesson of the day." She planned on teaching the twins the importance of thinking and speaking up independently. She'd have to be careful. A valuable lesson, one that could expand and strengthen a young mind, it would surely clash with Nazi edicts. "Let's go inside, shall we?" She opened the door, and her breath hitched in awe. Before her was the grandest room she'd ever seen. Thanks to her father's teaching, she easily recognized the oak and walnut parquet flooring, though she couldn't discern the wood variations that composed its inlaid border. Three of the walls were lined with mahogany bookcases. The fourth wasn't a wall, but rather a huge picture window with a view of the gardens, set off against rolling hills.

Fritz trotted toward the center of the room and draped himself over a large globe mounted on a brass stand with a gilded metal base. The spherical fixture stood beside a four-legged round table with an inlaid border. "This is where Teacher taught us."

"Mutter says you're to teach us now—and here," Wil added.

The boys reminded her of her sister, Krista. Unlike these boys, she and her sister did compete against the other, but there was never a doubt in their minds that they loved each other and supported each other as Fritz and Wil did. Where was Krista now? Elsa thought day and night of her sister. She prayed that Krista was treated well by her safe house hosts and the other children hiding from the Nazis. Had she been ratted on and swept off to a camp? Was Krista using an alias like her? Was she even alive? Tears stung Elsa's eyes. She never wanted to see this world again, filled with people daring to call themselves human.

Someone tugged at her hand. "Elsa?"

Wil. This was not the time for self-pity. Now in charge of two little boys—innocent children who had done no harm to anyone—Elsa made herself open her eyes.

"What's wrong?" Wil leaned toward her, took his glasses off, and studied her. "You look funny, like a ghost in our storybooks."

She definitely needed to change the subject and move away from talking about herself. "This is a grand room. What is better than a library to learn and to study?" Elsa eyed the semi-circular set of bookcases, each with electric light sconces mounted on the section dividers. "This is quite different from where I learned my lessons."

"Where was that?" the boys asked in unison.

Despite her determination to remain in the here and now and focus on the twins, her attention drifted back to Krista, and how the two of them had often sat at the kitchen table with their mother, reviewing the day's lessons from school. Often, Mama had hurried to one of the bookcases in their Berlin house, removed a book, and expanded on the lessons from earlier in the day. No matter where they lived, they were always at a fingertip's reach of books. But this wasn't the past. Gone were happier times when her family was together before her father disappeared and her mother put her and her sister into hiding. Elsa thought quickly before revealing her past to little boys who were not yet versed in discretion. "The town school."

She continued her visual tour of the room. A brass and crystal chandelier added brightness and cheer from its center place. A spiral wooden staircase led to a second floor. She imagined that was where the Herr enjoyed his privacy. She turned to the boys. "Will you be able to learn your lessons in this fine room and not be naughty when I turn my back and run up these stairs?"

"Vater says we're not allowed to. He has important books up there." Wil's eyes grew wide with mischief. "Unless you let us, Elsa." He approached and planted one foot on the first stair. "May we go up?"

"Your father, not I, makes the rules. So, no."

"What about the ostriches?" Fritz asked as he sat down at the table tucked under the chandelier. Wil sat across from him. Like university scholars, they identically folded their hands, though their grins showed their anticipation.

"Let me take a peek to see what books are here so we can begin our lessons." Hopefully, there was a simple book about animals. Elsa stepped to the closest stack of shelves to get a sense of what order the books were in. Erich Ludendorff. Rheinhard Scheer. Erich von Falkenhayn. According to what her father had shared, Erich von Falkenhayn was one of the main architects of the Great War. Known as the blood-miller of Verdun France, he had planned to kill enough French soldiers so that France would have no choice but to surrender. Except, there had been no clear winner due to high casualties on both sides, and he had been replaced. Sweat broke out on the back of Elsa's neck. These books were definitely not suitable for five-year-old boys.

She moved to the next set of books on the neighboring shelves. As if she traveled the world, the titles invited her to the Soviet Union, Poland, England, America, and other countries spanning the globe. These books also weren't what she'd hoped to find. The previous teacher must have brought her own textbooks and picture books more suitable for young minds. On the following shelves were books on economics and German businesses. The shelves below contained books on Jews. Titles ranged from *The Social Damages from Jews* to *The Jewish Economic Burden* and *The Risks Jews Harbor*. They were written by authors she'd never heard about. Based on the cover blurbs, they were a means to influence the general population to hate Jews. If these writers and publishers despised Jews so much, were there other groups of people that they targeted as well? Was this what her parents whispered about at night when they thought she was asleep, leaving out keywords just in case they'd reach her ears?

The room swam before her. Her belly flipflopped and bile raced to her throat. As if the air was pulled from her lungs, Elsa stooped over. The boys hollered, but she couldn't make out their words. Suddenly, a firm hand grasped her shoulder. Had Herr Friedrich arrived home and caught her roaming through his library?

"Elsa," came a calm and gentle voice. "Let me help you sit."

"Is she okay?" one of the boys asked.

"The books..." Elsa blinked back her focus and saw Erich. "I didn't mean to pry. Honestly."

"No concerns. You were simply looking at the books." Erich put an arm around her waist. "We can talk later. Hold onto me and I'll help you to the table." He instructed Wil to pull out a chair. "Here you go. Sit. Catch your breath—no explanations necessary."

"But—"

Erich lifted a hand to stop her. "Mutter told me how you're the twins' new teacher. Hearty congratulations. However, evidently, you remain weak from your foot injury. Shall I help you back to your room and then tell my mother that you need to wait until you're stronger to resume teaching?"

"I'll be fine—I need to build up my strength and cannot do that if I remain idle, tucked away in my room." She didn't want his good wishes; she wanted to flee from this house. Yet, with her bum ankle, she could barely walk, let alone stand for a long time. "I was trying to find a children's book about ostriches."

"Ostriches?" Erich repeated, his tone playful and his green eyes bright with big-brother love. "Did the boys put you up to this?"

Elsa shook her head, relieved the dizziness was gone. Erich had been nice enough, but she reminded herself that he was one of the sons of the mysterious Herr Friedrich—now her boss—and she needed to be wary, not careless. And certainly, she should not become distracted by Erich's handsome looks. "I thought a lesson about a bird that's nearly three meters tall is a good one for young children." She averted her eyes, but his warm touch upon her hand pulled back her attention. She looked into his eyes.

"There's a section around the corner for the twins' reading and lessons. Our father saw to it that his sons were not neglected when it came to a decent education."

"That's good to know."

"Fritz, Wil—why didn't you show Elsa your books?" When the two shrugged, Erich ordered them to go to their special shelves and select a book with a subject they'd like to study. He then leaned closer to her and whispered, "As a reminder, with the Allied forces bombing

Germany, my father has seen to the twins' private education since public education is now out of the question. You do understand?"

As each day crawled by since Germany had declared war on the world, Elsa increasingly comprehended little. This house, with this particular family living in it, within the style of luxury despite wartime, was no exception. Elsa looked at Erich and made herself chuckle. "Fritz and Wil will soon learn to never fool a teacher again." She waited for Erich to return a laugh, at least to make a clever statement, but he remained quiet. Elsa, uneasy, shifted, carelessly moving her bad ankle. She groaned.

"Is your foot acting up? Are you sure you wouldn't like to postpone the boys' lessons?"

"No, I'm fine. I just moved the wrong way."

Erich pulled his chair closer to her. "They'll be back in seconds—so listen to me." His tone was low and firm. She gripped the table's edge so as to not flinch. "Those books you were looking at belong to my father. His reading choices are, well, let's say, grim."

"Terrifying," she said, and then, catching herself, stopped before continuing.

Erich gave a slight nod. "Do not discuss those books you've found with the twins. They get enough of their own brainwashing. And don't bring up the topic with my mother."

Brainwashing? "Might it be best if we do not take our lessons here, in this room?"

"Although this library is where they've studied previously, it's probably not the best place. Mutter wouldn't care one way or the other. As long as you keep Fritz and Wil out of her path, she'll be fine. Let the boys grab a handful of books, then retreat to their room. Understand what I'm implying?"

She would always fail to understand prejudice, and that was what this hideous collection of "knowledge" detailed. But she couldn't tell Erich—son of an apparent Jew hater—her beliefs.

"I know what you're thinking."

She grasped the V of her neckline. "I don't think you do."

"On the contrary, I believe I do." He stared into her eyes,

expressionless. "You looked awfully lightheaded standing before the shelves of Nazi books, and combining this with the dribs and drabs of conversation with my mother, how could I possibly be mistaken over your alarm about living in a house that has pledged its allegiance to the Nazi Party?"

"Your father is a..." She couldn't finish her question. Didn't want the taste of that four-letter word in her mouth. Besides, she didn't need verification of the obvious.

"At this point of the war, Elsa, aren't all German non-Jewish men involved in the Nazi Party, to one extent or the other?"

8

Vienna, November 9, 1938. The one lesson Adela—formerly Vonni— had learned several months earlier on March 12, the day the Germans stormed into Austria to annex the country for the Greater German Reich, was that the world existed simultaneously with the worst and the best of people. Never the naïve one, she'd witnessed hints of the horrific in her hometown of Bratislava: the unfounded prejudice against her people, accusing them of being lazy, preferring to live in filth, and lacking the desire for education. The tragic irony of these untruths was that the rest of society forced the Roma to live in squalor compared to their own comfortable lifestyles by not offering employment, labeling them as work-shy. In this world, Adela and her loved ones were forced to live in encampments away from the *gorgios*, who unlike them, enjoyed the luxuries of hot running water, weekly income, and public schools for their children. They deemed temporary places as perfect for the Roma since there was no reason for a wanderer to need a permanent home.

After Adela had fled Clara's house on that cold and windy early March day, she guardedly asked the few people she'd met in the township of Bruck an der Leitha whether they'd seen a man that matched her father's description. The handful of folks she'd met kept silent; the nervous glint in their eyes spoke volumes. Then, she stumbled across three people who replied, but she wished they hadn't. A woman, wearing a tattered scarf around her head and a skirt with an unstitched hem that dragged on the ground, yelled "*geh' weg von hier!*" That suited Vonni fine—the sooner she got out of there, the happier she'd be. Then, two pipe-smoking, unsmiling men insinuated that since she was looking for someone with a Roma name, she should go directly to the Burgenland. She asked for directions to this place. The silver-haired one peered at her as if she'd asked for the directions to hell. The bald man simply pointed south and said it was Austria's easternmost and least populous region. "You won't have difficulty finding your way—it's obvious you belong there." Without thanking them, she began her journey toward Burgenland.

She spent the nights taking shelter where she could, often in half-abandoned barns with the biting wind hollering through holes and missing boards. She took off during the pre-dawn hours before she could be discovered. In a grove of trees, she hunkered under a coat she'd snatched from a garbage can, apparently tossed because of a large rip down the back and bloodstain on the front. She fell asleep trying not to think about what might have happened to the poor person wearing the coat, or his or her urgency to discard it. On the third evening, she'd slept in an old bus pulled up alongside a fire-damaged business. She managed to avoid people and their questions. As if the barn, the coat, and the bus were people, she'd fallen asleep with the words *don't ask about me and I won't ask about you* circling lazily in her mind until she floated into a dreamland of faraway places that she couldn't recollect upon awakening the next morning.

Despite the strained and stressful times of living in various Roma *vistas*, Adela wasn't prepared to see impoverished villages. There were masses of Roma—Gypsies, as they were called here, whether by choice or by insult from others. At one point, she'd heard an amazing figure of 8,000 people. For years, job after job was taken away from these people, leaving them to resort to begging and thievery. Although a Roma herself, in this place, Adela couldn't stop peering over her shoulder out of fear of who might be watching her. She found it impossible to ask about, let alone search for her father and sister. Hearing rumors about how the Germans might combat what they called "The Gypsy Problem," Adela received strong advice from these destitute strangers that looked at her with furrowed brows of competition over daily food and care. The non-verbal urging for her to leave Burgenland before she couldn't—before it was too late—was as real as if pickpockets had extracted the identity papers she kept tucked within a pocket.

She began her trip north again. This time, she traveled during the dark and moonless hours, sleeping during the day. Not ready to give up her search for her family, she resisted veering east and crossing the bridge back to her home in Bratislava.

Adela reached Vienna—or Wien, pronounced with a V, as Austrians, whose native language was German, called the city. Without a place to call her own, she lived on the streets, certain she'd find work to pay for a rented room within a day. She was young, willing to work hard and, though she hated to admit it to herself, her non-Roma looks might prove an advantage, for once. One rainy April morning when Daniel Ostrów opened his printing shop for business, Adela staggered wearily around the corner from an alley the shop shared with a bagel bakery, where she regularly scavenged the stale breads tossed nightly into trash cans. That was the moment Daniel pushed open the glass shop doors of his print shop and witnessed her collapsing to the ground in a fever. Rather than turn his back on her, as other Wieners did, he summoned his wife, Lara, offered her the spare bedroom in their flat over the shop, welcomed Adela Pasek into their family, and taught her the necessities of running a print business. No questions were asked. She was accepted for who she said she was.

Daniel and Lara were originally from Poland and had lived in Vienna for ten years. When not working in the shop, assisting Daniel with a print order or waiting on customers, Adela helped Lara care for Miriam, their one-year-old baby girl, and Irene, when she wasn't attending the public kindergarten. For the first time in months—or possibly longer—Adela enjoyed life. One day slipped seamlessly into the next. She missed her family and hoped by now her dear father and Antonina had arrived back to their *vista*. A constant visual replayed in her mind, one, when she temporarily slipped back to her true identity of Vonni and imagined a movie that showed in public theaters. In this particular reel of her family, she saw her father arriving home before her sister. Oh, how Matka would make a fuss. *Lash, you made me ill from worry.* She'd cup her face as if in pain, yet a huge smile would brighten her eyes and the room itself. *I wouldn't know how to live without you—I will shout my thanks up to the stars tonight.* Lash would tease her. *Queenie, the way you're carrying on, the stars already know.* Then, he would grow serious, kiss her, pull back, and tell her he was a lucky man to have her in his life. And, Antonina? In Vonni's mind-movie, she saw her sister arriving home days later, a bit on the sheepish side as she confessed that she'd used the excuse of searching for Lash when instead she'd become engaged to her boyfriend. Antonina would then address her parents. *How I wish my sister was here so I could give her a big hug and tell her I want her to be part of my wedding.* That's when Adela would shake the fictitious reel from her mind and remember she was no longer Vonni and no longer home in Bratislava. She lived in Vienna. Happily, with Daniel and Lara and their two adorable little girls. Each time this happened, Adela renewed her vow to herself to never give up the search for her father and sister because there was a good chance that, unlike in her daydreams, those two were still missing. For now, she'd stay put and call this Austrian city her new home and the Ostróws her new family.

The months passed by, and November had snuck up on them. Exhausted from working and cold from the nippy temperatures, Adela retired to bed early that night on the ninth day of the month. A shattering sound, like seashells broken and crunched by many feet, shook her awake. A vibration came from deep beneath her room, as if the print shop two stories down had shaken. It must have been a dream. She blinked into focus splatters of faint orange and red light flickering on the walls as if dancing to a wild beat. A shrill scream slashed through the air. Lara. Her new friend was in trouble. Possibly, they were all in trouble, but from what or why, she couldn't imagine. Jumping to her feet, she bounded toward the bedroom door at the same time as Daniel barged into the room.

"Get dressed immediately," he shouted.

"What's happening?" she asked as she slid into a skirt and yanked a sweater over her head.

Daniel grabbed her arms to steady her. "There are youths, all wearing brown shirts, throughout the city. They're chanting threats against Jews and smashing the windows of shops and homes. Fires are spreading."

"And the police?"

He called the police a vile name in Yiddish, a language Adela was slowly learning. "They're turning a blind eye." They grasped each other tight when a shout came from outside in front of the shop. "Hear that?" he whispered in her ear.

Adela nodded but wished she hadn't heard the loud chanting from the street: "Leave Jews!"

With the crackling of glass shattering, Daniel yanked her to the side and ordered her to stay clear of all windows. He rushed to the front window, moved the curtain aside, and peeked out. "It's the dress shop across the street—they've smashed the two front windows to smithereens." He cursed. "The brown shirts are marching right past us—for now."

Daniel was the closest she had ever had to a brother; Lara, another sister. "Are Lara and the girls okay? What should we do?"

"Let's gather downstairs in the parlor, away from the shop and the windows."

Adela followed him downstairs. Lara had pushed the sofa to the center of the parlor, away from the windows. She and the girls sat on it. Irene was pressed tight against her mother's left side, a thumb in her mouth. According to Lara, the older girl hadn't done that since the birth of her baby sister. Miriam sat cradled on Lara's lap. Worry lines were etched across their young faces. The loud noises and their parents' tense emotional states were taking a toll.

Daniel looked at his wife and daughters. "They're too young to be this upset. No one should have to be troubled because others find them unsatisfactory."

"Do you think it's time to tell Adela?" Lara asked her husband, then gestured for Adela to sit on a nearby armchair.

Daniel knelt on the thin carpet before Adela and took her hand. "Lara and I have feared a day like this would come to Vienna. Because of their Jewish faith, our parents fled several pogroms in their native Russia and ended up in Poland. Now, with the annexation of Austria to Germany, we've been mentally planning for more actions against Jews. To the extreme."

Extreme. Adela didn't like that word. "What can you do? The borders are closed—you can't leave. We're trapped." After a glance across the room to the curtain-draped window, with the riotous chaos on the other side, she looked back at Daniel. "I can't imagine you'll be permitted to leave this city." Lara stood, settled the baby in Adela's lap, and knelt alongside her husband. Adela stiffened. "What's happening? What are the two of you planning? You're scaring me."

"We're also frightened," Lara said softly.

Daniel kissed his wife on the cheek and stood. "I'll let the two of you talk while I go outside and learn what I can." He glanced at Adela. "Not once have Lara and I questioned where you came from and why you showed up in Vienna alone. We've trusted you, and know that we can continue to do so. Can I count on you to help keep our family calm?"

Adela nodded, stunned beyond words. *Our family.* Daniel and Lara thought of her as part of their family. No matter what they faced in the next few hours, she'd offer her help unconditionally. "Of course," she replied, but Daniel was already in a gallop halfway down the stairs to the shop on the lower level. He'd worked hard for years to save enough to purchase the building a year ago from his landlord. He was not about to permit the Jew-hating hoodlums to destroy his means of income or the house his family lived in.

Irene, wearing a pink floral flannel nightgown, appeared tinier and younger than she already was. With her hands covering her ears, she called out, "Mama, I'm scared."

Lara patted the carpet to her right and invited her oldest daughter to join them. She wrapped Irene in a hug but set her attention on Adela. "My little ones have favored your gentle touch and ways since you came to us. And I'm thankful for that. Now, Adela, on this horrible night, I have a question for you."

The shattering of glass nearby, followed by hysterical shouts—and the lack of police whistles—had Irene diving tighter into her mother's embrace. Miriam broke into a wail. Adela feathered her fingers through the baby's tufts of hair, still sparse like on a newborn. She began to rock the child, so utterly dependent on an adult for all necessities and comforts to sustain life, softly whispering her name with what she prayed wasn't a false promise. "Miriam... hush... it's okay." Without thinking, she repeated these words three times before she caught Irene watching her, and Lara nodding with a smile.

"I'm right," Lara said, confusing Adela more. "And I'm relieved Daniel agrees with me."

"About what?" Adela asked guardedly.

Lara inched within a breath's distance of Adela. "Daniel and I believe this attack on the Jews of Vienna is just beginning and won't end soon. We fear that what's happening tonight could well be occurring elsewhere as we speak." Lara hugged her oldest daughter tighter. "You have this natural way with Miriam—"

Sensing too keenly what Lara was about to say, Adela rushed to words. "You're her mother—she needs you, not me."

"Daniel and I are Jewish. Our children are Jewish. Although we never asked to see such proof, you've told Daniel and me that you have identity papers stating that you are not Jewish, and no harm should come your way for this reason. Daniel and I are planning to leave this city."

Adela scooted toward the edge of her seat. "Where are you going? What place is safe?" The other question—when would they leave—

dangled from the edge of her mouth in refusal to let go. Truth was often unwelcome and hard to accept.

"Honestly, we doubt if any place is safe for us. But we do have relatives living in Poland. They may be our best chance of escaping this madness." Lara glanced at her children. Her smile of maternal love contradicted the fear clouding her eyes. "To answer the question that I know you want to ask but can't—tonight. We were planning to leave three days from now, but as soon as tonight's chaos began, Daniel confirmed with our contacts that if we move fast, they'd be able to meet us and, through their connections, get us back into Polska."

"During this devastating destruction of the city?"

"We think it's the best of distractions."

Aware of what was about to be asked of her, Adela struggled to breathe. She pushed out the necessary words. "And the children?"

"It would be more difficult to flee with a baby." Lara peeked at Irene. "An older child is more manageable for a long journey."

"How can I care for a one-year-old that isn't mine?"

Lara gently placed a finger over Adela's lips to stop her from speaking. It was then Adela saw the tears in her friend's eyes and absorbed the agony of the young mother. "This is the role of parents, my friend."

"To surrender one's child to a stranger?"

"To entrust one's child to a good person in the hope that the child will have a chance to live. This is a hellish time for Jews and whoever else the Nazis decide to persecute. For Daniel and I, the decision to—as you say—surrender our little one comes with heartache, a wound we know won't repair itself if we live." Lara squeezed her eyes shut, and tears trickled down her cheeks.

Unsure of how to comfort a parent forced to make a horrendous decision, Adela touched Lara's arm. "This is difficult for you. I'm sorry for your troubles."

Lara nodded and opened her eyes. "Daniel and I don't know what's ahead, whether we'll even live..." She smiled a little. "We have no choice. Choosing between our children comes at a risk. If we make it to Poland and have the chance to start over again, we face never seeing Miriam again. Daniel and I know that you love Miriam—both of our girls—as if they were your own. There's no one else we can trust with our little one."

Tears flowed from Adela's eyes but holding the baby, she couldn't wipe them dry. She shuddered. Why wasn't Lara reaching for Miriam? Didn't she want to hold her youngest one more time? Was it because if she were to take the baby from Adela's arms, she'd never give her up?

Adela groaned. Lara grasped her hand. "What is it?"

Adela couldn't take the time to explain her personal situation, not with the increasing danger they faced as each second ticked by. She shook her head, encouraging Lara to continue.

"We never expected this disaster. I need to know—now—will you take Miriam as your daughter and love her for us?"

"This night will go down in history," Adela murmured, more to herself than to Lara. She peered into her friend's eyes. "Yes. I will take care of Miriam, but only in the hope and expectation that you, Daniel, Irene, and Miriam will be reunited one day."

A loud clatter came from below. Daniel's summons for Lara robbed them both of words. Lara stood, picked up Irene, and headed downstairs. Adela, with Miriam tucked in her arms, followed.

Daniel leaned against the outside door, pale and panting. "The brown shirts have started to torch this section of the city. They're dragging people out into the road, making them march behind a sign painted with insults against Jews, calling us filthy and deserving God's wrath. They're forcing old women to scrub manure off the streets. We must leave right now."

Someone pounded at the door. "Come out, worthless Jew store owner," shouted a chorus of male voices. "Come out or we'll burn your business down. Stay inside and burn too, for all we care."

Despite Daniel standing only across the room from his wife and daughters, he may well have been an ocean away. He smiled a smile of love and adoration for his family and mouthed a silent goodbye to Adela. Without a word more, he turned, opened the door, and walked outside. Hoots, threats, and insults razored through the air. Adela watched helplessly as Lara ran after her husband with Irene in her arms, a wife not about to surrender her husband.

"Lara, wait," Adela called and started to race after the two people who had treated her as if she was one of their own. Miriam began to whimper, alerting Adela to a reality she didn't want to face. There was no other choice but to act in the interest of the baby's safety. That was her chief concern, her sole concern. The front store window shattered. Glass shards flew in all directions. She pressed Miriam tight against her chest and moved into the hallway. She had two choices: step into the madness on the street or to run to the back office and out the door that led to the narrow alleyway. From there, she could climb a short fence and flee with the baby. The smoke billowing into the room narrowed her choices to one. The brown shirts had got what they wanted—Daniel, and then his wife and oldest child—but the sick, cruel bastards had evidently torched the shop, despite their promise to leave the place alone if Daniel left the building.

Adela yanked up her shirt and draped it over the baby's head. "Hold on, Miriam," she said softly to the child in her sudden care. "Don't say a peep. We're leaving. I promise I will find us a place to live."

More glass shattered; the walls shook. Another chant pocked the air.

"*Keine Juden mehr. Keine Juden mehr.* No more Jews. No more Jews."

Adela peeked through the window one last time as Daniel and Lara were shoved down the street. Irene was not with them—gone as if she never existed. This was not about to happen to Miriam. As long as Adela lived, she'd see that Miriam would not encounter any harm. With the baby tucked under her clothes, Adela ran to the back office, out the door, scaled the fence and down the alley they went, disappearing into the cold night air.

Three days later, Adela crawled out of the ruins of a building that had become the hiding place for her and two other homeless women following the night that fundamentally changed daily life in Vienna for Jews and non-Jews. She again stuffed one-year-old Miriam under her clothing. This time, in addition to her shirt, she used a shawl she'd found draped across the sidewalk. Appearing heavily pregnant, she wore the shawl with two large pockets sewn onto the inside, making it easier to conceal the scraps of food she found on the streets.

The baby would awaken any second. The little one would wail in hunger, demanding food that was unavailable, and wouldn't calm until her tiny belly was full. Adela could manage with little food but for Miriam, she'd face the unknown of life on the battered streets to forage for food. Like the rest of the city's homeless, she too was now a beggar, and competed against countless others in the search of food scraps.

The one plus of going out in the street before the break of dawn was that the two strangers she'd squatted in the cellar with were asleep. Plus, lingering pro-Nazi rioters, thirsting to spread more agitation, as if the bedlam that they had already caused wasn't enough, were likely tucked under the warm sheets of a comfy bed, gathering their energy for the cause.

She took five steps and swayed. The consequences of giving most of the food she found to Miriam, leaving next to nothing for herself, must have finally caught up with her. She hooked her fingers through the chain link fence for support. A hand pressed against her right shoulder. She started and tilted right.

"Steady, now," a man said firmly in German. "Turn around. Let me help."

After what had occurred on this city's streets, she couldn't trust anyone. "I'm fine, thank you. Just need to rest."

He spun her around and her eyes leveled on his thick, groomed mustache. "I can tell you're not—" His gaze traveled to her plentiful midsection. Against her stomach, Miriam stretched, poked her head out from under the shawl, and yawned. The man's eyes widened.

Before she could explain, he acted faster than she anticipated and grabbed her upper arm. "Come with me. Now." He started pulling her to a destination that he was not sharing.

This was it. Her attempts at hiding and keeping both herself and Miriam safe from the Jew-haters and the growing legions of Nazis pillaging Vienna—possibly all of Austria—had now come to an end. She'd failed Lara and Daniel and had ruined the chances of a future for baby Miriam. She had failed her own mother by not finding her father and sister. Emotionally drained from jeopardizing lives, she felt that she didn't deserve to live. But, Miriam? The baby had her whole life in front of her. To grow, to learn. To marry, to raise her own children.

The stranger gripped her arm tighter; her skin burned from the pinch. He managed to pull her around a corner before she latched onto a lamppost. "Kill us now," she said in German, the language that Daniel and Lara had helped her to perfect as if it was her native tongue. "You're not taking me nor the baby to snuff our lives out with your hatred."

His brows slanted inward; he frowned. Heat slashed his cheeks red. "I'm going to help you," he said through tight lips. "But first, you must listen to me and obey."

Obey? Various scenarios marched through her mind. Did he think she'd become his new harlot? Surrender Miriam to him so he could sell her for a nice price to a couple wanting a child to raise and mold into an ideal Nazi? Or, tired from the protests, did he fancy her becoming an obedient servant to make his life easier? Then again, he wore no uniform, brown shirt or otherwise. Instead, a white shirt showed from under a rather tidy checkered gray jacket that he wore over black slacks. He appeared clean, unwounded, and not concerned about whether others were watching. Rather than utter a reply, she shifted Miriam's position to the outside of her garments, allowing the baby to look around in an attempt to preoccupy her before the hunger raging in her tiny body flared and prompted her to cry for food. She just hoped this man would speak up before she flirted with passing out again from her own hunger pangs.

"Tell me your name," he said. When she didn't respond, a scowl commandeered his face. "You will regret not answering me."

"Adela. You are?"

He smirked, as if offended or annoyed that she inquired. "Richard."

"Richard, are you a Nazi? I've witnessed a lot of brutality these past few days by the hands of those supporting Hitler." She glanced at Miriam, who had stuffed a piece of Adela's shawl into her mouth to suck. "My baby and I have suffered enough."

"And that's why I want to help you." He glimpsed at the baby nestled against her chest, then back at her. "Both of you."

She wanted to pummel her fist into his gut. She wanted to yell into his face that not one Wiener she knew had wished for the pogrom of broken glass—only Jew-hating Nazis. Most of all, she wished she could cry her heart out. Let him hear the agony he and the others had caused innocent, good people. People who were minding their own business and not causing trouble. Let him feel the pain, anguish, and suffering baby Miriam would have to endure for the rest of her life from not knowing her real parents or sister. That was, if Miriam was to live. It was Miriam's needs that made her snap out of a one-way fight that she would have been destined to lose against Richard, whoever he was.

"How can you help us?"

"I'm on my way home and want to take you back with me."

"Where's home?"

"Germany."

She wrestled free from his grip and took a step backward, but only managed to pin herself against the lamppost. "We're not going with you, not to Germany."

With one hand, he held her tightly against the post, and with the other one, he snatched Miriam. Adela cried out. He unpinned her but covered her mouth with his free hand.

"Keep quiet. Listen. I will help you—I'll give you food, shelter. Provide for your baby. But you will have to do what I say without question."

"How will I know that you won't hurt us? How do I know that by going with you, our situation won't be worse than now?"

"Worse than living on the streets? If you want to live like this and see death for you both sooner than later, fine. I'll leave."

"But I'm not living on the streets." An outrageous lie even to her own ears.

"Yes, you are. It's obvious you're living on the street—if you call this wretched existence as living." He glanced at Miriam and lifted his hand toward the baby's face. Adela tensed, tugging the child closer to her chest as if that would protect her from his inevitable blow. Richard's brows shot upward; his hands dropped to his sides. "Do you think I'd strike a child? I'm no beast." He reached for Miriam and feathered his fingertips against her left cheek. "She deserves to live in safety, in a healthy environment and not among rats—both the pest and human kind. You have no means to safeguard her welfare. I do."

"And if we come with you? Then what?"

"I promise you that you and your child will have it better than what you have now."

He hadn't inquired whether she was Jewish. Had he assumed that since she was homeless, she must be Jewish? A man of apparent influence and privilege, based upon his appearance, could be making a real offer to rescue her and the baby from this hostile environment. What's more, he didn't appear concerned about what the Nazis thought of his decisions or actions.

Adela stood straighter. "If I were to go with you, under no circumstances will you have your way with me. Understand?"

Richard pulled his fingers from the baby and streaked a finger down the right corner of his mustache. "That will never be an issue between us."

Adela nodded. "Then we will come with you."

9

January 17, 1943. "It's Werner," Fritz said in response to the knock at the bedroom door. "He's here to take us to Jungvolk."

Elsa, seated at a corner table with the boys, glanced up from the book she'd been reading aloud. Both boys jumped to their feet.

"You stay here, Elsa," Wil said, as if she needed clarification. "Jungvolk is just for me and Fritz."

"Of course." Elsa offered a smile despite the butterflies in her belly. After obtaining the teaching position, she had wanted to ask more about this group and the boys' involvement, but hadn't gotten around to it. "Have you attended the Jungvolk for a while?"

"No," Wil said as Fritz opened the door for the butler. "We're special because we're only five. Vater says he wants us to be good German boys."

"Oh, I see," she said to Wil, despite the growing anxiety at each mention of this Jungvolk. To be polite, she smiled at Werner as he entered the room.

The butler, ignoring her greeting, glanced at the boys and mumbled his apparent astonishment that they weren't in their uniforms. He then faced Elsa. "It would be in your best interest if you were to have the boys dressed in their uniforms before my arrival to take them to their group."

For now, she nodded and watched Werner, with a hand on each boy's shoulder, guide them from the room. She was taken back by not only this unfamiliar role but by the expectations that those who lived under the Friedrich roof had of her. More vexing was her own response—she'd launched into the pretense of understanding her role without question and carried out orders as if she knew better than to demand an explanation. Her parents had raised her to speak up for herself, to question authority. Then again, that was before 1938, when Nazis and assorted hoodlums ransacked and pillaged German and Austrian towns. That was why her family had fled Germany. When they boarded the *M.S. St. Louis*, the ship they'd believed would take them to begin life anew in America, they could not have foreseen the cruel twist of fate that had awaited them and sent them away. They'd landed safely and happily in the Netherlands, but Nazi Germany again reared its ugly head and her once intact, loving family was no more. She was now Elsa for a reason. And Elsa did what she had to do to survive. Well, at least until she had built up her physical strength.

There was no sense in remaining in the boys' room without Fritz and Wil to teach. With the need to rest, she headed toward her room, located on the other side of the house. Not wanting to test her ankle's strength, she walked slowly as she went from one hallway into another and then climbed the stairs to the third floor. Rounding the corner, she stopped upon seeing Adela leave her room. Thinking the servant had left fresh towels, she was about to greet her but gawked instead, not believing what this woman carried.

"Those are my belongings, not yours." Immediately, shame ripped through her like a hot flame. Except for what she'd worn when she first arrived at the Friedrichs', Elsa hadn't a stitch of clothing to claim as her own. For that matter, in the few short weeks she'd convalesced in the private room that she now questioned was still available for her use, she'd never gained one item she could call her own. A borrowed room in a borrowed house with a borrowed identity.

Adela set the small pile of freshly laundered clothes, a small basket of toiletries, and her notebook onto a nearby table. To Elsa's relief, it didn't appear as if Adela had snooped through the notebook.

Adela dropped her gaze to the floor. "Frau Friedrich has ordered me to move you to the servants' section of the house." She'd spoken in excellent German.

"Because I now teach the twins," Elsa said, unsure if she was stating a given or asking a question. Not that it mattered. As she was fast learning, the requests from the Frau were always granted. "Thank you, but I can do this myself." She reached for the clothing, but her weakened ankle rebelled, and she lurched forward, knocking over the light with a stained-glass globe as well as the clothes.

Quick in her reflexes, Adela grabbed the fixture before it hit the bare parquet flooring. She then grasped Elsa's arm and steadied her. "Good. Neither the lamp nor you are broken. Elsa, do you agree that we do not need to report this?" Elsa gave a quick nod. Adela scooped up the clothes that had fallen to the floor and placed them back on the table. "It's best if I retrieve your belongings after I help you settle into our room."

A flush steamed Elsa's face. "Our room?"

"Yes. Frau Friedrich has assigned you to my room. It now has an extra bed since..." As if she'd just received a blow to her stomach, Adela hunched over and wrapped her arms around her middle. When their gazes connected, Adela sidestepped away from Elsa's side.

"Perhaps I should be offering my assistance to you?"

"No, no. Just tiptoeing around a memory." Adela then blushed as if she'd said one word too many.

Confused as to which one of them needed the most support, Elsa grew more curious about Adela. She hoped that in due time, they'd not only discover more about each other but if her instincts stood correct, they'd unite as two like-minded women. "If we walk slowly, I'll be fine. Where is our room?"

"In the cellar."

"At least it's not in a hot, stuffy attic." Elsa thought back to her attic room in the last safe house she had lived in, wondering if her friend Maud, the girl she'd left behind, now resided in the attic room. Was Maud safe? Had she had to contend with more of Dirk's unwelcome intrusions? Elsa felt helpless. So much of life was out of control. More alarming were those people who sought to take advantage of that situation.

"The cellar is damp and cool, no matter the season," Adela said in a matter-of-fact tone. "At least we aren't homeless, dragging our frozen feet through snowdrifts."

At a loss of positive words to describe her predicament, Elsa nodded. With Adela in the lead, they began to make their way down the first flight of stairs to the second floor, where the Friedrichs enjoyed their private suites. Elsa appreciated how Adela remained close enough to her that if she should again falter because of her ankle, she'd have her ready support.

"Have you been here long?"

"Richard—Erich's brother—brought me here in December of 1938."

As soon as they rounded the corner to the next flight of stairs, Elsa asked another question that wasn't her concern, but the teenager she was couldn't resist. "You sound comfortably familiar with Richard —are the two of you dating?"

Halfway down the stairs, Adela crumpled into a heap, rocking. Elsa, reached for the woman's arm. "Are you—"

Adela glanced up with a grin stamped on her mouth.

Elsa leaned on the handrail and placed both hands on her hips. "Did I say something funny?"

"At times, it's best to smile rather than cry all the time." Adela pursed her lips. "Forgive me, but you asking about me and Richard dating was the most curious thing I've heard since arriving here, a long time ago, already."

"And Richard? Is it because you are a servant that the two of you aren't seeing each other?"

"That's the best way of understanding the complexity under this roof." Adela touched her index finger to her lips. "From this point on," she whispered, "we must not talk until we get downstairs to our room."

Elsa nodded. Quietly, they approached the formal dining room, with its open wide double doors, which teased her and made her stop and stare. Her mouth dropped open at the spectacular room, as if she were a child catching a glimpse of circus animals for the first time. Dark wooden beams crisscrossed the ceiling, bringing to mind a French chateau. Large windows arched from floor to ceiling with drawn-back green velvet curtains that draped to the floor and let in the late afternoon daylight. A walnut table centered on a plush green and white carpet easily sat ten or more guests. Who did the Friedrichs, a family of six, entertain?

"Let's go," Adela mouthed.

As they continued down the corridor, Elsa took in the oil paintings hanging on the white walls, each illuminated by mounted lights, highlighting the scenes of rolling hills, pastures, and rivers: capturing the essence of the German countryside. She sucked in a deep breath. Oh, Germany! Her homeland. So what if she was Jewish? She was German by birth. No Nazi could erase that fact no matter how hard they tried. This hatred was like a shadow that lurked during the brilliant sunshine of day or the still darkness of night.

They came to the kitchen. Two women, dressed in white jackets over black slacks, chopped up fresh carrots, potatoes, cabbage, and string beans. A man, wearing an identical uniform, trimmed the fat off of a thick cut of meat. A roast? Elsa could only guess since she hadn't seen, let alone enjoyed, this quality of meat in years, not even in the meals Erich had brought up to her in the guestroom. A fourth servant, a woman wearing a poufy white hat, spooned chocolate batter into a cake pan.

"Hello." Elsa waited for a polite acknowledgment. None came. Adela jutted her chin in an indication to move on. Just as well. Not one servant would partake of this fine food. The thought of what they might eat—probably well after the Friedrichs indulged—motivated her to turn away from the feast preparation. It was a tease, the same as waiting around in expectation that the kitchen staff would see her as a fellow worker and befriend her, recognizing her as worthy of attention.

Adela opened a door. "Only one more flight of stairs to your new home. The good news—this stair climbing will help to rebuild your leg muscles. Close the door behind you."

"Yes, best to build up my strength to escape this wretched place." Elsa had only murmured her words and could just about swear on her life that no one other than Adela had heard what she'd said. Still, Adela turned around so fast that Elsa thought she was sure to raise Cain and get them in trouble.

Instead, Adela proffered an expressionless face. "It's best not to have dreams without a way of action."

The two of them definitely needed to become the best of friends. There was no way Elsa would accept Adela's attitude of hopelessness. After all, she was a woman barely a few years older than her.

The cellar room was worse than Elsa had imagined. Not that there were mouse droppings or cobwebs. No pipes clanged and cold air didn't brush her face as it leaked through the one small window that was too dirty to look out of. It was just so...

"Bleak?" Adela suggested.

Elsa turned around and nodded. "You read my mind."

"I thought the same upon first stepping into this room—if that's what you want to call it. No concerns, though. You won't be in this room except to sleep." Adela sat on the twin bed to their right and pointed to the other bed across from her. "Yours." She then gestured to the one chest of drawers. "We are to share. The top two are mine, but if you prefer, I can move my clothes around to accommodate your injury."

"On, no. That's fine. I'll take the bottom two drawers." Elsa rubbed her hands together.

"I warned you that it's on the cool side down here, no matter the season. The only difference in the summer is the added dampness that makes your skin crawl. But this is January, and this is Germany. It's undeniably not summer. Unfortunately."

Elsa sat on her new bed and stared at her roommate, unable to keep back a tiny grin. This was the chattiest she'd heard Adela, a sign she was relaxing around her and might be encouraged into deeper conversation. "Is it unfortunately because it's January or that this is Nazi Germany?"

Instead of an agreeable smile, Adela's open eyes and flat mouth confused Elsa. Was the woman contemplating what she'd just said or remaining neutral? Was she covering for a person, a group, or a past event best not spoken about? Could her roommate be trusted? Truth be told, Adela probably wondered the same about her. Elsa had more questions than answers and feared she might never learn more. She looked at Adela, but the woman remained silent. Elsa ran her hand across the scratchy gray blanket. "Whose bed am I now occupying?"

"It no longer matters."

"It absolutely matters—all people in this world matter." Elsa sprang up from the bed and settled beside Adela, ignoring her lifted brows of shock. "Did a loved one perish here?"

"Enough. You're certainly jumping to conclusions." Adela narrowed her eyes, reminding Elsa of past school teachers chastising the class for unruly behavior. "Just as well. We're only roommates. I think it's best if we respect each other's privacy."

Elsa never did well with brush-offs. "Listen, you can talk with me. I sense a great sadness is weighing you down."

"Well, you sense wrongly. Besides, I can't imagine you caring about me—we're just strangers sharing a room."

"I know what it's like to lose someone you care about." Elsa sat straighter. "Besides, isn't that why there's a war—because people are choosing to make conclusions about others without getting to know them first and making them perpetual enemies?"

"You're quite strong in your opinions. You need to take your own advice and get to know me first before jumping to silly conclusions." Adela glanced at the window between the two beds.

Elsa had to smile as she recalled her mother often praising her determination not to abandon a cause. A different approach might achieve the same results. "Although I miss my friends, Adela, it's the loss of family I mourn the most." This was the truth. And it stung. The cold loneliness and ache for her family gnawed within her like the agony of a bad tooth. Let Adela think her family was dead, for surely, they were missing in her life.

"Believe me," Adela said. "I can appreciate your feelings."

"You do?" Here she was, trying to get Adela to open up and to share a little about herself, but it was Adela that had succeeded in coaxing Elsa to admit the truth about how she missed her family, a fact she'd buried for a long time now. She longed for her two loving parents and sister. She longed to live happily together under one roof. That was why she'd started those letters addressed to her mother—to make sense of the idea of family that once was as solid as an uncontestable line but now, riddled with holes, made no sense. She glanced at her new bed and then back at Adela.

Adela searched Elsa's eyes and shook her head. "I can't talk about it."

Elsa heard the silent words of her hopeful friend. *Can't talk about my personal situation. At least, not now. Perhaps soon. Perhaps never.* "I understand," she said tenderly.

Adela pointed to the old, windup wall clock that hung on the post between the two beds. "You stay here while I retrieve your clothes from upstairs. The twins will soon arrive home from Jungvolk. Believe me, you'll have a job and a half to help them calm down."

"They're just boys. Aren't they permitted to show enthusiasm over their special lessons?"

"Trust me, not from these lessons. Boys grow into men, and in this world, men declare war on others, either one-to-one, or with another country." Adela waved a hand as if swatting away her thoughts. "The Frau needs her meals to be quiet—and her sons can be a handful. It's no surprise she enjoys a glass or two of sherry with her dinner."

"And their father?"

A sneaky grin twisted Adela's lips. "Oh, he likes his beer."

"That's not what I meant, but I can tell you know that." Elsa wagged a playful finger at her roommate. "I think we're going to get along perfectly."

"These days, Herr Friedrich is seldom home. And when he is here, believe me, the atmosphere is quite different." Adela's tone had turned serious again. "Returning to the subject of Fritz and Wil, you need to know about their lessons. Between you and me—and I'm telling you this because you're now their teacher—they believe they are enrolled in the Jungvolk. But they're too young since it starts at the age of ten and goes up to 14. However, the Herr does have his... let's say connections. So, twice a week, after their lessons, with you, they go to a special, elite group session made up of the young children from this region whose parents' allegiance is with the Nazi Party. It's like a kindergarten before starting Jungvolk."

A kindergarten to shape young Nazi minds? Elsa might have asked aloud, but she didn't expect Adela to acknowledge the obvious.

"As far as the twins go, it's encouraged to let them think they are attending Jungvolk. The Frau thinks it will fuel them with the correct energy." A frown turned down the corner of Adela's mouth. "Not that they need additional persuasion."

"I see." Elsa recalled this political tactic of indoctrination during her younger days in Berlin. She was aware of youth groups forming around the allegiance to Hitler and Nazism. As a Jewish child, she wasn't welcomed into these groups that gobbled up both boys and girls, conditioning their ways of thinking and grooming them for future use. The boys were to become fighters on behalf of the Reich; the girls would give birth to Aryan children. As for the Friedrichs, she assumed the older sons, Richard and Erich, had also gone through this education. She needed to remain wary of Erich and his brother.

Adela stood. "Stay here. I'll gather your clothes and be right back."

"Wait. I have one more question." Adela stopped halfway toward the door but did not turn around. "And Erich and Richard? Why are they rarely home?"

This time, Adela did face her. "That's two questions about two brothers with busy lives that they keep from the help's knowledge. Understand?"

The only thing that was becoming clearer to Elsa was that the details Adela kept from her were tied to one or both of the older Friedrich brothers. "Yes, understood." For now, at least. Elsa watched Adela leave the room. She'd do exactly what she had just been cautioned to do, to keep out of matters that didn't concern her. Yet, she had an inkling that she'd soon discover more than she had bargained for.

———

As Elsa slipped under the scratchy wool blanket that evening, she tried her best to block from her mind that once again she would fall asleep in a bed in a house that was not her own. She never handled transitions well, unlike her little sister Krista who was an ace at adapting. When their father insisted they move from one Amsterdam neighborhood to another because of the risks of remaining in their old apartment, it was Krista who acted as if nothing more than a gentle breeze had tickled the back of her neck. Try as she might, Edith—Elsa—suffered from loss of sleep, energy, and weight.

After tossing and turning in the cold cellar room, the first sensations of drifting off to a place where dreams awaited finally greeted her like a long-lost friend. She turned onto her right side, facing the wall, reaching out to grab a pan of baked apples with slivered almonds that her grandmother was offering her, a loving smile coaxing her closer and closer to the pan of sweet dessert that was Oma's specialty. A pipe clanged. A door slammed. Footsteps shook the overhead joists. Oma and her dessert vanished.

So much for sleep. Elsa whipped off the blanket, stuffed her feet into a pair of socks, threw on a sweater over her nightclothes, and headed toward the door. With no idea of where she'd go or what she might encounter, she gingerly opened the door, tiptoed out into the hall, and quietly shut the door behind her. She didn't want to awaken Adela and explain that she had the gumption to roam a bit in the hope of clearing her mind from haunting memories of a yesterday that was no more.

Her dried lips and parched throat commanded a drink, and she saw no reason not to stray into the kitchen and help herself to a glass of water. Slowly, she made her way upstairs, relieved her ankle supported her weight. Once she exited the cellar stairwell and turned left to head toward the kitchen, she froze when she heard two male voices conversing in German. Neither sounded pleased.

"What are you doing here?"

"Vater, as far as I know this is also my home, or are you keeping things from me that I should be enlightened about?"

Elsa pressed against the hall wall. She deduced the first man was Herr Friedrich. She could see why his tone was described as hypnotic, demanding others to pay careful attention to him. But the other person? He definitely was not Erich. This man, though gentle-toned like Erich, had more of a clipped way of speaking. He sounded annoyed. Richard? A gasp teased her lips, and she covered her mouth. Had this oldest brother finally come home? Might she meet him? She imagined Adela would be pleased. The grating of chair legs against a wooden floor scissored her runaway thoughts in half.

"Sit down, Richard, before you wake the household. Collect yourself, if you can."

Ah, she was right. This was indeed Richard. Another rumble scratched the air with a darkness ripe with tension, the perfect setting for a father and son to be ripped apart.

"As always, Richard, you're wrong," the older man said in a guarded tone. "This is my house—one you usually prefer to stay away from, so I fail to understand your pretense of concern or sudden but lame sense of propriety. As lame as your true nature."

"Dearest Vater, I'll be leaving in a few minutes, so please spare me your insults." Silence ricocheted through the house. "What is this? You can only hurl insults at me and have nothing more to say?"

His father cursed. "Answer my question."

"I owe you an explanation as to why I'm here as much as you believe you don't owe me one expounding on why you believe you have the audacity to treat me like trash."

The sound of a fist pounding the table cracked through the air. "This again? You arrive home and already you're questioning me? After what I've done for not only our family but for Germany?"

"What? If you expect me to salute you, you're in for a huge disappointment."

A foul curse squeezed out from what sounded to Elsa like gritted teeth. "You have the nerve—"

"Yes, I know," Richard said. "If it weren't for your legal influence on people like me back when I was only—"

"That's enough nonsense. Your ways are wrong. Evil. Sick. We've been through this, round and round like a headache that refuses to leave. You refuse to repent of your wrongful behavior and that's why I did what I did."

"To enable the Nazi police to make me into a criminal for the way I was born, for what I prefer? Do you know there have been people like me who have been arrested, convicted of crimes, brutally tortured to extract a confession, whether true or not?"

"You and your friends aren't people, aren't—"

Another pounding on the table. "I breathe air. I consume food. I need shelter. I even relieve myself like you. I like a companion in bed with me, particularly on a miserable cold night when bombs are dropping left and right and I have no idea if I'll be alive the next morning. See, Vater, I'm just like you."

"Shut up. You aren't like me, not one bit."

"Regarding the fundamental needs of life, I am exactly like you."

"What's the smirk about?"

"I'm smirking because of the two of us—we're even like Jews. Did you know that despite what you and your merry Nazi friends would like to think, Jews also need air, food, shelter and companionship? Just like you and mother. Just like—"

A loud noise of furniture being overturned boomed out from the room.

"Before you tell me again to shut up—to never compare the likes of me to you and Mutter, I'll make it easy for you."

A throaty laugh erupted. "Yes?"

"I'll fetch what I've come for from my suite, and before you can throw another barb at me, I'll be off and not cause you any more embarrassment. No need to wake Mutter, though I'd love to see her. And the twins—"

"Keep away from your young, impressionable brothers—you're not to corrupt them. Get on your way and get out."

"Oh, yes. It's fine if Fritz and Wil are molded into killer Nazis— talk about being impressionable. But Vater, imagine if these words ordering me to leave were your last ones to me. My, oh my. Think of the damage you'd do to my emotional state. Or might your sick mind enjoy that infliction of pain?" A pause. "Look at you—you're practically seething. It wouldn't surprise me if you and your Nazi *Parteigenosse* have already planned my demise. I wouldn't expect anything less."

Footsteps jolted Elsa into action. She turned around, opened the cellar door, and slipped back downstairs to the one place she never thought she'd appreciate seeing again.

10

The next evening, as Adela was explaining to Elsa the protocol of handling the twins in preparation for their dinner, the servant bell rang twice. Adela covered her pounding heart. No matter how often she heard that jarring noise, it always took her by surprise. At ten minutes before the hour of six, it was a peculiar time for it to sound.

Elsa glanced up from her bed. "What's wrong? Are we about to be bombed?"

"Fortunately, no." Adela pitied her roommate whose eyes were scored with dark circles. "At this time of day, this notice is unexpected. Two bells mean the entire staff is summoned."

"Should I be alarmed?"

"Truthfully, I don't know. It's not typical for Fritz and Wil to be late arriving home from Jungvolk. Let's hurry upstairs."

"Can't wait," Elsa mumbled.

Later, Adela would have to straighten out her roommate's youthful and unguarded reactions more fully. For now, as they walked out the cellar room's door, she whispered words of caution. "You may be tired, but you are to stand at attention. Be silent unless directly asked a question." Adela held her breath in hope that Elsa wouldn't debate this or share her views.

"Fine," Elsa replied. Her one-word response reached Adela's ear on a discordant note. Apparently, she didn't necessarily agree, understand, or accept. She sensed that Elsa was eager to make a friend in her. On the other hand, she would have to watch day and night for signs of trouble that Elsa might cause.

As they made their way upstairs to the grand foyer where the servants always assembled, a thought came to her about Elsa. Might she be younger than she'd purported? She stifled a sigh. She didn't have time to babysit a new worker.

Adela was doubly cautious when she saw Werner standing by the front door, wearing his formal black butler uniform. When had he had the chance to change clothing? This signal might mean that one of the older brothers had picked up the boys from their youth group. But that wouldn't have made sense, not with Richard and Erich both out of town. She noted the servants' formal greeting line, which at last count consisted of 21 people, including the new addition of Elsa. This indicated only one possibility. She discreetly glanced at Elsa, silently imploring her to read her mind. *Act proper, be courteous, and ask no questions.* She steered Elsa to their appropriate places in the line that ran from the most prestigious jobs, like personal butler, to the lowest, the housekeepers. As a domestic server, and Elsa the twins' teacher, their positions were in the middle.

Wil, followed by Fritz, barreled through the door. Since they were an exception to the other boys in Jungvolk, they wore their custom-made winter uniforms of black shorts and dark blue tunics over the traditional light brown shirts. Accessorizing this uniform were the touches of a black neckerchief, a belt with a Hitler Youth buckle, a dark-blue ski cap that matched the tunic, and dark knee socks. Adela, adoring children, wanted to see the boys as precious darlings but could only see them as little Nazis in the making.

Wil stopped and flashed a greeting at the line of staff. He beamed. "Do you know who visited us today at Jungvolk?" Wil had addressed his question to the group of servants as if they were not individuals with personalities of their own.

"Vater is home!" Fritz said, looking away when Wil shot him a disappointed look for revealing the surprise.

Like an actor gliding across a stage following an announcement, Herr Maxwell Friedrich walked through the entranceway, took off his cap and coat, and handed it to Werner, the servant closest to the door. Then he proceeded past the others on the line without a glance. His brown eyes, unsmiling mouth, and short dark hair without a trace of silver framed his clean-shaven face and made for a rather plain appearance. Yet, his tall, slim build exuded intimidation.

"Do you know what we did today?" Wil asked. If he wanted the attention of a particular person, he didn't wait for a response. "We learned a new song!" As he started to sing, his tortoiseshell glasses slipped down his nose and gave the illusion of an old man. Fritz joined him, their voices loud and excitable. "Jews are swine. Jews are swine. Hear them oink. Smell their stench..."

Herr Friedrich clapped his hands. "To your rooms, boys. Ursula will see to your dinner."

"Vater," Fritz said quietly. "Ursula's gone. We don't have a nurse anymore."

"Mutter says we're too old for one," Wil said more loudly. "But now we have Teacher Elsa."

"Enough, boys. Go to your room and await your teacher, then." He waited until the twins had marched upstairs, then scanned the line of servants.

"Teacher Elsa?" Adela sensed her roommate tensing. Herr Friedrich pinned his attention on the new-to-him face of Elsa as if he'd identified a disreputable intruder under his roof. "Step forward, Teacher Elsa."

Elsa left the line and tottered. Adela hooked her roommate's elbow to steady her.

Friedrich perused Elsa from head to toe. "Are you a cripple?"

Adela released Elsa's arm and stepped back into the line. She held her breath as Elsa approached him. Adela might have reservations about this newest staff member, but she didn't wish Elsa a speck of harm and certainly not the Herr's disdain. She wouldn't wish his contempt on anyone.

"Nein, Herr Friedrich," Elsa said, her head tilted down. "An ankle injury that is quickly healing—thanks to your good son Erich's graciousness. He brought me here for medical attention. I'm a strong German woman."

Adela hoped that Elsa wouldn't speak a word more. One misspoken word would have distressing consequences for all. She also hoped that he wouldn't ask Elsa about her allegiance, expecting a *Heil Hitler*. The stars alone knew what Elsa might retort. She wanted to like her roommate, but her nerves warned her of the risks. Curse this war that made her think twice about meeting strangers, declaring a person guilty until innocence was proven. This war was not only founded on undeserved prejudice and hatred, but it pushed one to be wary of others, an attitude that wouldn't fade into the next decades or even the next century. It was an ironic byproduct of hatred —hatred produced more hatred rather than kindness.

"Welcome home, darling," Frau Friedrich said as she entered the grand foyer. She wore a form-fitting leopard-print dress that hung just below her knees, a striking difference from the heavy green woolen skirt she'd worn earlier. Her heels clicked, echoing in the stillness of the otherwise silent foyer like icicles plummeting to the ground. "Maxwell, I hope only good news brings you back earlier than anticipated. I grew concerned when I learned that you were picking up the twins and then arriving home."

Friedrich bent from his towering height and kissed both of her cheeks. He then dismissed the staff, thankfully not pursuing his questioning of Elsa. As Adela turned to steer Elsa back to their quarters, she heard the Herr reply to his wife, "I'll share my news after dinner. It's not what we were hoping for. Do expect company later this evening."

Adela stopped short. The back of her neck prickled as if she'd just received electric shocks.

Elsa glanced over her shoulder. "What's wrong?"

Not now. Adela couldn't afford to have Friedrich single her out for questioning, accusing her of disobeying his command to exit the room. She met Elsa's gaze. "Nothing," she mouthed. *Nothing that you would want to hear*. And, with Elsa picking up the pace, she continued behind her roommate and left the foyer. She'd return with Elsa to the twins' bedroom, paste on a smiling face to greet Fritz and Wil, and then instruct Elsa on how to get the boys ready for dinner. Then, she'd retreat to her cellar room, but only temporarily. This was no ordinary night, not with the Herr home unexpectedly. It was time to contact Richard. With the way he traveled about, keeping his plans and routes secret out of necessity, she just hoped she could reach him, the one person she could trust.

11

If Elsa thought Fritz and Wil were excited to show her their father's library when she first became their teacher, the enthusiasm she witnessed now as the boys arrived home from their version of Jungvolk was near pandemonium. As she leaned against the door of their bedroom, Fritz jumped on his bed, singing the awful lyrics of the song about Jews he'd sung earlier. Meanwhile, Wil chalked a picture on a small blackboard nestled in the corner of a play area. At first, she thought it might have been a budding artistic interest that had prompted the golden-haired and dimpled boy to sketch, but then a picture of a pig blossomed before her, with the word *Juden* scrawled under the animal. She clutched her stomach as it rebelled. Last night's conversation between the Herr and Richard replayed in her mind. Might these young boys take after their father? How much of an influence did other children have on the boys? They were all conditioned to despise Jews and other non-Aryans. Still, she believed that if they saw a stray puppy in need of food and lots of love, they'd want to take it home with them. This proved that there was a modicum of inherent goodness within the boys. She needn't give up hope for morality to continue on.

The boys' dinnertime with their parents was fast approaching and Elsa needed to simmer them down. She summoned memories of how her mother had cared for her and her sister, as well as her mother's anecdotes from her work at the crèche where she handled unruly children on a daily basis. She clapped her hands to capture the boys' attention. As two pairs of impressionable eyes landed on her, she tried to concentrate on what she needed to do, dismissing all doubts and boosting her self-confidence.

"Tell me, Fritz and Wil, why are you so excited?" She smiled widely and aimed for a bright, carefree tone, emotions she couldn't summon in sincerity. "Was it our earlier lessons about the solar system? During dinner, you might like to tell your parents about the sun and the—"

"We're not allowed to talk during meals." Wil tossed the piece of chalk to the floor and sat on the bed opposite his brother. "We learned better lessons at today's Jungvolk."

A case of jitters zipped through Elsa, and she barely managed to hold back her trembling. The thought of sitting beside either child on his bed, or companionably pulling up a chair between them revealed the horrid truth: she was frazzled because she didn't want to be close to either boy. With her ankle beginning to throb, she limped to the chair where she had earlier taught lessons to the two children. "We must get you out of those"—she was about to say dreadful but caught herself in time—"uniforms and ready for dinner. Since it will be best to greet your parents more calmly, share with me your Jungvolk lessons." She wasn't keen on hearing about these lessons but thought it was a way to exorcize the franticness out of the twins' system, at least for a short while.

"You're silly," Wil said. Elsa was taken back by his serious tone, more suited to a stern adult than a mere child. "But I'll tell you." He looked at his brother for an explanation; the longer she was with them, the more she noticed how the twins relied on each other for support and approval.

"We learned lots," Fritz began, already calmer. "We heard stories about what good Aryan boys like about the Führer and how to please him by doing good things for Germany. We also learned what to do if we meet other boys and girls who don't like the Führer."

Elsa pulled at her collar. "What do you mean?"

"We must start a fight with children who disagree with us."

"Oh, my. Wouldn't your parents be upset with you?"

Wil grinned. "Elsa, you're both silly and funny. Mutter and Vater like our Jungvolk lessons. Just like when Richard and Erich went to Hitlerjugend."

"They tell us they're proud of us," Fritz added.

Richard, as well as Erich? When Elsa first met Erich, she couldn't tell which way he leaned politically, though it was safe to suspect that since he was Aryan and from an influential family, his allegiance slanted toward Hitler. His words came back to her from when he'd found her in his father's library. "At this point of the war, Elsa, aren't all German non-Jewish men involved in the Nazi Party, to one extent or the other?" She had assumed then that he was a practicing Nazi, like the rest of his family. And his absences from home were an indication of his service to the cause and not the pursuit of scholarly studies as he'd originally stated.

Her thoughts traveled back to her first meeting with Erich. He'd showered kindness upon her, bringing her to his home and getting her medical attention. When he lugged his phonograph to her room and entertained her with music, it was as if he might be flirting with her. His clean-shaven look made her want to feather her fingertips over his smooth face—a desire she'd never experienced before. His sandy-colored hair and twinkling green eyes made him quite appealing. Lately, she'd enjoyed a few dreams about him. Hand-in-hand, they strolled by a river, listening to birds singing, sharing goals and secrets, laughing at silly jokes. After a short car ride, they explored a quaint town and found a café with outdoor seating that offered a choice of delectable foods she hadn't enjoyed in years. And then, while waiting for their meals, he leaned over the table and whispered into her ear what he'd love to do with her when they were alone in his bed or on a picnic blanket in the middle of the woods where they would enjoy tranquil privacy. And there were the other dreams. Dreams that would make her blush if she ever were to share them with anyone. But now, as her suspicions about Erich became clearer, disgust toward not only him but herself for having those fantasies brought her to the point of nausea.

There was a war ravaging Europe. She was a Jew, he an Aryan and without a doubt, a Nazi. Separated from family and friends she was alone, despite the people around her. And she would turn 18 this year, though she led others to believe she was 19. More than ever, she needed her mother. One she didn't have. One who had abandoned her, one who said goodbye when she needed her the most. If Erich discovered the truth about her, he would despise her, for what was a man or woman short of their beliefs? This relationship between the two of them could never develop. It was doomed before it could begin.

Fritz called her name, reeling in Elsa from her dark, tangled thoughts to the here and now. A place she most definitely didn't want to be. She glanced at Fritz, confused about how she should view him. "Yes?"

"On Saturday, we go to Jungvolk with the older boys. It will be our first all-day Jungvolk because we're good boys that agree with the Führer."

"Is that why you're excited?" Elsa asked, bracing herself for his reply. Would she ever be able to see Fritz and Wil as mere children rather than Jew-haters-in-progress? And if they were learning how to despise Jews, then who else would they inevitably learn to detest to the point of categorizing them as an *Untermensch*, a subhuman socially and racially inferior?

"Yes," Fritz and Will squealed in unison.

"We're going to hike and march and sing songs," Wil added. "Just like the older boys."

"And play Capture the Flag." Fritz smiled widely. "Only one country can win."

Wil pushed his glasses up his nose, pursing his mouth in a too-serious look for a boy of five. "And it must be Germany. Always Germany."

If she lost her composure, she would undoubtedly say more than she ought and risk bringing the wrong attention to herself. Elsa stood. Her ankle was on fire. She latched onto the chair to steady herself. The boys flocked around her, asking what was wrong.

"Just me moving faster than my leg permits." When confusion clouded Fritz's eyes and Wil's forehead furrowed, she rushed on, taking control. "Now, before either of your parents come looking for us, let's hurry you out of those uniforms into nice, clean dinner clothes, and get you downstairs to eat." She opted for her sterner tone. "Enough Jungvolk talk."

Elsa thought that by the time she and the boys showed up, the Frau would have been standing guard outside the dining room—the room that Elsa had nearly drooled over when she first saw it. She expected the Frau to snatch her young sons and eject her into the snowy outdoors. Instead, as she tucked in Fritz's white shirt and patted down Wil's tie, the last strands of conversation between Frau and Herr Friedrich reached her ears.

"At the luncheon conference I attended yesterday, Hitler stated it was the duty of German soldiers to sacrifice themselves for the Nazi cause."

"What exactly did he mean, Maxwell?"

"It's the obligation of each man at Stalingrad to die for his country."

"Die? What's so vital about Stalingrad?"

"Whoever controls Stalingrad has control over the Caucasus oil fields, and of the Volga—the river that supplies its people with industry and transport and the—"

"Transport of oil."

"Correct. We must invade deeper into Soviet land and take the oil fields, sparing neither expense nor the lives of our soldiers."

Outside the dining room, the boys pulled away from Elsa and barged in on their parents. The Frau told her sons to stop running and walk like proper well-behaved boys. The Herr reminded them to sit down quietly and to remain that way throughout the meal, saying to his wife that she needed to instruct the new teacher to calm the boys' behavior. His other news would keep until after dinner. Elsa recognized the cue to leave—and fast. Tiptoeing backwards, she retreated toward her room, eager to speak with Adela. Her roommate had a lot of explaining to do and Elsa was determined not to let her get away from the questions she was prepared to hurl at her. With each step she took, her dear, intelligent father's words haunted her: "Hatred and the love of money fuel and rob many souls in this world."

12

"I understand. Safe travels." Adela hung up the phone and breathed easier. Although the Friedrichs were presently dining, content with an array of food that most Europeans, including German citizens, could only dream about, she assumed the air was thick with tension. Whenever the Herr arrived home earlier than expected and stated he had news to share, it meant bad news for both family and staff. It had been a feat for Adela to sneak into Richard's private suite of rooms without anyone noticing. He'd shown her the hidden passageway into his bedroom where he kept his phone, telling her to use it whenever she needed to alert him to developing events. If anything merited a phone call, the arrival home of Herr Friedrich most certainly did. As if a knife tip scraped the back of her neck, her skin prickled when she heard the door creak open. The hallway's light shot into the dark room, illuminating Elsa.

"Adela? Are you okay?"

"You followed me." Not a question, but a statement. There was no way Elsa could have found her otherwise. According to Richard, no other servants knew about the secret passageway he'd pointed out to her when he first brought her here. The words that he'd murmured to her on the sly when she first arrived at this house from Austria echoed in her mind. "I doubt my parents know about this entrance to my suite. The only other person who knows is Erich, whom I trust with my life." Despite Richard's trust of his brother, Adela was wary of Erich, though she seldom saw him. Her focus turned back to her roommate. She sprang from the bed, strode to the door, pulled Elsa into the room, and quietly closed the door behind her. "Did anyone see you leave our room and make your way here?"

Elsa shook her head.

"Are you certain?"

"I would not lie to you."

Would Elsa not? As much as Adela was aware that her roommate wanted to be her friend, she knew better than to let her guard down. "You are not to say a word about the way I arrived at this room, or for that matter that you and I were here." Suddenly drained of energy, Adela stumbled onto the armchair beside Richard's bed, its plush red velvet cushion with a diamond-tufted back a welcoming comfort. "What did you hear?"

"Nothing."

"Please. We don't have the luxury of time. Tell me exactly what you heard me say." When Elsa remained quiet, leaning against the door, favoring her stronger leg, Adela should have offered her a seat but couldn't chance them getting too comfortable. Instead, she narrowed her eyes at her roommate. "Go on. Speak."

"Well, I have a hunch you were talking to Richard. Is this his room? I heard you ask... whoever it was if the plans were going well. And when he was coming home. That's it. I'd arrived at the door after you had started speaking, and I swear, I'm not stretching the truth. You must believe me."

Adela stifled a groan. So, Elsa had stood outside of the door and listened to the conversation before making her presence known by opening the door. "I must take us back to our room where, under no uncertain terms, we must remain for the duration of the night."

"No."

Adela blinked. "Pardon?"

"First I must ask you several questions, and you must answer me."

"And why must I answer to you?"

"Because I overheard the Herr speaking when I brought the twins down for dinner. I've reached my saturation point for playing the dumb servant who keeps quiet, as well as the just-a-roommate for you to disregard." Elsa crossed her arms. "Exactly whose house do we live in?"

"You overhear a lot. Perhaps you're the one that I—and others—need to question." Adela sprang from the chair. In three strides, she reached Elsa and clutched her arms tight. Elsa winced. Adela couldn't remember the last time she'd held another so firmly, if ever. Living in Nazi Germany had changed her. Here, she was away from her sweet, gentle family and the people who defined the world in bright colors of joy. Hot shame encased her like a cloud of biting flies hovering over a filthy swamp. Had she gripped Elsa so hard because she was trying to steady her own life? She stared at the younger woman and released her.

"Is that your version of an apology?" Elsa said through gritted teeth, rubbing her arms, watching Adela.

Adela pressed a finger against Elsa's dry lips. "We will talk once we get back to our room."

"We better."

About to retort, Adela caught herself in time. With not a second to squander, she slowly opened the door, peered both ways, and stepped into the hallway. She glanced back only once to ascertain that Elsa followed. The only sounds that accompanied them through the secret passageway back to their shared room were the clangs and creaking of an old house and an odd whistle that reminded her of the wind. At least, that was what she convinced herself. Better to think that way than to imagine her deceased loved ones crying out to her about possible dangers.

As Adela opened the door to their room, Elsa rushed at her with a shaking finger lifted in a teacher's reprimand. Adela stepped backward as if shoved, collapsing onto her lumpy mattress. "Judging from your speed of movement, I see your injury is healing."

"I've learned to tolerate certain things in the interest of surviving." Elsa sat beside her, surprising Adela with a grin. "Including pain levels, though I have my occasional bad moments. What I won't accept is your bold attitude toward me. I've only ever treated you nicely, as an equal. Becoming injured and then practically dragged here, to this house wasn't why I'd fled from..." Elsa gasped, then covered her mouth with a hand.

What was this? They had more in common than either had perceived initially. "I hadn't a choice, either, to come to this place." Adela couldn't utter the word "home." This was no home. The grand rooms full of fine appointments, lush gardens and expansive land with its scenic views could never outdo her family's three-room home. At least they had lived together happily. Singing under a full moon. Telling stories around the campfire. Sharing ancestral stories. Life had been good. Her family and community were what mattered. She should have been reunited with them by now. This separation again tore at her heart, which she'd thought was beginning to mend. Adela took a deep breath then rushed her words before she chickened out. "Look at me."

Elsa shook her head.

"Please. I'm sorry I was hard on you, but you scared me."

"I scared you?"

"Although it might make sense to start from the beginning of what I'm convinced are long and sad stories, let's jump to your concerns. You said you have questions for me. Ask. I'll try my best to answer, but I may not be able to tell you what you want to know." Adela sighed. "Besides, we won't be leaving this room again until dawn breaks. Keep your voice low. There's no lock on our door to stop others from barging in, and there's no telling if anyone is on the other side, listening."

"Understood," Elsa murmured so softly that Adela had to lean forward to hear. "Answer my question I'd asked minutes ago—whose bedroom did I find you in?"

"Richard's."

"Are you two lovers?" She blinked in regret. "Sorry. I've asked this before. It's none of my business."

"No. Richard and I will never be lovers, though he's a sweet, dear man. The best, kindest one I've met."

"Is this a Nazi family's house we're living in?"

"The Herr and Frau most definitely are members of the Nazi Party. Blindly, without question, they are devoted to Hitler and Nazism and are raising their sons that way."

"But their two oldest sons are adults. They have a mind of their own."

"You're too innocent, Elsa. That's why you believe people have a good heart but can choose a bad side if they are inclined. This is Nazi Germany—there is only one belief to follow, and it has become a matter of life or death."

Elsa's eyes widened. "Are you implying that you believe in the Nazi cause because there is no other option if you want to live? Am I rooming with a Hitler follower?"

Adela cringed. "No, I didn't say that. I used to believe in innocence, but now..." She shrugged. "Certain things have shaded my thoughts like dark clouds. Listen, just get on with your questions—as long as they're nothing personal about me. We need to respect each other's privacy if we are going to live together in this dungeon."

"At least we agree about where we've been assigned to live."

"Believe me, I've known many to live in far worse conditions."

"Yes, unfortunately you're correct. I'll return to my questions. Please tell me how a mere court judge has standing in the Nazi Party."

Adela smiled weakly. "Judges can change the law to accommodate a government, or a person who wants to be king of the world and will not stop until he accomplishes it. They are not necessarily on the side of an average citizen or impartial."

"No matter who is destroyed."

"Is that a question, Teacher Elsa?"

"A statement." Elsa sighed. "You have a lot of names for me."

"Well then, you are correct about who gets destroyed." Adela paused to study this baffling girl-woman rooming with her, who was becoming more intriguing by the second.

"My father told me that Hitler despises judges."

"It depends. From what I've learned, Germany used the Western way of thinking when it came to making and upholding laws in the respect that it should be separate from government. Hitler changed things. He has his favorite judges who will do what he says, like Herr Friedrich. If he tells them to clear a path to discrimination and hardships that will make others despise certain groups of people—"

"Like Jews?"

"Yes. And others. There are several others that you're likely not aware of that would shock you. As for Hitler, if he says one thing, you can bet your life that his followers will obey."

"Is this what Richard told you about Hitler, about his own father?"

"It doesn't matter."

"Oh, on the contrary. It does matter. And I'll find out." Elsa gave an odd smile. "I suspect you'll be the one to tell me. But as you were saying?"

With tension tightening her muscles, Adela ordered herself to relax, as best possible. "Like we are servants to this household and willingly obey a command, these judges willingly give their allegiance to Hitler. No matter what. No matter who gets hurt. No matter the consequences."

"So, Herr Friedrich is one of a host of obedient judges that has manipulated German law to pave the way for Hitler?"

"The Herr is a top judge—right below Roland Freisler. Both were appointed by Heinrich Himmler. They serve the Reich Ministry of Justice. Have you heard of Freisler?"

"No. Nor this Ministry of Justice."

"Well, both—the Herr under the tutelage of Freisler—influence the Nazification of Germany's legal system. As for the Herr, back in 1940 when Germany took over the Netherlands..." Elsa's sudden pale complexion alarmed Adela. "You look ill. Do you need to rest? I can leave you alone—I have books to read."

Elsa waved a hand. "Just thinking. At times I think and remember too much."

"Don't we all?" Adela said gently. She breathed in deeply, deciding to continue. "I was going to say that the Herr traveled to Amsterdam—"

"Amsterdam..."

What was it with Elsa? Had she lied about her native German origins? "Yes, Amsterdam. He went there to attend a party with Arthur Seyss-Inquart, the Nazi who took control over the country, squeezing out the Jews and the others one by one, then by the hundreds, then by the thousands. Now who knows how many non-Aryans the Herr has helped to eradicate from the face of this world." Adela watched as Elsa swallowed repeatedly. Her poor roommate was going to be sick to her stomach! "Want me to stop?"

Elsa held up a hand. "No, I'll be fine. I have more questions."

"To be fair, if I were new in this household, I would also have additional questions."

"Tell me about these other groups of people on the Nazi elimination list."

"Elimination list? Hmm. You're more perceptive than I originally gave you credit for."

Elsa soured her face in apparent feigned shock. "Looks like you're as straightforward as I am." Her facial features then softened to a smile. "We all say regrettable words in the heat of the moment."

"Yes," Adela agreed, surprised that Elsa's thoughts had merit after spending the past five years not caring what others believed, with Richard being the one exception. Already, in the short time that Adela had known Elsa, she was impacting her life. Her old inclination said it was for the better. She hoped she wasn't wrong. "In addition to Jews, the people who aren't considered humans by the Nazi Party are the deaf and the blind—in other words those who might require the aid of government funds to sustain them, though many of these people are quite capable of living good, independent lives. Then there are those labeled communists, free-thinkers, homosexuals, alcoholics, and those of other faiths, like Jehovah's Witnesses." She stiffened. "And the Roma."

"Do you mean Gypsies?"

Adela didn't trust her mouth filling with angry words over the derogatory word choice, or her eyes filling with painful tears for the same reason, but she saw in Elsa a younger version of herself, and recognized a desire to learn. A memory of one of the grandmotherly women of her *vista* came to her: "Vonni, don't spend time being angry at others when they're in need of lessons you can teach them on our behalf."

"Although Gypsy is the most common term used, these people you speak about prefer to be called Roma. The German term is Sinti. To most of them, the label "Gypsy" embodies the stereotypic perception of beggars and thieves who are nomadic, refusing to settle down, to work, and to take care of themselves."

With the tip of her index finger, Elsa tapped her bottom lip. "Is that why the Herr was concerned about my supposed cripple status? Because he thought I'd be forever work-shy, and as a Nazi would see me, worthless?"

There was that other foul term: Work-shy. The damning accusation and insult to the Roma. And why bother with them when they wanted government handouts, wanted to live in filth, wanted their children to go unbathed?

"Adela? You're now the one who appears ill. Can I do anything for you?"

"No, thank you," she said, hopefully loud enough to be heard. She was drained of energy and didn't want to repeat herself. "Where did you hear the term work-shy?"

"It's an old term and has circulated for a while. It is an awful and prejudicial name, a false assumption—an accusation—just like the Nazis think all Jews are rich, and as long as they're around, there will not be enough money for the Germans to enjoy." Elsa hugged her middle. "I see that I've made you upset."

"It's not you but it's anyone who puts themselves first before considering the next person as equally deserving of the basics of life."

Adela smiled. "Looks like, Elsa, we have a lot to discover about each other."

A siren screamed, a rising and falling signal. Like a person alive one second, then falling dead the next.

They both jumped to their feet, shouting the two words that both Aryans and non-Aryans had come to dread: "Air raid!"

13

Elsa clutched Adela. This was a life or death moment. They needed each other. Barely able to think straight with that siren screeching, she pushed the necessary words out. "Where's the shelter?"

"I'll show you. First, we have to get Fritz and Wil."

"But—"

"No buts. They're two little boys. They might be tucked in their bedroom, but they're away from their parents and aren't safe." Adela wiggled free of Elsa's hold but encircled her fingers around Elsa's wrist and started to pull her out of the room.

Despite the added risks of not leaving immediately for the shelter, Elsa understood and agreed with the need to find and protect Fritz and Wil. Now fully aware of the Herr and Frau's political allegiance and better understanding why the twins were excited over Jungvolk, her view of them as precious and cute had changed a little. Still, they were children who deserved adult protection. Along with Adela, she would do anything within her ability to save their lives. She rushed through the hallways with Adela to the boys' room.

The boys' bedroom was empty.

Adela exhaled sharply. "Good. Shirley—the overnight nanny—must have already moved them to the shelter. Let's go."

"Is it safe to step outside? Where is this shelter?"

"We're not going to the town's shelter. This house has two—one for the family, one for the servants."

"But because the boys weren't with their parents, they're closer to ours?"

"Yes. I'm assuming that's where Shirley took them—she's a sweetheart. Hold strong—we're almost there."

Elsa followed Adela around the corner and through a door leading to a back stairwell that she'd never seen before. "You're quite caring and brave to check on the boys, considering your position here."

"My position, filling in when needed, even if it means disposing of the trash or worse?" Adela kept moving.

"Oh, dear. I didn't mean to misspeak. When I'm nervous I tend to babble. Sincerely, though, I see you as the admirable one. Perhaps I, the teacher, need to take lessons from you."

"It's a time of grave danger, go easy on yourself, if you want my unsolicited advice. And I shouldn't have snapped—I know better." Adela said over her shoulder. Her pale complexion contrasted with her bright blue eyes. She then uttered something unrecognizable.

What language had she spoken in? Then, Elsa recalled Adela telling her that Richard had brought her to the Friedrich house in 1938, though she had never mentioned from where. Before she could think further about this, they bolted around a corner and her bad ankle twisted the wrong way. Fiery arrows shot up her leg. A groan flew from her mouth. She leaned against the wall. "Wait. Please."

"Oh, my. You can't move any faster than a wish." Adela hooked Elsa's elbow. "Let me help you."

"Thank—"

"Later," Adela said and tugged her onward.

Their footsteps clanged on the metal stairs as they descended to a door marking the entrance to yet another flight of stairs. Evidently, there were several hidden passageways in this old house. This estate was not only the perfect living arrangement for a family with secrets, but Elsa could well imagine it as well suited for ghosts to roam and wail. The day when these Nazis would be reduced to harmless apparitions couldn't come sooner.

God help them if they were bombed—deeper than a coffin in the ground was the bomb shelter. If a catastrophe would occur, they'd never be found. "Where's the family's shelter?"

"On the other side of the house—it's a more secure room than ours, with a few more luxuries." Adela opened a thick metal door. "Here we are. Go ahead."

Elsa hurried in, but after her eyes adjusted to the dim lighting, she stopped so suddenly that Adela collided with her. Before her, Erich sat on the lower bunk of a three-tier bunk bed unit, his arms around Fritz and Wil. "I'd invite you to tea," he said, looking directly at her, "but I left the necessities upstairs."

"Understandable," she managed to reply, her mouth dry. She hadn't seen Erich since he'd come to her aid in the Herr's library a week earlier. Now, she was again dazed by this young man with sandy-colored hair and green eyes, a shade that reminded her of sea foam and evoked a sense of freshness and nature. *Dummkopf*, she silently called herself. And that's what she would be—a stupid person—if she got carried away by his looks.

"Fritz and Wil," she addressed the boys, "I'm relieved to see you both here."

Fritz bobbed his head. "It was a scary noise, but when Erich helped us down here, it was better."

She glanced at Adela, then at Fritz, trying her best not to look at Erich. "Shirley didn't help you?"

"She did," Wil said, jumping in for Fritz. He pointed across the crowded room at a gray-haired woman in a neat white uniform who looked more like a nurse than a nanny. The poor woman's face was white as chalk. She huddled with two other women, appearing to listen as she chewed her nails. "But then Erich found us. We were in the hallway. Erich picked us up and told Shirley he could move faster than she could."

"Concerning the tea, not my most tactful of lines," Erich mumbled.

A sense of awkwardness sent Elsa's gaze to the cement floor. "It's good that Erich showed up and thought of the two of you first."

Erich suggested to his brothers that they scoot onto the top level of the bed. He patted the now empty space to his left. "Have a seat, Elsa. It's best for your hurt leg."

Adela touched Elsa's arm. "It's not exactly a cocktail type of atmosphere, but I'm going to chat with Shirley." She stared at Elsa's bad foot. "You might want to take Erich up on his offer."

Elsa watched as Adela joined the small group of women. She then looked about the room; its white walls and black-painted concrete floor constricting and adding to her emerging headache. The staff crowded inside didn't help the squeezing, choking feeling around her throat, and she pulled at the collar of her blouse. She imagined that where the Herr and Frau hid, they enjoyed—if that was an applicable word one could apply to being in an air-raid shelter—ample space.

"I'm not a monster," Erich said. "I promise not to breathe fire like a dragon."

There were only two choices: sit beside Erich on the bed or sit on the floor. She chose the hard concrete and hugged her knees to her chest, staring straight ahead at a patch of blank wall.

"Suit yourself."

It was a toss-up between whether he sounded gruff because of her or the situation. She searched her mind for an acceptable topic. "It's nice that the twins have a bunk bed to rest."

"Have you ever taken shelter from a bomb?"

"Of course!" Not caring that she was the gruff one now, Elsa hoped her annoyance resonated with Erich. "How might I have lived thus far during this miserable war if I hadn't?"

"A good answer to a ridiculous question."

"If it weren't for…" She slapped a hand over her mouth before she could assign blame. *If it weren't for you, for your Nazi family and friends who want to take over the world. Or your dearest buddies who want to kill anyone who isn't a loyal Aryan willing to live, breathe, breed, and die for the Nazi cause.* She was painfully aware of the many things she couldn't say. "I've taken shelter in places like this, but they always unnerve me. I can't get used to this type of surrounding."

"None of us was designed to live in fear, waiting for our lives to be snuffed out when a bomb explodes on top of us."

"Is that supposed to comfort me? If so, it's not working."

"I see that—hear it in the shakiness of your voice." He gestured with his chin to the place beside him. "Are you sure you don't want to get off that drafty floor and sit beside me?" He grinned for the barest of seconds. "I've been told I tend to throw off excess body heat when I'm nervous, so that might be a plus if you're chilled."

As fast as her mouth had dropped open in reaction to his reference to body temperature, she snapped it shut again. He'd just admitted to his own case of nerves. She inched toward the bed, yet remained on the floor.

"Good," Erich said. "I was just being polite. I need space to think, so this semi-privacy is fine with me."

Here she was, resting on a cold floor in a cement room buried underground. They were a sitting target. Their lives might end any given second. And she sat in proximity to a person she wanted to like but couldn't because of who he was—an ironic reversal of the prejudice the Nazis used as a calling card. Her insides twisted, the fear battling with shocking shame coiled within her like snakes. She wrapped her finger around a strand of hair and began to twirl it in the hope she could pull her emotions together. She did not need observant eyes on her, either from Erich or his father. The latter, even if the Herr wasn't in the same room, still had a significant presence since he was the one with the ultimate say of what occurred under his roof. The one who could also extinguish her life, like a bomb, if he were to find out her true identity. She was Edith Weber. A German-born Jew. And if Hitler had his way in this country of hers— in this world—she wouldn't get to live.

Erich's hand enveloped hers and he offered a gentle smile, yet his brows were bunched. She looked into his eyes, then at his fingers wrapped around hers. He slid his hand to her shoulder, gave it a little pat, and then rested it on his lap.

"I'd ask how you are, but considering our surroundings, I'd only worsen a silly conversation," he said quietly, just for her to hear. "If you'd like to talk, I'm here for you. If you look about, the majority of folks penned up in this shelter are chatting. Humans need each other's company."

"This, coming from someone whose family..." Before she'd make a mess of the circumstances, she stopped herself from ranting against Nazis. Never before had she imagined that she would teeter on the brink of becoming an adult by watching her mouth to prevent adding fuel to a fire. "... whose family lives quite nicely but removed from others in town." Aware of how lukewarm she sounded, she didn't dare look his way. She wished she could curl into a ball of feathers and float away. She'd ride the currents to America and search for her mother's friend Zofia, the one she'd met on the ship. She might find Zofia's friend, Aanya. Or, she'd float to Iceland, where she could watch the aurora borealis paint the night sky with waves of electric green, yellow, violet, and red. Images of other foreign and exotic places flashed before her and enticed her like sweets tempting a child.

A firm voice yanked her back to the here and now, a place she didn't want to be. "I don't know what your grievance is with me since I've been quite pleasant to you, but I just came home after a receiving a shock or two myself. What I don't need from you is short-sighted assumptions."

While she had several grievances with his family, the present state of her beloved country of Germany, let alone the upside-down condition of the whole world, an inkling made her think that it was best not to take offense. She batted her lashes, expecting to see the red of anger heating his face, or a grayish wave of regret washing over him. Instead, sorrow swam in his eyes. He was a human too. "I'm sorry for your trouble."

"I'm sorry too," he said. "I shouldn't have snapped. We're both unnerved."

"Yes." She paused, searching her mind for how to phrase her next words. "Since it's quite late, and you just arrived home, I imagine you've traveled through an area that is seeing its own misery. That must not have been easy to navigate, physically or emotionally."

"You have that right," he murmured. Yet, his tone was a bit softer, less accusatory. "I'm not up to talking about it."

"I understand." She looked away, debating whether to leave his side and join the group of women servants that Adela chatted with.

"Three friends were killed."

Erich's sudden disclosure, jolted her upright. "That's horrid."

He swore under his breath, but it reached her ears. "I've known them since we were ten."

The same age, Elsa recalled, at which her father had told her that good German non-Jewish boys joined the Hitlerjugend. Was that where Erich had met these friends? "That must be quite a shock, mingled with a bit of guilt because your life was spared."

He remained quiet for so long that she didn't think he'd respond. Suddenly, a soft squeeze came to her shoulder. She looked his way and saw a smile. "You're astute." Again, there was a long silence between them. When she glanced across the room to see what Adela was up to, Erich cleared his throat. "Back when we first met, the four of us were trying to be good sons and make our parents proud by doing what we were taught was right: great and patriotic accomplishments for our country."

He'd used the word "taught." Had he had a change of thought since those days? She drew her knees up again, relieved her ankle didn't complain. "As a teacher, I'm curious about this teaching bit. Did you boys question or immediately take these lessons to heart? That is, if you don't mind me asking."

"It's fine. I understand you're just passing time."

This time, she was the one to reach out to him. She touched his arm, rubbing it for a brief few seconds before pulling back. "I'm both curious and trying to learn more about you."

"Me?" An odd grin twisted his mouth. Then, like a magic trick, it was gone, replaced by a grimace. "The four of us were first taught what it meant to be a good German child. You know—to respect one's parents, one's flag, one's responsibility to one's country." His tone dropped so that she had to lean closer to hear him. "We weren't taught the moral quandaries of what could happen to the people we'd been instructed to view as different from us."

"Different?"

"Different races. Faiths. Backgrounds."

She sucked in her breath. In his mourning frame of mind, an unintended revelation might have slipped out. There were differences between Erich Friedrich and his parents. She'd seen it before. Like his expressed concern for her health. He'd taken a huge risk to bring her over the German border from the Netherlands, let alone to his home. And for goodness' sake, here he was, talking with a servant of the household, his brothers' teacher. He could have chosen to ignore her, categorizing her as one not worthy of conversing with.

She pushed on. "Did the four of you—or just you—make choices that set..."

"That set us apart from the new standard of behavior sweeping across the country?"

That was certainly one way of labeling budding evil. "Yes. That's what I'm thinking."

"Let's just say that my friends and I reached a different opinion on how we were told to think and act. Sorry good that did. Now Arno, Günter, and Walter are dead. Killed, if you want to know the awful truth. And I'm not."

"I'm glad you're alive," she said so quickly that her words caught her by surprise. She rubbed her frosty hands then shoved them under her legs for warmth. "So, you had just arrived home when the siren blasted? Adela told me about your parents' separate shelter that I'm guessing you couldn't make it to fast enough."

He glanced upward. "What are Wil and Fritz up to?"

She glanced up to the top level of the bed. "They're asleep, amazingly."

"Those two! It's unbelievable what they can sleep through."

"Just as well, don't you think?"

"Yes—to both your questions about the twins asleep and me arriving home. I literally walked through the door when the siren pierced the air. Thinking my parents might have been tipped off before the alarm sounded and had time to hurry to their shelter, I rushed here since it was closer."

She wanted to know how and why the Herr and Frau might have been warned. Had one of their guests informed them about the pending matter upon arrival this evening? Did they not have enough time to gather their twin boys into their protective hold and carry them to their shelter? Exactly who was upstairs keeping them company? Instinct screamed at her to heed caution when it came to Erich or any Friedrich family member. Curse her curiosity. She peeked at him in the hope he'd tell her more.

"I was on my way home from Cologne. I had business matters there to take care of."

She bobbed her head. "Since I've been here in this house, I've overheard bits and pieces of conversation saying that several bombs have struck the city over the past few months."

"More like since the war began. The summer of 1942 was ugly. Talk about near devastation. It's amazing anyone survived."

1942. She and her family had lived in Amsterdam for nearly three years by then. That was the year she went by her birthname of Edith and lived with her mother and sister, with her father missing. If Adela thought of her as innocent and naïve, how would she have labeled her back then when all she desired was to stroll to the shops in Rembrandtplein she hoped to see a certain boy? That was the time when their mother met that woman—Johanna, who happened to be married to Walter Süskind, the man who helped put Jewish children into hiding. He was the one responsible for convincing her mother to say goodbye to her. Were the Süskinds alive, or had they, like other captured Jews, been shoved onto a cattle car and deported to a camp far from those they loved? If so, may they rest in peace. Their actions may have saved her life, and hopefully her sister's, though for now she mostly felt like she had lost her family.

"You're right about 1942. It was an ugly year," she said. "Was it then your friends lost their lives?"

"The summer months of '42 were particularly bad for Cologne."

She assumed he hadn't heard her question or had chosen to block it and its significance from his mind. She thought it wise to let him continue however he felt best, especially since the topic was the loss of friends. "That was when the 1,000 bomber raid by the RAF began." He looked at her quizzically. "What? You do know what RAF stands for, right?"

"Of course, Britain's Royal Air Force."

He nodded. "3,000 buildings were destroyed, another 9,000 damaged. Then they moved on to Essen and Bremen. 20,000 German lives were lost in Cologne alone."

"Those are too many grim statistics you're carrying around. They must weigh you down from time to time, if not constantly." The way he stared at her she couldn't quite place his thoughts. Had he imagined her more as an enemy plane that had just found its target or as a dove delivering a peace offering? More startling was her wish that it was the latter. "Warfare is a sadistic beast, wouldn't you agree?" He lifted a brow; whether in question or agreement, she couldn't tell. He was hurting, understandable after the death of friends. Concerned that her last words would leave him brooding, she sought to clarify. "No matter which side one is on, whether fighting on behalf of Germany or against, to lose a family member or a close friend is never easy. Against the backdrop of war, with constant misery and the threat of death, these losses significantly carry a punch and I'm very sorry for your suffering."

His gaze met hers for mere seconds before he glanced away. "Thank you," he murmured.

Images of her mother flashed before her and she sighed. "This war! Why does it take the killing of others to stop the killing of others? This madness spawning more madness is plain crazy."

"Yes, quite ironic. Should I be quiet?"

"No," she said, sincerely. "I was just thinking about my mother."

Erich scooted off the bed and asked her to move over. "If you won't sit with me on a more comfortable surface than this miserable floor, I'm sitting next to you." As he sat beside her, she scanned the room. "Let them think and say what they want, Elsa. Who I am offers several advantages." He let out one lone chuckle. "Tell me about your mother. What was her first name?"

Erich's question about her mother in the past tense shook her as if a wave of icy water swept over her and began to tug her into the ocean. Then she remembered she'd told him that her parents had died. Was it safe to tell him her mother's name? He had no reason to investigate the truth. "Herta."

He winked. "Ah, a good German name."

Torn between snarling and laughing, she let out a little tee-hee. "German born and German married."

"Well, what were you thinking about her? Good things, I hope."

"How she was a brave woman when it came to dealing with adversity, and how she got that way. It was what my *oma* advised my mother when she was a little girl." She jabbed the bridge of her nose to concentrate on choosing the correct words from her memory. "Anger in the form of retaliation or revenge makes matters worse, not better. Hatred only and always begets more hatred. What this world needs is love and kindness. And that's what we need to spread between us—this love."

"You're absolutely correct." He stared at her and grinned. "Why are your eyes so wide? You never expected to hear that from Herr Friedrich's son?"

As she debated with herself on how to best reply, the ground shook. She grabbed onto Erich's arm. "Did you feel that?"

The room grew silent. Was death imminent? Should they be uttering prayers, confessing their sins, and asking for God's forgiveness? Then, collectively as one, murmurs of speculation began about what would happen next.

Beside her, Erich straightened but continued to hold onto her. "You're not imagining it, this place shook. Probably the vibrations of a strike off in the not-too-far distance. Are you afraid?" He wrapped an arm around her and pulled her tight against his side, an unexpected, safe feeling washing over her, the complete opposite of what she felt seconds ago. "You don't have to be brave each second of this war. I know I'm afraid."

She pulled back to look at him. She'd been frightened continuously since the days following Kristallnacht. "You're the only person who has told me that it's okay to be afraid since this war began. It's exhausting to always put on a brave face."

"Exhausting is too minimal of a word," Erich said.

She nodded.

The door to the shelter opened. Werner, the butler, stepped in, ringing a handbell. When all eyes fell upon him, he stopped the clanging, as sweet as it was to hear. "The town has blasted the signal —a continuous note of the all-clear siren. You can return to your rooms."

A few thank-God praises swept across the room, along with smiles and several emotional sobs. Fritz and Wil jumped down from the top bunk, a look of confusion and fatigue blanching their faces.

"So," Erich said to his little brothers. "A nice loud bell is what it takes to wake you two up."

Fritz nodded, but Wil spoke for them both. "There are no bombs, right? We don't like bombs."

"No one does." Erich picked them both up and set one on each shoulder. "Let's get you upstairs to your bedroom."

"Wait," Elsa said. She reached out to the twins and tousled their hair. "You two have a good night's sleep. We grown-ups will watch out for you."

"I'm glad you're with us, Teacher Elsa," Wil said.

Erich mumbled that his brothers were getting heavy. Over his shoulder, he said to Elsa, "I'm glad you're with us, too."

Before Elsa could ask for an explanation from Erich, Adela made her way toward them. She looked directly at Erich and waited silently, apparently believing he would hear her unspoken question.

"Yes." Erich set the boys down and told them to wait by the door. "He's fine. You can breathe easy."

Adela worried her lips. "Is he? Will he?"

Erich gave the slightest of nods. "As planned."

Adela patted her heart.

"Adela?" Elsa said.

Adela would not look her way. "Let's return to our room, shall we? Tomorrow will come soon enough with a full day of work for both of us."

Although Elsa agreed, by the time she dropped into her bed, ready to gamble that sleep would come for her faster than she could spell the word, she couldn't nod off. Glancing at Adela, who was sound asleep, Elsa tossed off her blanket, pulled a sweater over her nightclothes, and pushed her hand under her mattress to where she kept her notebook and pen.

Dear Mama,

It might have been a while since I last penned my thoughts to you, but I think of you each day. Papa and Krista as well.

We saw this awful time brewing way before Kristallnacht. This war contradicts what the Aryans believe they are—invincible. Death comes to both good people and those who are not. Persecution and the killing of others is not a solution as the Nazis believe! I hope there will be happier times for our family again.

My heart is lighter now that I've shared my thoughts with you. I'll write more as soon as I can.

But how should she sign the letter? Sincerely? Yours? Love? Did she feel any of those? And with what name? Edith? Elsa? Like many things she'd lost during this war, she no longer knew her identity.

14

A nerve-splitting jangle buzzed through the cellar room. Weary and emotionally drained from the air raid threat a mere three hours earlier, Adela was tempted to ignore the servant's summons. She wanted to sleep and continue dreaming about her parents and sister and of campfire tales of visits from the ghosts of deceased relatives. She'd even welcome the awful dreams she'd had sporadically since arriving in Monschau. Dreams of walking by the shops in Bratislava, despite she was forbidden to explore what goods were sold on the other side of the threshold due to her being Roma. Curse it. She'd had it with the trite nonsense the older generation tried to heap onto her about accepting the parts of life she couldn't change. No longer was she a naïve and hopeful girl. Led by wanderlust, she'd believed she could go wherever she wanted to and accomplish her dreams. An 18-year-old she was no more.

Adela threw the covers off and sprang out of bed. She glanced at her roommate. A lone snore rolled from Elsa's mouth as she turned over onto her back.

"Oh, my. Elsa, get up immediately."

Elsa cracked one eye open and shot upright. "Another air raid?"

"Fortunately, no." Adela approached Elsa's bed. "Are you well? You're as pale as—"

"Someone who was trying to sleep after an air raid a mere few hours ago and fearing another one?"

Adela let out a deep breath. She rocked back when she took in Elsa's sudden smile. "What?"

"You care about me—I had you worried, didn't I? Is that what spending time sheltering together from a bomb does? I'm flattered."

"Don't be," Adela said a bit too gruffly. Judging by another silly grin on her roommate's lips, Elsa hadn't taken it as an admonishment. "Let's get ready for work."

Elsa groaned and sank back against her pillow. "Can't we stay here and chitchat about how we both enjoyed listening to our grandparents' stories, the lessons they had to teach us, or the cooking tricks we gathered from watching our mothers in the kitchen?"

Evidently, her roommate had enjoyed similar pastimes as she had in her *vista* days. "Not with the Herr's two littlest ones in need of your attention."

Elsa tossed off the blanket and scrambled out of bed, rubbing her arms against the room's chill. "Is the whole household back to life as normal—however you choose to define normal following a bomb threat? Or, for that matter, whatever normal means in Germany these days?"

"Shush." Adela pivoted and strode to the dresser to withdraw her day's work clothes of a black skirt and white blouse. "You best hurry," she said over her shoulder as she brushed out the knots in her thinning hair. She might be eating better here than if she had remained in Vienna—or home, in Bratislava—but unlike the Herr and Frau and their children, the servants lacked certain nutrients. She squeezed her eyes shut. That too may change. Soon. If she could just hold on a little longer.

"Adela." Elsa's voice startled her, and she jumped. "I see your unhappy reflection in the dresser's mirror. What's wrong?"

"I'm preparing to start my work day, that's all. I'm grateful to have this employment."

"Truly?" Elsa stepped up to her. Rather than wait for a reply, she pulled open one of her drawers and withdrew a brown skirt and white blouse. She snarled at the clothes. "These clothes resemble the uniforms of the brown-shirt Nazi boys."

That was enough. Adela spun around fast. About to shake a warning finger at the impulsive girl, she held back, aware that the only difference between the two of them was not what they thought and believed in but that she had learned the art of stifling her thoughts. In contrast, Elsa spoke what was on her mind. Was that the difference between an adult and a child, or the brave brilliance of individualism despite the consequences? She shifted from foot to foot as her admiration for Elsa blossomed. But they couldn't afford to take chances. "Be careful your mouth doesn't get you—or both of us—in trouble one day. Understand?"

Elsa pursed her lips and gave a quick nod. "Can I take a bath first? I'm as grimy as..." She glanced about. "As grimy as a damp cellar. No reflection on you, however."

"When you marry a nice Nazi boy and become his Frau and he builds you a castle, you can take baths whenever you wish. But for now, throw on those clothes you just made a face at, gobble down a bowl of porridge, and greet Fritz and Wil with the biggest smile you can muster."

"And you, my friend?"

Adela had begun to walk toward the door but stopped at Elsa's choice of words. "Friend." It had been a long time since she had been considered one, other than by Richard.

"I'm reporting for duty. If there are no servant call-outs today from those claiming an illness—then believe me, there is always an item or two that needs cleaning. I'll keep plenty busy, as should you." She opened the door and slipped out before Elsa could seize her once more with a word of hope.

After nibbling on a biscuit and gulping down a few sips of real coffee —one of the few perks of living in the Friedrich household—Adela began her work day. Surprisingly, the comfort in the daily routines of work and chores overtook a mass of morbid thoughts. Just as well. Adela had no objections to working by herself. The mundane task of polishing silver candlesticks, or an equally boring task, would supply ample time to imagine what the next few days promised and how she could best prepare for them.

At mid-morning, she needed a bathroom break and excused herself to the head housekeeper. After freshening up, she walked out into the hallway, and a wave of grief slammed her against the wall and carried her back to Vienna. The child cried. Her little arms hugged her tight as they ran through the night in search of shelter. Her eyes clouded. Her face paled. Signs of fear no child should ever have.

Adela staggered downstairs toward her bedroom door. Upon discovering she had the room to herself, relief unknotted the tension in her shoulders. Hurrying to the dresser, she pulled out the top drawer and slid her hand to the right corner where she kept her private stash. She withdrew the three pictures of Miriam, handling them with tender care as if one slight move would scare away the memory of this precious child. She propped each photograph, taken by Richard as a means to appease her heartache, against the mirror. The headshot showed the one-year-old's golden locks, bright blue eyes, and an open-mouthed smile. If one were to see the expression, they'd never imagine the child in dire hunger or missing her mama or papa or big sister. The photo on the right showed Miriam hugging a rag doll, its tattered limbs poking out of an equally worn and faded red dress. The last image always snatched a piece of Adela's heart, threatening to never give it back until they met again, hopefully, in the near future. This photograph showed Miriam resting against a pillow on the bed that Elsa now used. Beautiful Miriam showing her lower front teeth in a big smile. Not a trace of fear scored her face but rather, total trust in her, the one who never did her harm—until moments after that photograph was taken.

That was when Miriam had called her mama for the first and last time.

Adela pushed past the tears that dangled total hysteria before her eyes, ruining the last chance of hope for her. As if Miriam was before her, she summoned her wits for the child's sake.

"Hello, my sweet *bebelus*. Are you a happy baby now?" She shuddered as if a blast of wind had gushed through the small cellar window that was fastened shut. "Forgive me, Miriam. Are you happy, my big six-year-old girl?" She choked on the last word and pressed a finger against her mouth to block the sobs pushing to escape her mouth. A warning from Adela's mother shifted to the forefront of her memory: "Words lift into the air and trail their way to ears that may or may not need to hear what is said. Always be strong and of good cheer." Adela needed to calm down. She had to comfort the child, not scare her.

She took a deep breath and exhaled slowly, keeping her eyes on the photographs. "Sweet Miriam, how are you and your foster parents getting along? Are you enjoying school, learning lessons about this world we live in? What do you think about the blue sky and how it holds the murmurs of your ancestors? Do you hear the whispers of my family as well? Do you have a meadow of the greenest grass where you can sit with friends and play dollies, or do you busy yourself trying to catch butterflies? Here's a secret, my love: catch the fireflies of the night. Hold them gently, and lift them to your ear, and you will hear them tell century-old tales. That's what my grandmother always told me and to this day, I believe her." She chuckled. "Not that I have time, the opportunity, or the energy to chase down fireflies at night."

"Adela?" came a shout from the hallway.

Werner? What did he want? Might he have news of Richard? She darted out of the room. No one was there. How odd. The butler had a distinct accent—no one else in the household sounded like him. Adela ducked around a few corners, but didn't see him. Then, she remembered she'd left the photographs of Miriam on top of the dresser. She retraced her steps to her room, but stopped cold when she heard the Frau's voice coming from within. She pressed against the wall, heart pounding, and hoped the Frau hadn't seen or heard her.

"What are you doing away from my boys, Teacher Elsa? Where are they?"

"Fritz and Wil are fine, Frau Friedrich. I'm sorry to have given you concern. Shirley stepped into their bedroom suite where we were studying the lessons of—"

"Get to the point." Impatience and boredom rang in the Frau's tone.

"I needed to freshen up and..."

"Yes?"

"I apologize, Frau Friedrich. Since I was also in need of monthly supplies..."

"Supplies? Oh. Of course. Those. Well, then, hurry back to my sons without delay."

Quietly, Adela ducked around a corner she doubted the Frau would travel. She was correct. After a minute or so, she peeked around the corner. The Frau was gone. Adela rushed into the bedroom and saw Elsa leaning against the dresser. The photographs were not there—Elsa must have seen them. The risk of leaving them exposed had consequences. Up to this point, Adela had managed to keep this secret hidden from all eyes, with the exception of Richard and one other person. Fear pocked her skin with gooseflesh; anger over her ruined plans followed, heating her body and chasing away the chill from seconds ago. Yet, she couldn't further delay her plans. She willed herself to remain calm and gently closed the door. "Where are they?"

"The boys?" Elsa wrapped her arms around her middle. "Or the photographs?"

So, she definitely had seen them. "Don't play games with me."

Elsa lifted her chin to look directly at Adela. "After that scare of the Frau barging in, rather than unleashing your anger at me, you better spend your time thanking me for shoving those photos into one of my drawers. If the Frau had seen them and was itching to make a stink, I'd have taken the blame instead of you."

"Oh," Adela mouthed. She was unnerved. The Frau had ventured into their room, which always carried consequences. The Frau knew about Miriam, but not the photos, though she probably would have simply dismissed them as overly sentimental. However, if Elsa had actually fibbed and claimed that the photos were hers, the Frau's suspicions of them both might have ruined Adela's plans for later that evening. And to think Elsa was prepared to fib about the photographs, taking great risks to protect her. She looked into Elsa's eyes. "Thank you," she said softly.

"Why was the Frau here?" Elsa asked.

Adela shrugged. "She definitely is free to go wherever she wants in her own house. I wasn't expecting her, not that she shares her itinerary with me." She lifted a brow in concern. "Did you need sanitary products again?"

"No. I couldn't think of a more convincing excuse—one she wouldn't question me about." Elsa frowned. "What were you doing, standing outside the door and listening?"

"I almost walked in on the two of you, but when I heard her, I thought it would be best to stay out of the room."

"Who's the sweet *bebelus* you were addressing?" Elsa's face turned apple red.

Adela matched her roommate's stance, arms to her side and chin up. "What were you doing—standing outside the door and listening?" she said, repeating Elsa's exact words.

"Sorry. Yes, I was outside the door about to walk in, but when I heard Werner say your name, I ducked around a corner." She paused, her eyes growing narrow. "What language is the word *bebelus*? Is Miriam your little girl? Your daughter? What happened to her?" Elsa glanced at the bed she'd been sleeping in since rooming with Adela. "Is that Miriam's bed I sleep in? Is Miriam the one you call to in your sleep?"

Too many questions, though Adela sensed she owed Elsa an explanation. "The word you're asking about is in a language that has become dead to me." With that one sentence, Adela was seized by a tidal wave of emotion she'd suppressed for years now. "Stop saying her name. Please. I beg you."

"Beg?" Elsa said softly. "Why?"

"Because she's not here right now."

Elsa took a step closer toward her. "That's not the real reason. Please, I want to know."

"What is it to you?"

"I care."

Adela couldn't escape the truth a second longer. "It hurts too much."

Elsa tenderly steered her to her bed. "Sit, my friend. It will be fine."

"You know nothing about what you speak. It will never be fine. Not with distance between Miriam and me, not with this war going on with more and more people willing to rid this world of others they deem inferior and unworthy to live."

"May I sit beside you?"

Adela nodded, aware of how badly she needed a friend to understand, accept, and reassure her that yes, the bumps in life would eventually smooth out, despite her not believing that nonsense. She hadn't seen her family in years. Were her parents, her sister, her beloved extended family in her *vista* alive? Richard had told her about other Roma taken into Nazi captivity, invading their encampments in the middle of the black night. They might all be gone, existent only as haunting, restless spirits. She shut her eyes against the thought that her loved ones might no longer be alive. That included her second family: Daniel and Lara Ostrów, Miriam's parents. And what had become of Miriam's sister, Irene? If Irene was alive, she'd be ten years old now. The worst part was that with each delay in leaving this monstrous Friedrich estate, she might never secure the answers she so desperately sought.

"Adela, I can understand what it's like to lose a dear loved one."

Adela opened her eyes and sat taller. "Do you speak from

personal experience? Tell me. I want to hear. But later tonight since the Frau is expecting you to return to the twins."

"That would be fine." Elsa stood. "Later, we'll have a conversation that I believe is a bit overdue."

Adela watched her roommate exit the room. She was beginning to see that her first reaction to Elsa had been undeservingly cool. From what the younger woman intimated, they might indeed have a lot in common. Their similar histories could smooth the paths for them to become emotional supports to each other. Dare she dream they might even become friends? What was she thinking? That was a chance she couldn't afford to take right now. If luck graced her, Richard would soon return, and by tonight, they would take off together. She and Elsa would never have this discussion, let alone see each other again. That was the way it must be.

15

The hours traipsed on. Overall not a bad day, Elsa thought. Considering they'd taken shelter from the threat of bombs and had less than a handful of hours of sleep—a mere nap—no disasters occurred, though she came pretty close to a row with Adela, who was in a mood. Elsa's gut told her she'd get to the root of her roommate's gloomy state of mind, that the two needed each other's friendship badly during this dreadful war.

The somber day perfectly matched the gray January sky, with its heavy clouds teasing a snowstorm. As for storms, at least she could deal with the weather. She didn't even have to worry about Fritz and Wil's Jungvolk that afternoon since it had been canceled for the day due to the air raid. They were droopy and difficult, and she'd spent a good deal of the day beside herself, trying different ways of calming them and getting them to focus on basic math. She'd even stooped to the level of acquiescing to Wil's demand that she explain the example of addition and subtraction in terms of the number of tanks minus the people they kill. If years ago, she'd been told that she'd be teaching a five-year-old that kind of lesson, she would have laughed. Now, she wanted to cry. She rubbed her throbbing temples.

"Teacher Elsa?" Fritz pointed toward his brother drawing on the chalkboard tucked into the corner of their bedroom. "Wil drew a sick woman. Are you sick?"

Wil set down his chalk and faced them. "Mutter is sick with a headache and is staying in bed today. Says it's from all the noise last night."

Ah. She'd go with that excuse. "Yes, I too have an ache of the noggin. I think there's a few of us like that today." Elsa stood from her desk chair with her mind made up to stretch the truth for the sake of convenience. "Since it's approaching dinnertime, and you've done quite well with today's lessons, you boys are dismissed." Before they could become boisterous, she gestured with a repeated downward push of her hands for them to simmer down. "Please remain quiet for the sake of your mother's poor head—and mine—and stay here in your room. I will alert Werner to our situation, then retire to my room. Will you two behave?" As they bobbed their heads in perfect sync with each other, she left the room to find Werner. Except for an occasional ache if she moved the wrong way, her ankle had healed, and she was relieved to be able to move quickly.

After Werner assured her that he'd look after the twins, she excused herself to head back to the cellar room she was reluctant to think of as a bedroom. The path to go there meant walking down the grand staircase from the second floor, where the family's suites were, to the main foyer where guests were received, and the staff assembled for the Frau's daily inspection. Fortunately, from what she'd heard murmured in the kitchen earlier, Herr Friedrich had returned to wherever good Nazis stalked when away from their estates. His company from last night also long gone.

"*Guten Tag*, Teacher Elsa."

She did not have to turn around to ascertain that Erich stood behind her, not with his rich voice, the one that visited her in her dreams.

"Or, considering the lateness of the day," he continued, "I should greet you with a *Guten Abend*."

She turned to face him. "Hello would do nicely."

He narrowed the distance between them and smiled. "Well then, hello. Would you be returning to your room?"

She tensed. "Your brothers are fine. I left them in Werner's care."

"That's not what I asked." He clutched her upper arm and tugged her closer to his side. "It's time to drop your guard, don't you think?"

She lifted a brow. "What—we have a conversation in a bomb shelter, and like long lost friends, it's good between us?"

He motioned for them to continue walking. She hadn't anticipated an escort by one of the Friedrichs, but she certainly couldn't protest. This was his home, not hers. She was a servant, a depressing fact made clear each morning when she awoke to the annoying buzzing of a bell, summoning her to work. Once she and Erich made it past the kitchen, away from prying eyes, she heard a distinct sigh coming from him. Of relief?

He held the stairwell door open for her and motioned her to step forward. Once inside, he again clutched her arm, drawing her against the concrete wall. "Let's talk for a moment, yes?" With no choice, she nodded and waited for him to continue. "I'm home, unable to return to Cologne as planned due to a nasty storm dumping meters of snow and heading this way."

She didn't think Erich was striving for idle chitchat about the weather. The little she knew of him, she could tell he was a highly intelligent person that didn't act without a reason. "Have you heard from your other friends and acquaintances since last night's air raid? Are they accounted for, and are they well?"

"Yes. No worries there."

"But there are other concerns?" She winced. "Sorry, that was too personal to ask."

"That's fine. I appreciate how perceptive you are."

She mustered a little smile. "That's what my father always said about me. I mean, not that I'm comparing you to him or to other men his age, but—"

"Understood. I have concerns, though, to discuss with you and Adela."

She tensed and started to step away. He pulled her back toward him.

"Before anyone else might stumble across us here, permit me to continue." He eyed her but didn't wait for an acknowledgment. "As for you, earlier today I made a few phone calls to my various connections. Starting in Berlin."

Her stomach buckled and she wrapped her arms around her middle. "About?"

"Grant you, Berlin is a major city, but in the last 50 years, there is no trace of a woman by the name of Herta Hoffmann."

She wasn't about to admit guilt or defeat. Nor would she raise her voice in anger, and she certainly wouldn't reveal details about her family that could incriminate them as wanted Jews and put them in harm's way. "Do you have such great concern about me that you've gone out of your way to inquire with people who know little about me? If it's my teaching your brothers, I will strive to do better." Since she'd spoken in a relaxed tone, she expected a little grin or even a stern expression that shouted that he was the Herr's son and could do as he chose and get away with it. Instead, the most serious look she'd ever seen on Erich's face radiated trouble.

"From the beginning, Elsa—if that's truly your name—I've had difficulty accepting your story of why you were walking the streets in Nijmegen." He reached toward her. She stepped back. He inched closer, and this time, streaked a finger across her cheek. She froze like a cornered animal. "You had a black and blue eye and a bad ankle. I took you here and had a doctor summoned." He swallowed twice. A look of pain slashed across his face. "The doctor pulled me aside—away from my mother—so we could talk, you know, man-to-man."

This conversation had jumped from odd to horrible. She covered her mouth to keep spiteful words—or was it vomit—from rising up. Carefully, she spoke around her fingers. "What did the doctor say?"

"He did a full examination of you."

"When I was unconscious?"

Erich nodded. "He said you'd been recently violated. A bit

different from the explanation that your friend's boyfriend almost raped you."

It took her several seconds to process his words and to mull over how to respond. "And what now? Will you label me a slut? Have me arrested? Thrown into a camp?"

This time, he flinched. "I doubt the Nazis have a special jail cell or camp for women who have been raped or mistreated. They're not into humanity."

"Is this a sick joke for you?"

He shrugged. "The only thing I can bank on is that I don't want harm coming to you. Not in any form or degree or by anyone's hand or by anyone's command."

She refused to look away. Let him recognize that he wasn't dealing with a mousy wimp. "So, you've tracked me down just now to tell me that you've discovered I might have told an untruth about my mother and what had happened to me?"

"Did you hear what I said? Let me repeat it: I don't want harm coming to you."

This must be one of his tricks. He was the Herr's son. Like father like son?

Erich grasped her arms. She squeezed her eyes shut; a groan slipped from her lips. He let go of her. "Have I hurt you?"

"No." His hold on her had been oddly comforting, like a shawl wrapped around her shoulders for extra warmth on a chilly night. A strong sense of loneliness engulfed her and she began to shake. "It's me. I detest the person I've become—suspicious of each person I meet. Here I am, despising prejudice against others who are born into families and faiths that others see as deplorable, and I'm treating you horribly because of the family and circumstances you've been born into."

Slowly, gently, he lifted her head with his fingertips. "You didn't deserve what that worthless rapist did to you. Nor the heartache you and your family suffered at the hands of this monstrous war. This is a tragic time with people pitted against each other. There's not one person I know that wouldn't tell a lie in the name of survival. I'm not here to jeopardize your existence. If that was the case, I wouldn't have brought you here." He grinned. "By the way, that's the truth, not a lie."

"There's nothing like a nice Nazi home to bring protection and comfort to a woman walking aimlessly on the streets."

He stuffed his hands into his trouser pockets. "My family is who they are. I'm the son of parents who pledged their allegiance to Hitler. I couldn't pick and choose my family or this miserable time of chaos, just like you couldn't pick and choose your own family or when you were born. But, evidently, I can't persuade you to separate me from my parents' actions or beliefs. I guess that means I will have to suffer your condemnation. So be it. But I wanted to let you know that I learned a little about your past. If I did, and easily, then others—like my father or his friends—may be able to do so as well, if they haven't already investigated. You must be more careful."

She couldn't get overwhelmed by what he was implying. Instead, she focused on the man beside her. "What I don't understand is what you plan on doing with this information. It's not conclusive. So, what if a woman by the name of Herta Hoffman can't be found? As you're fond of saying, this is wartime. Mysteries occur all the time." She chuckled bitterly. "It might just be well that we don't understand about some of the things that happen before our eyes."

"Here's the thing. I don't know either. Don't know why I've bothered to find out what I could about you except that I was curious."

Curiosity could go two ways, either on a positive or negative path. Positive curiosity between a man and woman could indicate attraction or respect. But, with Erich? And, here, in Nazi German during the war? He was the Herr's son. This curiosity would certainly not end well for either of them. She wasn't about to explore that quandary, at least not right then and there. She rubbed at her temples. "I'm afraid I have a headache. You caught me on the way back to my room to rest."

This time, he offered a smile. Although she thought it was sincere, she looked away.

"I must speak with Adela," Erich said. "I'll walk you to your room and hopefully find her there."

———

Adela was in the room, but from what Elsa could surmise, she appeared less frantic than she'd last seen. Still, Elsa had experienced enough to understand that how a person chose to act didn't necessarily mean they were not full of fear, regret, or misgivings. She stared at her hopeful friend and smiled gently. About to ask how she was, Erich came up behind Elsa, stopping short.

"Pardon me," he said as he rested his palms on Elsa's shoulders. The touch was firm, necessary in the name of preventing a collision, yet distinctly comforting.

Adela sniffled and blotted her wet cheeks with her sleeve. "Elsa? Erich? What's wrong?"

Elsa stepped aside and cleared her throat. "Would you like me to step outside and give you two privacy?"

"No," they both answered in unison.

"It's an unwise choice," Erich added.

Elsa blinked. She'd intended her question for her roommate, but both had responded. She nodded and leaned forward to listen.

"You first," Adela said to Erich. She glanced at Elsa's bed then back at Erich. "Sit, if you like."

"I'll try to make this brief." Erich accepted the invitation to sit. "You can relax. No bad news about Richard."

"What then?" Adela asked.

"It's a delay to your plans due to the weather. Nothing more. I had my men secure this information. Richard will aim for tomorrow night. Same time. He doesn't believe there have been leaks—"

"Spies?" Elsa said, interrupting.

Erich pursed his lips, his right brow lifted higher than the left. "Yes. Looks like you're also learning a thing or two about how the Nazi hate-machine operates. Believe me, when it's discovered one plan doesn't work well, a solution pops up fast, whether it's a material item, an improved directive, or a change in personnel."

"A change in personnel," Elsa echoed.

"When it comes to the extinguishing the lives of one section of the population, it's the goal of the Nazi Party to carry on until only the Aryan race alone is alive and thriving. Apart from certain Aryans who have fallen foul of the Party." Erich stood from the bed and strode toward Elsa. He extended his hand to her. "You're looking too pale to ignore. Come join us and the three of us will carry on this conversation."

"But how can I trust you?" she blurted out.

"I tried to explain this moments ago," Erich said, his tone gentle, caring. "But it didn't go as smoothly as I'd hoped. Richard and I are not the brutes that others think we are."

"Elsa," Adela said. "We'd both be dead, in a camp, or homeless by now if it weren't for Erich and his brother."

Elsa grasped Erich's hand and permitted him to lead her toward Adela. She sat to Adela's left; Erich sat opposite of them. Before either Erich or Adela could speak, Elsa started to tremble. Erich stood, gathered the blanket from the bed where he sat, and wrapped it over both her and Adela's shoulders. Elsa nodded her appreciation and was taken aback when Adela pressed into her side.

"It's cold," Adela murmured. "We can share more heat this way."

Elsa smiled. "That sounds good."

"I'll tell you the little I've found out," Erich continued. "My brother should be here at two tomorrow morning. Adela, while Elsa remains here, Richard expects you to—"

"I don't like the sounds of this," Elsa said. "I remain here? You two —well, three, if you include Richard—are about to go off on an adventure—whether a good one or dangerous—and you expect me to stay here and follow orders to help the Friedrichs live happily ever after? What if Frau Friedrich corners me in regard to your whereabouts? Should I shrug? Tell her I don't know? I guess I could do that, considering you're leaving me in the dark." Elsa looked hard at Erich. "I'm wondering if this trusting business is pure malarkey."

"Far from it." Erich leaned forward, his elbows balancing on his knees. "Richard has one of the biggest hearts considering what he's up against. Hmm, I can see you're perplexed by this. Let me try to explain."

"Please," Elsa said. "Keep it simple, my head's swimming enough."

"Well, my brother's heart is both a boon and a drawback. He's taking huge risks right now on Adela's behalf, but he's committed, and there's no going back for him until he carries out his mission. As for me, I'm involved in another operation of sorts. At times, our lines of communication cross over. That's all I can say for now, perhaps for good. Because of our positions and risks to ourselves, Adela, and now you—and our family..." He paused when Elsa's mouth sagged open. "Yes, even our Nazi family counts, which makes it more difficult, not easier. Richard and I are the sons of two parents who try their best to love us. You and others may see them as ruthless Nazis, but my brother and I have been loved by them, as well as our two little brothers who know nothing apart from what they've been taught by our parents and select teachers. We do not condone our parents' choice of beliefs, which puts enormous pressure on us. They believe what they do as much as we believe the opposite. We cannot risk our plans and other lives being jeopardized. Our time to leave is tomorrow. Adela and I need you to remain here, or events may turn sour fast."

He stood and patted Adela on the shoulder. "Are you set?"

"Yes, as planned."

"I am too." He rubbed his hands together. "I'm going to check on a few things. Unless there's another change, you won't see me until tomorrow night."

"Thank you," Adela whispered.

Without responding, Erich strode out of the room. As soon as the door was shut, Elsa faced her roommate. "If you cannot tell me about this mission that you and Erich are on, you are going to tell me who you are and about your past."

"And you will tell me the same."

There was no going back now.

16

As soon as Erich stepped out of the room and shut the door behind him, Adela once again wished she could dissipate into thin air and transport herself to another time and place when life was beautiful.

Elsa slipped out from the blanket they were sharing, sprang to her feet, and began to pace the room.

Adela jabbed her temple with one hand and with the other clutched Elsa by the elbow. "You're making me dizzy. Sit next to me and we'll talk."

Rather than oblige, Elsa sank onto her own bed. "I'm making you dizzy?"

Adela crossed her arms. "You sound like a brash teenager."

A smirk lifted the corners of Elsa's mouth. "Because I am a teenager, and I learned a long time ago that it's fine to stand up for what I believe is right. I'm rather disappointed that you think I'm rude or overbearing. I was hoping you'd see me as an equal because I've come to respect you."

Adela didn't quite know how to respond. On the one hand, she was curious about this girl-woman. On the other hand, she'd learned the painful way that it was best not to know the truth about others. The less attached one was to another, the less it hurt when the inevitable separation came. "How old are you? Tell me about your true identity and why you are here."

"Will you answer your own questions about yourself after I reveal things that I shouldn't be telling anyone?"

As she thought about leaving the household, Adela took comfort in the one thing that Erich and Richard had ascertained for her was that her roommate wasn't a spy. She rested back on her elbows. "I'll say what I can."

Elsa surprised her by plopping a finger into her mouth and starting to chew a nail. "My name is Edith. I'm Jewish by birth and not ashamed of it, though I've become terrified of identifying myself that way to strangers. My family's faith has destroyed my family." She paused. "No, that's not quite right. It's other people who refuse to acknowledge my family's faith and their right to worship as they choose that has destroyed my family." She did a double take when Adela nodded. "Adela, are you also Jewish?"

"No. But my family too was destroyed. You'll see. Continue."

"As long as we're in this house, please use my name—Elsa—the one I took on when my mother abandoned me in a safe house in the Netherlands."

"Abandon? I've heard about the Dutch putting their children in these places because they didn't have any choices. Abandon is a harsh word, isn't it? I would think that your mother put you into this protective situation because she loves you so much. I imagine that it broke her heart to do it."

Rather than resume chewing her fingernail, Elsa shoved both hands under her thighs and started to rock back and forth. "She first abandoned my younger sister, then me."

"And you resent your mother for wanting to give you a chance of surviving this war? What would you have done if you were in that situation with a child you loved?" Heat flushed her face. "Oh, dear. Please forgive me for asking a sensitive question since no one is truly prepared for a catastrophe before it strikes, especially war."

"Put that way, I don't know," Elsa replied. "When I arrived at the first safe house, I was willing to die over never seeing my mother again. Now, I admit I'm quite confused. I've been suspecting my reaction was severe because never seeing my mother, father, or sister would be awful. It was the four of us, you know. Just us against the world. We tried leaving Germany—yes, I'm a native German, though fat good it does as far as Hitler and his machine of hate go."

"What happened?" Adela asked, relieved she hadn't alienated her roommate. After tomorrow they wouldn't see each other again, and she'd come to respect Elsa. If it were another time and place, might they become friends and enjoy each other's company? She sighed inwardly. This was a world war. Nazi Germany wanted to be the world's supreme ruler, making inhumane rules about who got to live based solely on who benefitted and propagated the best to the supposed Aryan race. Oh, how she wished she could spit out the vile taste in her mouth, but she didn't want to rattle Elsa.

"We made it to Cuba," Elsa continued. "We were supposed to travel on to the United States., but they didn't want us, neither did other countries, except for the Netherlands. So, we sailed back there and were just beginning to live happily ever after—"

"When the Germans occupied the country?"

"Yes." Elsa huffed. "Occupation. What an odd concept. War is war. On paper, it's one thing; in life, well, reality, as I suspect you know, it's a whole different matter."

Adela stroked the scratchy blanket. "How did you get here, to this town, to the Friedrich estate?"

"I was raped by the owner of the safe house."

Adela gasped. "I'm so sorry. How awful." Elsa, a confessed teenager, and she had much in common—they both had no choice but to overcome what they shouldn't have had to think twice about. In need of better, kinder thoughts, her mind drifted back to the days of sunshine and birdsong and campfire stories. Of laughter. Of life's only problem being competition with her older sister, tiptoeing around their mother not to make her upset, carrying on the hard work of gathering firewood, cooking for hungry faces, and ignoring the insults hurled against them because they were Roma. Beautiful, good people. Once upon a time, happy men, women, and children who, if they wanted to, could dance down a road and not worry about what others thought of them.

"I had to get out of there, the non-safe house," Elsa said, luring Adela back to the awful present. "After I fled, luck ran in the opposite direction and I twisted my ankle. That's when Erich found me. The pain was horrific and I passed out. When I woke up, I was stretched out in the backseat of Erich's car, and we were in Nazi Germany, the one place I didn't want to be."

"You had to make the best of an awful situation because you have fight in you."

"I had no other choice."

"One always has a choice. In your case, you chose to stand up for yourself rather than let that jerk at the safe house dictate how you were to live. That's certainly admirable—what strength and determination you showed." Adela stood, crossed over to Elsa's bed, and sat beside her. "You've braved Nazi Germany despite the odds stacked against you." A chuckle escaped her lips. "Even put up with becoming the twins' teacher."

"I try."

"I believe you always do the best you can."

"Thank you." Elsa bunched fistfuls of the blanket. "What's your story?"

"Because it's getting late and we should check on our duties, I'll have to give you an abbreviated version." Adela waited for Elsa to protest, but she didn't. "My real name is Ivona, Vonni for short, though continue to call me Adela. I'm Roma." She took in Elsa's gawking. "Yes, I have blonde hair—natural blonde hair. I used to think I was a freak because no other Roma that I know has blonde hair, but according to Richard, there are a few of us around." She blinked. "Well, I hope the others are still alive."

Elsa nodded. "I know exactly what you mean. Where are you from?"

"Bratislava."

"That's a long way off."

"In some respects, yes. In others, it's like my beloved native land is around the corner."

"Probably because it lives—like my Berlin—in your just-yesterday section of memory?"

"That's right," Adela murmured. She could almost taste the slice of life she remembered as sweet, not only when devouring *xaritsa*. The thought of the fried cornbread made her mouth water. The same with *xaimoko*, rabbit meat. "One day, my father went missing. Life changed. My older sister went to search for him, but because of my mother's fear of the bad news the bird brought—I'll tell you about our superstitions another time—I too went out searching for my father. I got lost in Austria. I encountered people I wish I hadn't. The Anschluss happened, and Austria gladly gave itself to Germany. I made it to Vienna where I was practically adopted by this most beautiful Jewish family, with two of the sweetest little girls."

Elsa turned sheet-white. "The photograph of the girl, of Miriam. Kristallnacht."

No questions. Statements. Her roommate understood. "Yes."

"While you faced that horrid night of destruction in Vienna, my family faced it in Berlin."

"Brown shirts grabbing people and dragging them away, making them clean the streets."

Elsa nodded. "Store windows shattering. Cries. Synagogues turning to ashes."

"People screaming. People crying. Families ripped apart."

"Yes! That's why we had to escape. But Adela, you aren't Jewish."

"Doesn't matter. I was living with a Jewish family. Anyway, the Nazis hate the Roma. In their pea-sized venomous brains, we are worthless vagabonds."

"And Miriam?" With the tips of her fingers, Elsa wiped the tears from Adela's cheeks. Tears she'd been oblivious to.

"Her parents only took the oldest girl because they didn't think they'd make it back to Poland—where they were originally from—with a baby." Adela could hardly breathe as her life in Vienna flashed before her. "They begged me to take Miriam. Richard found us living on the streets. See, your mother wasn't the only one who had to give away a child in the hope of saving a life." She hadn't meant to sound severe, but the thought of Miriam's family fleeing to Poland, only to have Germany—and Russia—invade Poland in September 1939, was too much to endure. They probably weren't alive. They had most likely perished in a camp, working so hard and starving that they wished they were dead. It was just like what may have happened to her own family, according to Richard's informants. And that was why she had to find out for herself, even if it meant getting caught herself and winding up in the same dreadful circumstances.

"But I'm sleeping on Miriam's bed. What happened to her?"

Adela willed herself to calm down and breathe. "I can't tell you now. I want to tell you. It's just that—"

The bedroom door slammed open. Frau Friedrich stepped in. Dressed in a black skirt, a brown silk blouse with a flappy tie fastened in a bow, a black jacket with wide shoulder pads, and her customary lack of a smile, she appeared taller than her real height and radiated Nazism with a capital N. "Come with me right now. Both of you."

17

Elsa intuited straight away that the Frau summoning her and Adela spelled a distinct disaster, though unknown to her. Elsa failed to understand, however, why the Frau peered warily around each corner of her own home as if she feared or suspected an unknown terror to seizing her. She couldn't ask, or keep up with the woman's pace. A glance at Adela showed she too had to compete with the Frau's fast clip. The creases across her roommate's forehead revealed worry and intensified Elsa's rattled nerves. When they reached the main level of the house and started in the direction of the formal dining room, with guests on the way, Elsa thought that this was simply the Frau's way of getting extra pairs of hands for dinner preparation. Yet, if that had been the case, it wouldn't have been for the Frau to personally summon them. This whole situation definitely did not bode well.

Once past the dining room, the Frau glanced over her shoulder. "Continue to follow me upstairs to our private suites. Quickly. Quietly."

The only times Elsa had been on the second floor of the house had been when she busied herself with Fritz and Wil, in a distant wing from the Frau and Herr's collection of rooms. There was a separate stairwell she and the other servants were expected to use. This moment reminded Elsa of the days preceding Kristallnacht—terror was brewing but when disaster would strike was impossible to predict. Was she about to receive an admonishment for leaving the boys to Werner's care earlier, shirking her responsibilities? Would she be told to leave the house immediately, tossed outdoors into the stormy winter evening? That made no sense. Not with Adela by her side. If she was going to be told to leave, the Frau could have done so downstairs in the cellar bedroom. Elsa shuddered at the images parading through her imagination of the Frau shoving her to the front door and pushing her outdoors, a wicked snicker flying from a mouth, the witch in a fairy tale.

As Elsa climbed each stair, she snatched sideway glances at the original masterpieces by artists she'd studied from her father's personal books before her family had fled Berlin, the moment her life became marked as Before *Kristallnacht* and After *Kristallnacht*. Vermeer's *The Milkmaid* pouring the beverage from a pitcher to a bowl. Monet's *Women in the Garden* with the four women in white and ivory dresses, making her wish she was one of them. Then there was also one portraying melted timepieces strewn across a table surface. She had a hunch it was a Salvador Dali. Were these framed paintings originals or copies? The only thing Elsa knew was that with most Germans and others throughout Europe and the rest of the world suffering from a lack of food, fuel, and medicine, she didn't want to know where the Friedrichs obtained these artworks.

She felt a poke to her right shoulder blade. Elsa glanced at Adela's narrowed eyes. She understood her friend's stern but unspoken warning: keep your eyes ahead and hurry like your life depends on it. Elsa couldn't help but lift her brows in question. What's happening? What should we do? Is this the beginning of the end for us? Adela seemed to understood and replied with a shrug.

The Frau whipped around a corner and made swift strides down a rich burgundy runner. Prepared to follow the woman around yet another corner, Elsa nearly plowed into her when she halted before a shut door.

She faced the two of them. "This is my personal suite. You are not to say a word while I do the talking."

Elsa and Adela glanced at each other, nodded, and followed her in. Right away, Elsa saw Erich pacing before a desk, its surface strewn with loose papers. The desk drawer was pulled open a crack. It was a mystery whether Erich or his mother was the primary user, but Erich didn't have guilt stamped across his face upon seeing his mother enter the room. He wore casual black slacks, a thick, emerald-green shirt, and a dark brown buttoned sweater vest. He paused by a desk chair with his heavy tartan brown beige coat draped over its tall back. It was the same coat he'd worn when they first met in the Netherlands and made her wonder if he was preparing for another trip.

"About time."

"It will be fine, Erich," the Frau said, shocking Elsa with her tender tone and reminding her that the Frau was a mother first and foremost. "You can trust me. As I've already told you, I've seen to the final arrangements."

"I do trust you. Not others, but definitely you." Erich flicked his attention between Elsa and Adela. "Due to the stormy weather, there's been a drastic change of plans. I encourage you both to listen carefully to what my mother has to say."

The Frau invited her son, then Elsa and Adela, to have a seat on the sofa to the right of the desk.

Disregarding the Frau's strict warnings, Adela leaned over Elsa toward Erich. She shielded her mouth and whispered, "She knows everything?"

"Of course I do," the Frau replied before Erich could address Adela's concerns. "It's my house, my business. Now please, we do not have the luxury of time. Be quiet and let me tell you what is to happen." She paused as Adela pulled away from Erich. "Last evening, our dinner and subsequent meeting with our special guests were interrupted by the bomb threat. Fortunately, there was no bomb. Unfortunately, these honored officers have been invited back here to another gathering tomorrow. Karl Renner, for one."

Erich swore, jumped to his feet, and resumed pacing. "That Austrian pseudo-leader? He'll be here?"

Elsa had heard how this Austrian leader advocated the Anschluss in 1938 that united the country with Germany. She had also heard how vehement he championed antisemitism. Who were the other guests last evening? She could barely breathe.

"Yes, but I'd watch your tongue," the Frau said. She motioned with her chin for Erich to sit and waited until he resumed his place next to Elsa and Adela. She wrung her hands as if she was the one who had to worry. "Now, getting back to the subject of the weather—I talked with Richard earlier this afternoon. Due to the snow, he's stuck in Vienna, but an unexpected snowstorm is to our advantage. I've learned from my husband that German meteorologists rely on barometers and that customary tools can make fairly decent predictions up to 72 hours in advance. That is, if Mother Nature doesn't trick us with a surprise storm."

"Which is happening right now," Erich said without disguising the glee in his tone. "For once, I'm happy about our miserable weather."

The Frau rocked back, whether from hesitation or amazement that her son had interrupted her Elsa couldn't decipher. "The other plus is that Germany's enemies' bombers and other aircraft are likely grounded. In other words, if you have to cross this country and get into others, like Austria, this would be a most ideal time." She looked at her son. "Werner will drive you and the girls to Richard. In good weather, it would be a 13-hour trip. With the roads dicey from the storm, it will take longer, and you might have to lodge somewhere overnight. I have confidence, though, that between my car and Werner's driving skills, you have a better chance of success than if Richard was to make the trip here. After Werner arrives safely in Vienna, he will return home. Alibies are arranged." The Frau gave Erich a pointed look. "I understand about your activities in Cologne, but I need you to put that aside for now and help Richard."

Erich's forehead furrowed. "The way the RAF and their

Mosquitos have been bombing the city in past weeks, our efforts have turned fetid until we can enlist new recruits. Of course, I'll help."

"Excellent," the Frau said. "Adela, Elsa, it's time to get you on your respective journeys."

"Pardon? I don't understand." Elsa leapt up from her seat. Did the Frau dare to think that she'd go one way, Adela another?

The Frau motioned for Elsa to sit and waited until she did. "It's been brought to my attention that it's in your best safety interest not to remain here."

Elsa crossed her arms and glared at Erich.

"This is based on tomorrow's dinner guests and a few concerns I've heard from my husband." The Frau stared at Elsa. "Time is short and of the essence—it's best not to waste minutes with details. I've made arrangements for you. Upon arrival in Vienna, you will be redirected. Under no circumstances will you hinder my sons or Adela."

Redirected? How? As in on a transport to a work camp? To one of the death camps? Then again, the Frau had just said she was acting in the interest of her safety. What did this woman know about her? And why or how would she hinder Adela or Erich and Richard? "You can count on me not to become an obstacle. To anyone. I will not be sent another way as if I'm a misplaced valise." It had been a feat not to spout off on the inhumanity of packing cattle cars with people and depositing them in camps. As the war progressed, it became common knowledge that rather than work camps, these were places of slaughter. Aware this wasn't the time or place to get into it with the Frau and wanting to prove she wouldn't delay her son or Adela, she remained silent.

"Elsa will remain with me," Erich said. "I'll take full responsibility and see to her safety."

A grin lifted the Frau's lips, but she quickly covered it with her hand.

"Mutter?"

"I was hoping you'd say that, but I needed to hear it." She looked at Elsa. "If you should change your mind, you can take advantage of the safer options I've arranged for you in Vienna, a place you will discover is a point of no return in your journey." She paused, her gaze sweeping across to each of their faces, then lingering on her son's with a concern Elsa had never seen before from this woman. One consequence of war was that one could not accept what was seen or heard as the truth. She reckoned the Frau's stern persona was a cover.

"I can't ensure no harm will come your way," Erich's mother continued. "These are awful times. Son, I know I don't have to emphasize this to you, yet as your mother, I'm obliged to. You'll be taking two additional people on your journey who aren't accustomed to the sights you may encounter."

Question after question stormed through Elsa's mind. What kind of activity had Erich been involved in, yet he was willing to take the time to help his brother and Adela? And put up with her coming along? For that matter, what was Richard up to in Austria? She glanced at the Frau. What kind of mother approved of her son's efforts and shooed him out the door, in the middle of a snowstorm, into a country fighting a war with the rest of the world? A son that she might not ever see again because she—and this estate—was a sitting target for a bomb or other military combat. The answer nearly lifted Elsa from her seat: the Frau was a mother willing to take risks to ensure the welfare of her children, like her own mother. It was becoming clear to Elsa that each day she lived, she had lessons to learn.

"Thank you for understanding," Erich said.

The Frau nodded. "Despite the short time I've had to plan this trip for you, I've seen to packing supplies that should persuade the most hot-headed but hungry German who is eager to defend the Fatherland to look the other way. In the car's trunk you will find extra clothing, food, and drink." She pressed an envelope into Erich's hand. "Here's some money that should help if you are questioned. You'll find a crate of Sturm cigarettes and lighters to make any military personnel happy."

"Interestingly," Erich said, taking advantage of his mother's pause,

"Hitler is opposed to cigarette smoking. He has banned it throughout Germany, but it's the one mandate of Hitler's that is heavily ignored."

"Best to be healthy so one can kill others," Adela mumbled.

"Also," the Frau continued, "in the car you'll find fresh eggs, cheese, and chocolate—the essentials of bartering."

Erich kissed his mother on the cheek. "Excellent planning. I appreciate it."

The Frau motioned for them to stand. "Return to your rooms, gather the necessities, and get out of here before my husband surprises us by returning home earlier than expected. This time, I believe he's bringing his friend Arthur Seyss-Inquart home with him."

Elsa gasped.

"Do you recognize the Reich Commissioner's name?" the Frau asked.

"Mutter," Erich said. "Who doesn't know Arthur's name?"

Elsa shot Erich a sideways glance. He too was seemingly on a first-name basis with the wartime leader of the Netherlands—the man who'd destroyed her family and the way of life for millions.

The Frau cast a tender look at her son. "Point well taken, son. All right then. It's time for the three of you to hurry off before you can't."

Elsa crossed her arms and stared directly into the Frau's eyes. "Not until you tell me your first name."

Again an odd grin toyed with the Frau's lips. She gave Elsa a quick nod. "My name is Edith."

18

The Frau knew! Seated beside Erich in the back seat of his mother's luxurious car, a car that only the wealthy in Germany could afford, Elsa couldn't still the thoughts that swirled like a tempest in her mind. The way the Frau had divulged her name—Edith— accompanied with that peculiar grin—she had to know they shared the same name. Without a doubt, this signaled that Frau Edith Friedrich had more information about Elsa, including her family name Weber. She must know Elsa had lived in her house under an assumed identity. If the Frau had knowledge about her, didn't that mean Erich also knew? And if so, why would he play the game of pretending it was a mystery? Then again, why had he gone out of his way to warn her to be careful when they met on the stairs? Did this indicate that the Frau also knew that she was a Jew? Was she being brought to Vienna to help Adela or was it a more sinister plan that could cause the end of many lives, even the end of her own life? Perhaps they'd use her as a pawn to their own advantage. A human swap—one life for another? She hated how she'd become so mistrustful, yet sensed that it was best to be careful and constantly look over her shoulder for danger.

If these thoughts and images weren't heavy enough to bear, she struggled with more confusion as thoughts of her mother clouded her mind. After the Germans occupied the Netherlands, she'd watched her own mother change before her eyes. Herta Weber slipped from being a once cheerful and optimistic person. She became like others who struggled to live in an upside-down society controlled by those whose sole aim was to extinguish the lives that were deemed unnecessary.

Miserable flames of shame twisted through Elsa as guilt filled her for her wrongdoing against her own mother. Her mother was wise, not foolish. Wartime had changed both of them, exposing emotional weaknesses and resilience. Gone were the days when Elsa believed life hinged around boyfriends and the longing for elegant blouses and skirts. She could now see that her mother only wanted the best for her daughters, wanting them to live through this dreadful time and to see many tomorrows.

Erich pressed into her right side. "Are you hurting?" he asked in a hushed tone.

Elsa thought of the encounter with Erich on the stairs, remembering his words of not wanting harm to come to her. She looked into his eyes, unsure of her relationship with the man before her. "No. Why?"

"Because you just groaned. Is it your ankle?"

She rotated her foot, accidentally brushing against his. Were they sitting inappropriately too close? "My injury is no longer a burden. Don't worry, it won't slow us down."

"Honestly, I wasn't thinking about you as a burden. But I'm glad you're not in pain."

Elsa wasn't expecting his considerate words and navigated the awkwardness by looking at her other two traveling companions. Werner's fixed attention was on the road ahead—between the snow falling and the headlights picking up the snow like missiles hitting the windshield, visibility was poor. Adela, her head slumped against the passenger window, appeared asleep. Elsa's self-consciousness lessened. "I have a few things on my mind."

"I can imagine," Erich said. "We have a lengthy ride ahead of us and I have two good listening ears if you'd like to share your concerns."

"I'm more confused than ever," she said softly, wanting to keep this conversation between the two of them. "I don't know what to think of your mother." About to voice her concern about the likelihood of the Frau's awareness of her identity, she again wondered about the possible coincidence of it all. She lost her nerve and pointed out the window. Despite the snow, and the lack of streetlights —likely as a precaution against enemy bomber planes—she recognized the town they were now driving through. "This is Monschau, is it not? The town you first drove us though en route to your family's home? I can just about make out the charming half-timber houses."

"Yes, you're correct. I've always thought this town was a pleasant place. At least on the surface."

She remembered what he'd told her about the Jewish children removed from the town on the Kindertransport and how it was no longer typical to see children on streets throughout the country. "What's become of this town's Aryan children?"

"Most German children under the age of ten, and many of their mothers, have been settled into *Kinderlandverschickung* camps, KLV, for short. They're scattered in what are considered safer places in Germany and Austria. Locally, these children and mothers were sent to camps in Essen, Cologne, and a few other cities. And before you ask, no, I'm not involved with the KLV in Cologne."

"I wasn't about to ask," she said softly, more as reassurance than defensively, though, the thought had crossed her mind.

"A few were sent to Hungary and Denmark too," he continued. "In the name of expanding the good German name, you know."

"To verify, only for Aryan boys and girls?"

"Yes. It's Nazi-Youth oriented. Werner Würschinger—a senior official with Hitler Youth and an acquaintance of my father—is expecting to have these camps full by the end of this year."

"How many children would that be?"

"About three million. Others have projected five million. We're talking about a million of these camps."

"Whew," she exhaled. "That's a lot of children. I'm glad I'm not a teacher at one of those camps—I wouldn't have managed to hide my disgust." Immediately a wave of guilt flooded her. Yes, he was the Herr's son, but he was also plain Erich Friedrich, the young man who had offered his help when no one else would give her the time of day.

He grasped her fingers and pulled her hand down to her lap. "I'm glad you didn't end up in one of those dreadful camps."

Dreadful?

"The KLV might be sending the children of Germany to safer places—relatively speaking—but despite Würschinger's goals, parents want their children back. It's understandable." He watched her nod in agreement. "Mothers and fathers don't appreciate how this short-term project that should have only lasted a few weeks has grown into months or even years, considering it started up in 1940. My father's hearing lately that the movement might be abandoned later this year. At this point, who knows if KLV will see the start of 1944."

"For now, it's probably for the best. At least the children are safe— that is, they should be safe—from air raids. Yet, no place in Germany, not even charming historic towns like Monschau, have managed to go untouched by this war."

"Make that no place in the whole world has gone untouched by this war."

"You don't sound pleased, especially as the Herr's son." Why did she say that? "Pardon. I didn't mean to be rude."

Erich waved away her apology. "Yes, I'm Maxwell Friedrich's son. But that's the extent of it." He leaned closer to her. "Perhaps if I tell you a bit about myself, you can learn to trust me. I'd like that. And if you want to reciprocate and tell me about yourself, that's fine as well. If not, no concerns." He called out to Werner. "How long do we have to our first stop?"

Werner lifted his eyes to the rearview mirror. "I'm hoping we will make it to Frankfurt, ordinarily a three-hour drive from Monschau.

But who knows in this weather? We might have to find a place to stay overnight if the road becomes slicker."

They began to cross the bridge over the Rur River, the noise pinging through the metallic grates undampened by the snow. Elsa glanced at Adela. Her head pressed against the door showed she remained in dreamland. As for Werner, he was now humming softly, probably in an effort to keep alert and calm while driving through the horrid weather. She returned her attention to Erich. "I'm all ears."

"Good. Considering we've only traveled a handful of kilometers, we have time to kill."

This time, she sighed. "Let's try not to use the word 'kill' as we progress through Nazi territory."

"Good point," he said. Then he remained oddly quiet.

"Mulling over where to begin?" she prompted. She glanced toward the front seat, then back at Erich. "Are their ears off limits?" she whispered.

"No." His soft tone matched hers. "I fully trust both Werner and Adela. What I have to say is complicated."

"I suspected it might be."

He stretched his arms, then his legs, reminding Elsa of a cat awakening from a long afternoon nap. "You read people well."

"My little sister would say similar words to me on occasion." She couldn't keep the affection from her voice. "Although, not wanting to admit I might be correct, she'd tease me that I was either psychic or had a vast imagination." Elsa paused as she saw Krista's sparkling eyes and golden curls before her. She heard her singing like a robin on a spring day as she helped Mama with the dinner dishes. And observed her compassion when she helped one of the older women from their apartment building down the slippery front steps on a winter day. They'd bickered over sweaters. Laughed over Papa's jokes. Cried together when Krista left their family to go into hiding. Krista. Where are you now? Are you happy and well? Will we see each other again?

"I can tell you miss your sister," Erich said, jolting her out of her reverie.

Slowly, she lifted her gaze to this man just a few years older than her. "How?"

He fanned a fingertip from the corner of her right eye and trailed it down her cheek. "Tears make excellent clues."

She pressed her fingers to the side of her damp face where he'd touched her seconds ago. "I wasn't aware I was crying."

"I'd cry too if I was never to see Fritz and Wil again, as bratty as they can be at times. I hope you're reunited with your sister, and soon. How old is she?"

Since Elsa had told Erich she was 19, she didn't want to make him suspicious and did a fast readjustment of her sister's true age. It would be best to switch subjects, focusing more on Erich. "My sister's 14—five years younger than I am. Just like the age difference between you and Richard." She sniffled. "Are you thinking that our trip may be your final departure from your little brothers?"

"One never knows. I don't think so, though. Let's hope not, for all our sakes."

"Minutes ago, you alluded to a strained relationship with your father. That can't be pleasant or easy."

"It wasn't in the beginning."

"Oh, right. I'd forgotten you told me that this is your mother's second marriage. Was she widowed?"

"Yes. My biological father perished in a—"

"Only tell me if you want to."

"In a road accident in the middle of a snowstorm." He glanced out the car window. "He wasn't driving, though. He was crossing the road and was struck by a vehicle that skidded on an ice patch." He swore. "The driver was too young and reckless to be out in that weather, according to the police. Didn't comfort my mother that it was a random accident."

"I'm so sorry. How old were you?"

"Three, but old enough to have a memory or two of a man who was like a king to me and a Prince Charming to my mother. You know, this may sound silly, but I can still hear my father's laughter."

"That's not silly. Kind of nice, special." She thought of the word endearing but felt too self-conscious to say it. "What did it remind you of?"

Erich pulled at his chin. "Circus clowns, playing with a puppy on a rainy day, and the thrill of sledding down a big snowy hill but knowing you'd be fine because he'd be there to lift you onto his shoulders and carry you home to hot cocoa beside the fireplace." He stared into her eyes. "The latter was my last memory of my father."

Elsa patted his arm only for seconds before pulling her fingers away. "I'm glad that you have the memory of pleasant times with a father who sounds like a good and loving parent. From what you've shared, he sounds like my father."

"If I remember correctly, you said your father had passed too."

"Yes," she said, praying it wasn't true.

"I'm sorry to hear that. Richard was age eight, so he felt our father's passing worse. Then, one day Mutter met Maxwell Friedrich, and the two fell in love overnight. They married, and I had a complete family again. Life was good."

"Until?"

He huffed a breath. "There's that keen insight of yours. Not bad for a 19-year-old."

About to correct him that she was only 17, she clamped her lips in time. "And 20 is wise-old-man territory?"

"Didn't say that," he said around a grin. "I believe I have lots to learn, though the lessons I've been learning about life—about how people behave—haven't necessarily been pleasant ones. Returning to the subject, both Richard and I couldn't find fault with our mother's new husband, who became a true father to us. Maxwell was kind and considerate. Until the political landscape began to change in Germany."

Elsa lifted a brow. "Meaning, when Hitler came to town?"

"How many Wild West cowboy stories did your mother read to you and your sister when you were youngsters?"

She gave a little chuckle. "Enough to entertain large and hungry imaginations."

He reached for her hand, gave it a squeeze, and then as if he'd done an untoward act, planted his hand back on his lap. As if Werner had rolled down his window, her hand instantly became cold. She wished Erich hadn't let go.

"Yes, life changed for us when Hitler became the supreme leader of Germany. I was ten. Richard 15. Vater, once jovial, a doting father and husband, became a serious man who embraced Nazism and championed Hitler to help get Germany out of the sinkhole it had fallen into. Richard and I were both enrolled in the Hitlerjugend before it became compulsory for Aryan children in 1936."

"But you stayed in the Hitlerjugend?"

"I had no other choice. When I was 16, I secretly became an Edelweiss Pirate."

"A what?" As she'd asked that two-worded question, Elsa had looked about for a reaction from Werner and Adela. Despite her loud voice, neither Werner nor Adela had stirred.

"See, I warned you that my story was complicated."

"I'm afraid I don't understand."

The car slowed. Adela stirred awake.

"What is it, Werner?" Erich asked.

"I don't think it's a good idea to drive further." Werner stopped the vehicle and pointed out the windshield. Three intense lights fixed on a guard shack spotlighted two uniformed men approaching the car, each with a rifle strapped to his shoulder. "However, we've reached our first checkpoint. Take out your identity papers and don't volunteer information you aren't asked for."

19

Adela nearly stopped breathing. With her nerves already a jumbled mess, she warned herself to speak German, not Romany, if either of these two men working for Hitler asked her a question.

She felt a hand on her shoulder. Elsa leaned toward her from the back seat. "We will be fine. Stay calm."

Adela wanted to question this young woman who wanted to be her friend. How can you possibly know? What do we do if we aren't and our travels are over? And then it came to her, this new reality that was like an unexpected gift. What do I do if they separate the two of us from each other?

Werner's narrow-eyed glare shorted them both of words. He rolled down his window. "Hello, officers."

"Identity papers," the shorter, pale-faced guard said while the other trained his rifle on Werner. Likely no more than 20, he's spoken with a snap to his command that made up for his scrappy appearance. "Do not delay."

Adela handed Werner her papers, followed by Elsa and Erich. He fished out his own from his jacket pocket. Despite her fellow passengers' drawn faces, Adela held back her worries about her false papers. She was willing to assume that all their documents stated changed names, ages, and backgrounds. It was a bonus that Erich's father ranked high on the Nazi list. By default, since they were traveling with Erich, they should be fine. She banished the lingering fear to the back of her mind.

With the first guard examining the papers, the second officer gestured with his rifle to Werner. "Out. We'll search the car."

Werner opened the driver's door and stepped out. "Yes, of course. While you search, do you mind if I have a smoke? I have plenty of extra cigarettes if you gentlemen are inclined." He pointed to the car's trunk. "They're in the back. May I get them for you?"

"*Fein.*"

With both hands lifted to show he wasn't handling a weapon, Werner proceeded to the rear of the car, opened the trunk, retrieved a handful of cigarette packs, and as Adela, Elsa, and Erich emerged from the vehicle, plodded through the deepening snow toward the front of the car. He handed the packages to the guards. "Enjoy."

Adela winced when both officers perused her as if they hadn't seen a woman in too long.

Erich stepped up to her and clutched her elbow. "Officers, thank you for carrying out your duties responsibly. My fiancée would thank you too but she is under the weather with a flu."

The two uniformed guards stepped back and consulted with each other. They stole glances at the four of them. The guard who had read the documents handed back the papers to Werner. "Where are you going?"

"Frankfurt, then onto Vienna."

"The roads are bad. Find a place to stay until tomorrow before going onto Frankfurt."

Werner slipped the papers under his arm and rubbed his hands together. "*Ja*, good suggestion. It is certainly cold out." He glanced over his shoulder toward the open trunk. "Would you like to look through it?"

The taller guard strode to the car's rear, slammed the lid shut, and banged it twice. "Hurry before you can't."

After a painfully slow 20 minutes, Werner stopped the car, but kept the engine running.

Adela glanced at him. "As the guards said, we won't make it to Frankfurt tonight, will we?"

"I'm not ready to give up. Despite what those two guards advised, we won't be stopping at the first town either."

"Why is that?"

"I learned a long time ago to never do exactly what a Nazi wants you to do, unless they're aiming a gun at your head. Right now, without one of the sick morons and their guns in the car with us, we're going to travel a bit further on."

"Do you think there's a chance that they'd ambush us?"

"They are already aware of the smokes we have to offer them—they're probably eager to learn what else we have." He chuckled, his voice lowered by a sardonic twinge. "There's nothing like a snowy deserted road to find out. Erich, let's get the chains out from the trunk and onto the tires. I want to make it to Frankfurt, or as close to Frankfurt as road conditions warrant."

"I'm more than willing to drive," Erich said. "You've done plenty for us. Let me be of help."

"Help? Right now, help me set the chains before the rear wheels." As Erich trudged toward the trunk, Werner looked at Adela then Elsa. "Do either of you ladies have any driving abilities?"

Adela shook her head but lifted a brow of surprise when Elsa nodded. "Yes. Sort of. I might have been awfully young, but back in my childhood, my father did have a car for a short while and gave me a few lessons."

"Perfect," Werner said. "Erich, you watch the left, Elsa, the right, and shout out to me as I creep forward if I'm about to miss my mark."

Thankfully, the chain wrapped smoothly around the tires. They piled back into the car.

"This is like Clara and Bruck an der Leitha, all over again," Adela murmured.

"Who is Clara?"

Adela peered at Elsa. Apparently, she hadn't spoken softly enough. Then again, the more time she spent with Elsa, the more she learned that the younger woman was quite perceptive. Adela was relieved that someone cared enough about her to pay that close of attention to her. Without a doubt, she had Richard to watch her back, but despite his vow to help her in her quest to find her family, their mutual support, as close as it might be, would never be more meaningful than a true sisterly friendship between women. She glanced up at Elsa. Who was she fooling? Upon reaching Vienna, her journey would continue, not end. Once Elsa learned of her true plans, she wouldn't want to venture on with her and she couldn't blame her. This was wartime. Nothing pretty would await either one of them.

"Sit beside me," Elsa said when Adela didn't respond to her question about Clara. "Though I want to talk more with Erich, there's bound to be time ahead. For now, we can catch up a bit more with each other." Before Adela could respond, Elsa faced Erich and asked him if he'd mind sitting up front with Werner. He said that since there was more heat up front, he'd be more than happy to oblige. "See, Adela, that works out just fine."

Torn between wanting to keep the chilling memory of Clara away from her thoughts and sharing with someone who might understand, she nodded at Elsa and climbed into the back seat.

Elsa rubbed her hands together. "So, about Clara?"

Adela was relieved when Werner began driving. She settled into her seat. "Clara is a woman who lives in Bruck an der Leitha, Austria. She came to my rescue on a stormy night like tonight but turned out to be a person I wished I had never met."

"Were you stuck with her for a while then?"

"Yes, since it was a sudden storm, as nasty as could be. I'd just left my home country—for the first time ever—to search for my father and sister. I came across a barn and took shelter there. The owner of the property—Clara, an old woman, though far from a grandmotherly type—greeted me the next morning and invited me indoors. With her husband and son long gone, she eagerly wanted me to stay and wait out the storm. She offered me food, clothes, and decent company, and I thought I had run into good luck." She glanced out the side window, disappointed to see the snow pelting down. *Please, I just want to get me back to Bratislava,* she thought. *I want to see my people and my family again.* Adela rubbed the bridge of her nose. Hadn't she learned a lesson from this awful war—to question fate, to rule out hope? Then, she remembered that there were good people, her three traveling companions and Richard to name just a few. Yes. She wanted to cling to hope and certainly to a power bigger than her or the face of evil. She returned her attention to Elsa. "Clara's cat is the one I miss."

"Clara certainly sounded pleasant enough," Elsa said.

"She was, at first. But you know how it is—folks are nice upon the first meeting, especially when they're in need of what the other person has to offer. In her case, she was lonely and appreciated my companionship."

"Until?"

"Until she learned more about me, about my family."

"About your Roma heritage?"

Adela, once upon a time, Vonni, squeezed her eyes shut. She wished the war would end. She wished to see her father's smiling face, put up with her mother's fears and superstitious worries, and deal with the petty rivalries between her and her sister. Were they alive? Well?

"Vonni," Elsa said softly, gracing her true name like a musical note. "Tell me what you're seeing, what you're hearing."

With Erich and Werner talking to each other up front, Adela's self-consciousness lessened, not that she was nervous around those two men. Still, it was easier talking with another woman. She opened her eyes and shifted the blanket draped over her lap toward Elsa so she too could be warmer. A little smile tugged at her lips. "I heard the grandmothers of my *vista* sharing recipes. The old men talking about the town they came from in Poland and telling tales to the young children about the various countries our people have lived in over the past hundreds of years."

"Life was good, then?"

"Yes and no. We Roma never had it easy. We've had to fight against a lot of prejudice that made it difficult to step into the roles that the *Grunters*—non-Roma—wanted us to become."

"That's certainly ironic."

"Yes," Adela said. "But, right up to the time my father and sister disappeared, I knew who I was, what people I belonged to, where I lived. I knew what tomorrow would bring. And most of all, I had what I needed in life—people that loved me."

"When you stop and think about it, that's what each of us needs. It's greed that makes dictators control a country and set out to conquer other countries and to justify the ugliness of destruction and death." Elsa shook her head. "Let's return back to the subject of Clara —you have me curious."

"After the storm cleared up enough that one of her friends could visit, I learned which side she truly stood on—the Nazi side. Both she and Adelaide were against Jews, against the Roma, against anyone who didn't look Aryan. I had no desire to stay around and see if they'd come to their senses, so I left. I eventually made it to Vienna and met the Ostróws."

"And life was reasonably good until Kristallnacht?"

"And the fires of hell coursed throughout the planet? Exactly." Adela again glanced out the window. "Werner, will we be stopping shortly?"

"I had high hopes to make it to Frankfurt," Werner began. "Despite the tire chains, it's probably wise to take advantage of Frau Friedrich's arranged stopover in Koblenz, about five kilometers from here. Although it's two in the morning, they're expecting us. But be warned, I've never visited the city." He peered at Erich. "Let alone have clues about the connection to the people your mother has lined up, if you catch my drift."

"Yes, I do." Erich faced Adela and Elsa. "My expectation is full-force devotion to the Greater German Reich. Would you two be up to a Nazi salute?"

Adela wrapped an arm around her middle. "If it means achieving my ultimate goal, what choice do I have?"

"Elsa?" Erich asked.

"Likewise," she replied softly. "I might get sick to my stomach, though."

With his long-armed reach, Erich leaned over and patted Elsa's shoulder. "Myself, included. We have to put on the act, though."

"I'll try." Elsa drew the blanket she shared with Adela up to her neck.

"Good," Werner said. "We must put on a distinct persona at all times with these Hitler worshippers."

"I do know two facts about Koblenz," Elsa said.

"Ah, you've been holding out on us, Teacher," Erich said.

Adela took in Erich's adoring gaze pinned on Elsa, finding it at first surprising but then changing her mind. They shared common interests, like the love of family and their studies. Whether Elsa could ever forgive Erich for his family heritage and the weighty burden of his Nazi parents was a whole different matter. Aware of what Erich was up to behind his father's back, Adela wondered if Elsa's perspective of Erich might eventually soften.

"Do tell," Werner said in an energetic tone.

"First lesson," Elsa said. "During the French Revolution and at other times throughout the 18th century, the city had French royalists and other assorted émigrés living there. The yo-yo was nicknamed *de Coblenz*, using the French way of spelling the city with a C rather than the German way with a K."

Adela snorted. "Yes, I see how that is a significant contribution to the human race."

"And the other matter of importance?" Erich asked.

"Did you know that this Rhineland city of Koblenz dates back to the ancient Roman days, founded in 8 BC?"

"Hail, Elsa!" Erich said. Both Adela and Werner repeated his acclaim, mimicking his serious tone. "It's obvious you've attended a fine university or at least a gymnasium."

Elsa shook her head. "No, the war has seen to a drastic change of plans."

About to ask for clarification on Elsa's teaching credentials, Adela held back. When the Frau had asked Elsa if she was a teacher, she'd replied affirmatively. She hoped her friend continued to pursue teaching after the war ended. Children deserve an education no matter their race and faith. With her passion and energy, Elsa would make a perfect teacher. "Who taught you so well, then?" Adela asked her new friend.

"My mother," Elsa murmured, her throat catching. She turned toward the side window and looked out into the cold, stark silhouette of life around them.

Adela's attention trailed Elsa's out the same car window. "The snow! It's stopped!

How—"

"Here we go again," Werner said. He braked hard.

20

Erich, Elsa and Adela stared at the three uniformed guards blocking the road, their rifles aimed at the car. Lightning quick, the driver's door of the vehicle was yanked open. Werner was dragged out by not one but two of the guards. Erich flashed a stern look at Elsa and Adela: cooperate.

The third guard approached the car and commanded them to get out with a wave of his gun. They scrambled out, hands lifted in capitulation. He remained silent. Elsa followed, then Adela.

"Identity papers," the guard demanded. After he received the three sets of papers, he tucked them under his arm and gave a sideways glance at his fellow guards, who had shoved Werner to the snow-covered ground, ordering him to remain there.

Elsa winced and began to walk toward Werner when she was stopped by a resounding "Halt!" She stopped, more frozen than the temperature. Slowly, she turned around to face the guard. With his gun now directly aimed at her, he scanned the identity papers. "Are you Elsa or Adela?"

Elsa gulped. "I am Elsa."

"Why are you with the others? Where are you going?"

A groan from Werner distracted her.

"Answer me!" ordered the guard with the gun in her face.

She had no other choice but to tell him the truth, at least the version a Nazi would prefer hearing. "Frau Maxwell Friedrich is sending her son, Erich, to Vienna. She ordered me and her other servant, Adela, to accompany him, but I do not know why."

"That's what the driver says as well," shouted one of the guards standing by Werner.

The guard at Elsa's side trained his gun on Erich. "Why are you going to Vienna?"

"My mother wants me—us—to check on my brother."

"During a snowstorm?"

Erich grinned. "You know how mothers worry—mine is hoping that the bombers will hold off until it stops snowing, making for easier traveling. The snow easing is a good sign as for driving, but my mother—and my father, Herr Maxwell Friedrich—will now be more concerned whether we will be able to complete the trip safely."

The guard peered directly at Erich. "Best if you drive."

Instead of hurling her rudest sarcasm at the three guards, Elsa rushed to Werner and helped him to walk toward the car. Adela opened the driver's door, but Elsa continued to take charge. "Erich, would you prefer to drive or would you like me to? I haven't driven much, but I'm sure I can manage."

"I'll drive. Not a problem."

"Good." She looked at Adela. "Help Werner into the front passenger seat, he'll be more comfortable there than in the back. You don't mind sitting with me, do you?"

Adela kept a serious face, but her shoulders relaxed. "Of course not."

Elsa looked toward the guards. "May I fetch a blanket from the trunk?"

Rather than replying, one of the guards accompanied her to the rear of the vehicle. She opened the trunk and began to rifle through the delectable treats and provisions. In picking up the extra blanket, she'd uncovered the bricks of cheese. As if on cue, the guard's stomach let loose a growl.

"Oh, dear," Elsa said, in her best concerned tone, considering the circumstances. She handed him a hearty chunk of the wrapped Tilsit cheese. "You take this. I appreciate your hard work in defending the Fatherland. I hope you will enjoy it."

The guard gave a quick nod. Although he didn't reply, he did shut the trunk for her. Upon returning to his comrades and showing them the cheese, he saluted. The other two guards gave a salute as well. Then they waited.

"Heil Hitler," Elsa said and saluted, staring straight ahead. *Please forgive me, God*, she thought. *And keep me from vomiting on the snowy ground.*

Adela and Erich mirrored Elsa in her salute. Only Werner, crumpled in the front passenger car seat, remained still, though the guards didn't appear dismayed at his silence. The guards then hurried back to their shack.

Elsa rushed to Werner. "Here you go," she said softly, spreading the blanket over him, hoping to ease his trembling. "Shall we take you to a hospital?"

"Absolutely no. I bruised my hip. I'll be fine. Just need to rest."

"Let's go." Erich directed Elsa and Adela into the car, and they drove through the checkpoint without further delay. "We'll stop only for fuel and a toilet break in Koblenz, then will continue on to Vienna non-stop, weather permitting."

Elsa poured drinking water from a thermos into a cup, reached forward, and gave it to Werner. She was relieved when he took the cup in a sturdy grip and sipped slowly.

"Bunch of bored ruffians, they were," Werner murmured.

"You're holding back," Erich grunted. "More like moronic, soulless footmen of the devil."

"Did they say anything of interest?" Elsa asked.

"Got the impression that one was teaching the others how to be good Nazi." Werner groaned then sat up a little straighter. "Just drive. Get us out of here."

"All in the name of Nazism," Adela quipped and turned to look out the window.

Elsa's attention leaped to her mother. Separated from pen and paper, let alone the privacy of writing, she mentally composed another letter to the person she missed more and more with each passing second.

Dear Mama,

I hope you are well, and Papa and Krista too. May the three of you be together and safe! I hope you aren't fearing and wondering how much longer you will be alive. That's how I am right now. I admit, I'm terrified, but I try my best to push bad thoughts to a distant part of my mind.

My new friend, Adela, is helping me through this awful time. That's not her real name. It's funny that none of us are who we claim to be. Will the time come when this dreadful war is over, and we can be brave and proud of who we are again? Will there be a time when we don't have to live in fear of punishment, torture, or death? I'm mentioning Adela now because, like me, she is far away from her mother and the rest of her family. We both yearn so badly for our mothers!

We just experienced a frightful event that left me and my three traveling friends unnerved. My sweet mother, I want to apologize for ever having one bad thought against you and want to do so face-to-face. I hope you can forgive me. I wish this war was a horrid dream, but sadly, it's not. If I was granted only one wish, I'd wish to hold you in my arms and tell you how I love and need you. Because, Mama, I'll always be your loving daughter. I'm just sorry it took me this long to realize.

I want to share with you that I've learned that I can indeed be resilient. One must be strong and able to bounce back in times of war as well as when facing daily struggles. I never expected this change, this growth, to be an outcome of this awful war. I'm definitely not the girl I was just a few years ago. I hope I can live through this time and continue to put others first before I think of myself and my needs.

Elsa stirred from the deepest sleep she'd had in a long time. Adela was staring at her. A questioning look on her face made her friend appear older than she was. One irony of war was the rapid aging and exhaustion from the worry of whether or not one would live. No one escaped it.

"You were murmuring in your sleep, though I couldn't understand you."

"I'm fine." Elsa batted her heavy eyelids and sat up straighter. "I'm surprised I fell asleep."

"I was asleep too until you woke me."

"Sorry."

Adela waved her hand as if waving away a swarm of worries. "I think if anyone else experienced what we just did, they'd also be exhausted."

Elsa glanced upfront. "How are the men holding up?" she asked softly.

"As well as could be."

Elsa nodded. "How are you, my friend?" She liked how Adela smiled at her last two words.

Adela stretched her arms. "Good. Well, considering we had three Nazi lunatics aiming guns at us." She paused as Elsa nodded. "Matka always said that sleep is how the body restores itself and mends the soul."

"Matka? Is that mama in Romani?"

"It's my people's name for mother. And I call my father Tata." Her mouth flattened; her brows furrowed. "That is, before he disappeared. Before I became separated from the rest of my family."

Elsa reached for Adela's hand; her fingers were cold. "I understand. So many of us have disappeared, along with our old ways. In my sleep, I was writing my mother a letter."

"About disappearing?"

"More like how we've let go of our old ways so we can make it through our current, unthinkable circumstances. It's how we survive."

Adela softly smiled. "We'll get through this, you and I."

"We don't have a choice." After a pause, Elsa added, "I'd love to know more about the Roma way of life if you'd like to share."

"Before the war or after?"

"Odd how life has whittled down into this, the before and after part. But that's what I was just telling my mother in my dreams. That I'm no longer the little girl I used to be."

"It's just that it would have been nicer if one portion of society didn't change it for the rest of us by force, right?"

Elsa held back a sigh. "Correct."

"Despite the non-Roma's fondness for making us out to be a despicable people, the best way to describe my beloved Roma is to say that we always carry a song in our hearts. A song of hope, of sunshine."

"I like that. That's a good way to be."

"Yes. It's easier to carry around a cheerful song than a burden." Adela locked gazes with Elsa. "Don't misunderstand me, though. Fate has always carried a different way for us in its pocket. A twisted fate. Who doesn't want to be clean and educated and have a decent means of providing life necessities for one's family? You know, the basics, like food, clean water, warmth in the winter, clothes. Why so many have thought that we do not want these ordinary things, we Roma cannot understand."

"I know exactly what you mean." Images of her family's home in Berlin before they were forced to leave flashed before Elsa's eyes, contrasted with the simple but lovely apartment they enjoyed in Amsterdam, then the apartment when they moved to the Jordaan, smaller but still nice because they were together. "My own definition of grand once meant the luxury of one's own bedroom, a garden to stroll through. Then, little by little, it narrowed down to sharing a bedroom with my younger sister, but we still daydreamed about growing into adults with children and older women with grandchildren. We've gone from having to decide which dessert we want or which fancy dress to wear for a special holiday to wearing the same clothes until they fall to pieces." Elsa offered a tender smile to Adela. "And to think that the Roma—as you're saying—never had such opportunities."

"That's right," Adela murmured. "Most *gorgios* detested us so much that they made us live the poorest of the poor lifestyle, blaming us for not wanting to work while removing any chances for us to do so. It makes no sense. Hatred and prejudice never make sense."

"Oh, Adela... Vonni. I'm so sorry that I'd used that unfortunate word 'work-shy' following the staff lineup when the Herr inspected us. I'll never use it again. Forgive me."

Adela gave her a sad smile. "The two of us aren't different. I'm the one who also should be apologizing to you. There's no difference between Jews and Roma as far as the Nazis are concerned. In their eyes, we aren't people but pests that need to be vanquished." As if the last bit of energy had exited her body, Adela leaned back, exhaustion scrunching her eyes shut.

Bone-weary, Elsa also leaned back into the car seat and thought about what Adela had just said. They might have different ways of worshipping and understanding a Supreme Being, but they were two women with one common drive: the right to live equally and fairly like others. A peace washed over her and she let sleep lure her away. When she opened her eyes, she had no idea how much time had passed. She sat upright in time to see Werner stirring.

"Easy," Erich said to Werner. "I'm driving. You've been hurt but are hopefully well. We're in my mother's car, heading far away from those worthless guards you've encountered at that last checkpoint. You'll soon be back to your old self."

"To think that before I met those less-than-charming three men, I would have flinched at the word old used to describe me."

"I'm willing to wager that if you survive this war, you'll look forward to complaining about growing old," Elsa said.

Adela gasped.

Werner glanced at Adela. "Don't be shocked. Elsa speaks the truth. One doesn't miss certain aspects of living until it's about to be carted away before one's eyes."

"We were just talking about that, before we dozed off," Elsa said.

She drummed her fingers on the door. "Erich, let's make a bathroom stop?"

"That's not a good idea."

Elsa peered firmly into the rearview mirror, catching Erich's eyes. She gave him the same stern look she'd seen her mother give her poor father at times. "We don't have a choice."

Erich shook his head. "You don't understand. We're entering Nuremberg, a city that does not want to see the likes of me, nor do I want to see it ever again. We need to drive through it."

"Pull off the road," Werner ordered. "Now!"

21

Werner looked at Erich as he braked. "My mother taught me to never disregard a woman who says she's in need of a toilet."

"And my mother taught me to never trust a Nazi."

"Pardon?" Adela streaked her fingers through her hair. "Your mother taught you to be wary of Nazis? Explain."

"I can't. It's complicated."

"This is ridiculous," Elsa said loudly, slicing the bickering chatter into silence. She asked Adela to accompany her. "I'm in need of a toilet and right now the great outdoors will do just fine. Like it or not, we'll go down the bank, I'll do my thing, and then we'll be right back." She motioned to Adela to open her door, and the two scrambled outdoors. "Goodness," she mumbled as they hiked down the snowy slope. "I could understand if Nuremberg was in the middle of an aerial bombardment..."

"Don't think it or say it. I don't have to tell you which country we're in or that this is wartime. Do you think you've slept through it and that we're magically in a peaceful area ten years from now?"

"The war better be over way before 1953. Way before I see my 27th birthday!"

"Pardon?" Adela's forehead wrinkled. "That would make you—"

"Let's not talk about my this now." Elsa hadn't meant to reveal her true age. "Be a love and turn your back. Stand between me and the vehicle." She hiked up her skirt and squatted, trying not to focus on the stinging cold snaking up her legs.

When they returned to the vehicle, Erich was in the passenger seat under the same blanket that Werner had used. His hair looked unkempt and his shirt was misbuttoned. He held a hand over his mouth as if trying to avoid being sick.

"What's happening?" Elsa asked.

"Fräuleins," Werner said from the driver's seat, "please get into the car, and whisper so as not to disturb the ill—and contagious—Erich."

Elsa crawled into the back seat, followed by Adela. They exchanged glances but didn't say a word. They continued through the city, agreeing to stick to their planned story: they had been en route to Vienna when the son of Herr Maxwell Friedrich was stricken with an illness, which he likely caught from the coughing and sneezing patrons at the beer hall where they'd stopped off yesterday for a meal. Because it was essential to visit a dying uncle in Vienna, they still hoped to proceed quickly.

After they cleared Nuremberg's first security check, Werner bristled in place, squaring his shoulders. "I detest this city."

"We may be 170 kilometers, give or take, north of Munich, but it feels more like 17,000." Erich remained reclined in his seat as if terribly ill. "The sooner we're away from here, the better."

They were driving through the city's historical center, passing several fortified buildings.

"That's Nuremburg Castle," Erich stated. "It's historically meaningful to Germany, making it a likely target if you ask me. Probably just a matter of time."

"Aren't you the cheerful one?" Adela groaned. "Sorry for my sarcasm."

"Afraid?" Erich asked.

"More like terrified."

"What I find more chilling are the ghosts crying out," Werner said. "My grandfather told me handfuls of tales."

Startled by sudden chills running up and down her arms, Elsa leaned forward. "What do you mean?"

"Ever hear of the Rintfleisch massacres of the Jews?"

"Was that similar to the Russian pogroms?" Elsa asked.

"Massacre, pogrom," Adela muttered. "A slaughter of an ethnic group. Death, annihilation, evil." She sniffled. "May Jews and Roma be pitied and spared. May no harm again come our way."

Elsa noted neither Werner nor Erich reacted. They knew! Knew of Elsa's Jewish faith. Knew of Adela's Roma heritage. Knew that they were traveling with two women who could easily get them arrested or worse.

"My Opa," Werner began, "said it was during these times, on the cusp of the 13th century, that Jews were falsely accused of violating the consecrated host. During the next century, there were more of these massacres, occurring parallel to what we now call the Black Death. The Jews were either burned at the stake or booted out of the area. A marketplace was built where the Jews had once lived."

Adela wiped the tears streaming from her eyes. "It's like the plague drove them hysterical and they attacked each other."

"Blamed each other," Erich murmured.

"Werner?" Elsa hugged her middle. "Is it that Germany has a long history of hating the Jews or that this country has yet to learn from its history?"

Werner steered the vehicle around a left turn. "My dear, I'm sorry to say that as a collective people, we are guilty of failing to learn from what has occurred in the past. In other words—we've overlooked how we've wronged each other and have done significant harm to each other. Tragically, it has happened in every country. Civilization has failed to prevent these acts from happening again. Mark my words—I believe that the attempt to remove specific faiths or races or ethnic groups from this planet will perpetuate until the end times, only stopped by Divine intervention."

Elsa scanned the vehicle. To her right sat Adela—Vonni—a Roma on the run. Her people, like the Jews, were rounded up by the Nazis and subjected to much suffering. In the front seat sat Erich. Although he was the beloved son of a favored and high-ranking Nazi Party judge, he stood his ground opposing Nazism. It was an act for which he could pay the highest price. Still, he was willing to take the risk. He had joined the Edelweiss Pirates at the age of 16. Only one year younger than her actual age! Then, there was Werner. The more time Elsa spent with this middle-aged man, the more she suspected that Werner was also Jewish. They all wanted to get through this dreadful time, clinging to the hope of a brighter life. Somebody to love, a place to call home, access to food, and medical treatment. The freedom to worship without the fear of condemnatory and incriminating repercussions. It was these basic needs that fueled hatred between people and persuaded the masses to choose a leader that would champion this evil.

"Yes, Werner," Elsa said softly. "From what I've learned from my history studies, as well as what I'm currently seeing, the ugly parts of history perpetually repeat themselves because people weren't willing to change."

"It's easier to blame others than it is to take responsibility."

"Slow down," Erich called out, pointing a finger ahead. He slumped back into his seat and resumed looking pitifully ill. "Another damn checkpoint."

22

The first indication that danger had come to greet them at this checkpoint were the men wearing black uniforms with the badges of skull and crossbones of the SS.

"What do you think?" Adela said quietly to Werner.

"Could be a number of things. Everyone, get out your papers. Erich, stick to the story of suffering from influenza. Start coughing."

Werner pulled to a stop and cranked down the driver's window. Frosty air gushed into the car as if fans were working on revving up the biting wind. He presented his papers to the SS officer who had approached the car, while two other officers stood nearby.

"Where are you going?"

"Vienna," Werner replied.

Adela reminded herself to breathe. Her sweaty hands were shoved under her legs, concealing fingers shaking beyond her control.

A round of phlegmy coughing pulled the officer's attention to Erich in the front seat. "You! State what is wrong."

Erich waved his papers. "Do you want—" Not bothering to move the papers away from his face, he coughed again.

"Nein." I'm not touching those germ-infested papers was

probably what the officer was thinking. He switched his attention back to Werner. "What is wrong with him?"

"Influenza."

The SS officer eyed Adela and Elsa. They both held up their documents in an offering, but the officer signaled he didn't want to review them. He stepped back from the vehicle. "Hurry on. Do not stop, a convoy of troops is expected any minute, and you're in the way."

Without further delay, Werner cranked up the window and proceeded. Barely away from the guard hut, a shout caused him to swear as he peered in the rearview mirror. "What now? That Nazi is running after us with a handful of others following."

"You better stop," Erich said. He remained sunken into his seat as if he couldn't move to save his life.

Werner halted the car and rolled down the window. "Yes, officer?"

The SS agent waved folded papers. "Your identity papers, Herr Schulze. You don't want to forget these."

"Whew! *Danke schön!*" Werner took the papers. "May we move on?"

The officer nodded, stepped back from the car, and they traveled forward.

"My, that was close," Adela said.

Werner bobbed his head. "That's putting it mildly."

Elsa reached for Erich's shoulder. "You're awfully quiet. What's upsetting you?"

"Without one doubt, that was my father in the guard hut."

"Don't look at me like that—I know I saw my father."

Adela couldn't blame Erich for his defensiveness, yet he didn't have to act so jumpy with friends. "Were you expecting him to be here in Nuremburg?"

"One never knows where he might be." Now that they were a good kilometer away from the checkpoint, Erich straightened in his seat. "The majority of the time he doesn't bother informing my mother. Strategically speaking, it makes sense. It protects him, our family, and anyone else involved. None of us know what he's involved in on behalf of Hitler. Oh, we've known that he was instrumental in changing laws to benefit the Reich, but other matters? That was always top secret and kept from us." He faced Adela. "The way the Nazi command goes, though, mandates are not done randomly but instead planned and instrumented, and accuracy is my father's expertise."

From her talks with Richard, Adela could tell Erich wasn't simply glossing over facts. "I do not doubt you saw your father, or his devotion to the Reich."

"That SS imbecile," Erich continued, "revealed they're expecting troops to pass through any second. From what I see on the empty road ahead, they must be moving from a different direction than the way we're heading."

"But that doesn't mean they can't be behind us in minutes," Werner said.

"Right you are." Erich glanced to the sides of the vehicle, then looked behind them. "All good, so far. What we don't want is to be followed to Vienna by men fighting on behalf of Germany."

At these words, Werner accelerated.

"Herr Friedrich is an important man to the Nazis," Adela said guardedly, not wanting to prompt Erich into silence. "Have you a guess as to why he might be meeting the troops?"

"It could be to do with Stalingrad. The latest thinking is that this area and the timing is a turning point, a make-or-break juncture for the Germans."

"Although you don't think so?" Elsa asked.

Erich shrugged. "Hitler wants to control this area because of its oil riches. The crux is the number of German soldiers he's willing to sacrifice to starvation and disease. My father may be part of a plan to send in supplies from a different direction."

"Although you think there's something more behind your father's appearance?"

Erich looked at Elsa. "I think he got word of my—our—disappearance and is looking for me, for us. Best if we continue on to Vienna and find Richard before my father catches up with him, which I'm inclined to think is his ultimate goal. I can't imagine why he might be chasing after Richard but it's probably wise to get to Vienna quickly. Werner, can we circumvent Munich and head directly to Salzburg?"

"Most definitely."

"Good. I believe I'm miraculously recovered from my sudden flu. However, I can't imagine you're quite over your experience with those guards. How about if I take over behind the wheel?"

A distinct grin pulled at Werner's lips. "I'm doing reasonably well by concentrating on the driving. It's taking my mind off of certain people that only manage to inspire me to spit." He glanced at the backseat. "No offense, *sehr geehrte Damen.*"

Dear ladies, they weren't. At least she wasn't, Adela thought. Not with what she was planning to do if fate permitted. "None taken," Adela replied for both she and Elsa.

A memory zipped before Adela's eyes. Her sister, Antonina, at the age of twelve, her dark hair already long enough to reach to her backside. Herself? She was five, though she understood plenty—more than old people like her sister. Yet, once on an overnight trip with their father, as they waited for Tata to wake up in the camp they'd made in the forest surrounding Bratislava, Vonni had thought twice about her sister's limited knowledge.

"Antonina, how far to the Little Carpathians?"

Her sister hushed her, cautioning her to keep her voice down so as not to anger their father. Before Vonni could point out that she spoke no louder than Antonina, her sister pointed behind Vonni. "The magical hills are that way."

"Why do you say magical? Magical like our ancestors?"

Antonina bobbed her head then shook it. "It's not that our Roma relatives were full of magic, more like getting the *gorgios* to believe we were magical."

Vonni scrunched up her face. "I don't understand."

"Neither do I. But this is the what our Great Mami and her mother have told us. To make others respect us, we must respect them. We must, each day, make a *kintala*—the word means peace between us Roma and the *gorgios*."

"But why is this magic?"

Antonina reached out to Vonni and tousled her short blonde hair. "You, who are so different looking from the rest of our family, need to understand this lesson about magic and peace. If we do what others do, they'll see us as the same as them. And that's special magic."

"Antonina, that's not magic. That's telling a lie. We aren't supposed to lie about who we are because we're proud to be Roma."

"We may be proud, but we aren't stupid, little sister. People hate us, make up ridiculous things about us. You know what's worse? The multitudes of people eager to believe and follow vile nonsense."

Her sister's adult-sounding words confused Vonni. "Are there ever right reasons to hate?"

For the longest time, Antonina, with her knees drawn to her chest, remained quiet. Her lined forehead cautioned Vonni not to interrupt her sister's deep thought. She counted to 20, which was a ridiculous amount of time just to think. She had to know the answer. "Antonina?"

"Yes. When someone hurts you or a loved one and it makes you want to hate them. But, there's an exception. A big exception."

"Why do you say it like that?"

A shy smile crossed Antonina's lips. "Because that's the magical part. We have to forgive. That's what most people won't do. Tata says that's why little fights break out and big wars blow up like a volcano." Antonina lifted her hands from her lap and thrust them into the air, mimicking an explosion. "You don't have to approve of their wrongdoing, though. Like, if someone hits you—you don't tell them to hit you more because that's not good. But if you forgive a person for their wrong, you're a special person with strength—a special ability—that others don't have. Some people call this magic."

"What do you call it?"

Antonina patted her chest. "Heart-caring."

Copying her sister, Vonni sat up from her bedroll and hugged her knees. "Are people in the Little Carpathians the only ones that forgive others?"

"It's a peaceful area, so maybe a lot of forgiving happens there."

Now, seated in the back seat of Frau Friedrich's car, Adela—Vonni—was performing a feat of magic. She was disappearing. Adela looked about the car. All four of them were individuals with one common denominator: the desire and will to chase the freedom and right to follow the faith they chose, to love whom they wanted, and to embrace with respect their fellow human beings.

Werner cleared his throat. "If the weather holds up, we should arrive in Vienna in about three hours."

Only three hours to Vienna, which meant four hours from Bratislava. What would happen if her beautiful family was gone? If her beloved Roma had been rounded up and carted away to camps or had already faced the end of their precious lives?

Elsa touched her arm, offering a tender smile. "It will be okay."

Adela blinked back tears of fear. "And if not?"

"We'll make it better."

Adela gave a little nod. Elsa was in the same circumstances—away from her family and wondering if they were alive. They weren't at the Little Carpathians yet. She breathed deeply and absorbed the power of hope. Hope was, after all, the manifested competence of survivors.

23

As they drove southeast toward Salzburg, the woods thinned. This was the first time Elsa had traveled in this Bavarian section of Germany, and she couldn't make out where she was. It didn't help that it was late afternoon; the fading January sunlight promised darkness sooner rather than later. As they left behind yet another town, an expanse of freshly cleared open space flanked both sides of the road. In the far distance were fields strewn with construction equipment. Her stomach flopped. This was no agricultural land on which to plant nourishing food. She rubbed at her middle, wishing her imagination would simmer down.

Erich had changed seats with Adela after they'd left Nuremberg. He glanced over at her. "Are you ill?"

Elsa stared at her fingers as if they moved of their own volition. She willed herself to act maturely when in reality, she wanted to whimper and call out to her mother. "No worries. I'm fine." She glanced toward the front of the car where Werner and Adela were chatting and decided it was safe to converse without disturbing them. "Honestly, this place we're passing is leaving me with a sour gut. Where are we?"

"We just left the town of Mühldorf."

She sensed that he was cautious, answering her question with the precise information she had asked for and nothing more, an indication that he was protecting her, which couldn't be good. "Is this a site for a new prisoner camp?" He rocked back. Evidently, she'd asked the right question. "Be honest."

"Keep in mind that I have no way of verifying the truth of what my sources tell me."

"So far your information seems to be good."

"Unfortunately. Places like these make me want to do one of three things—swear, pound my fist through a wall, and launch a bomb at its center. I'm trying to keep my anger from you."

"Then it is a camp!"

"We believe it's a type of prison camp that the Nazis have designed to do more than exploit prisoners as free labor."

"Targeted slaughter?"

He exhaled a long breath. Had silent curses ridden on that sigh?

"Yes. The term is a concentration camp. On one hand, it's a bizarre phrase. On the other, it's correct that a massive number of people are gathered together—by force—to be processed."

"Processed," she repeated. She was painfully aware that in this sense, the awful word meant the systematic collection, sorting, and herding of people to their brutal death. It was evil incarnate.

"Like a line-up of cattle is..." Like the lives eventually lost in these camps, Erich's words had drifted off into the air.

"I understand," she managed to say. "That is, your explanation of the word processed. What I fail to understand is how a human can do this to another fellow human."

"The operative word here is human. In my mind, evil and human —humanity—cannot coexist."

"I agree." She tugged at his hand and offered a little smile when he stared into her eyes for longer than she had expected. "Do your sources believe this is an independent camp, separate from the others already in operation?"

"No. It's been leaked that it is one of several subcamps of Dachau."

Elsa gasped. "If I'm not mistaken, Dachau will celebrate a ten-year anniversary this March."

"Correct," Werner said, jumping into the conversation. "How do you know that awful fact? Many don't know about the camp, let alone how long it's been in operation."

It was information that too many German Jews had the displeasure of storing in their minds. Instead, she said, "My father was big on history and shared that fact with my sister and me." Elsa held her breath. Relief flooded her when no one questioned her about why her father would go to the trouble of educating his children about how the Nazis were destroying civilization.

"I've also heard about Dachau," Adela said, her voice pained. "It's a place for not only political prisoners but for Jews, Jehovah's Witnesses, homosexuals, the Roma." She met Erich's eyes. "Who is building this camp? When will it be completed?"

"Likely prisoners from other camps are hauled here to do the hard labor of constructing the camp. As to its completion?" He shrugged. "A few months? Next year?"

"Heavens!" Elsa wiped at a runaway tear trickling down her cheek.

Erich wrapped an arm around her and pulled her gently to his side. "Let's talk about a more pleasurable place than Dachau." He pointed out the window. "Look at this land that we're passing through. Isn't it beautiful?"

The healthy human mind was only capable of clinging to unpleasantries for a limited time. This moment was no exception. The snow-covered basin was majestic. "Yes, it's magnificent," Elsa said.

Erich leaned closer to her ear to whisper, "Accept it for what it is."

Understanding that he meant accepting the scenic beauty for what it was—and the need to keep it separate from the horrors to come at the new campsite they'd just passed—she sniffled then nodded. "I've seen photographs of the northern foothills of the Alps but never thought that this area would prove more impressive than the pictures."

"It's an amazing world we live in," Erich said. "The Alps start in France, clip northwestern Italy, and reach through Switzerland and Germany to Austria and Yugoslavia."

"Have you ever wondered how they might look from outer space?"

"*Ja.* Do you think space travel will be a possibility in the far future?"

Elsa rubbed her cold hands together, wishing it was warmer in the rear of the car. She smiled when Erich reached for the blanket that had fallen to the floor several kilometers back. He covered her lap with the thick green and white plaid material and inched closer to her. "I think space travel will be a definite. Stop and think about it. If man could invent the horrific means to..." The tears brimming in her eyes stopped her short from rattling on about mankind using its supposed intelligence to engineer the assembly-line production of killing others. She inhaled deeply, collecting her inner-strength. "I have no doubts that space travel would inevitably be up and coming if Germany or another country wasn't already working on a project of this magnitude." When Erich fished for her hand under the blanket, she smiled the best she could, silently thanking him for not uttering pat, useless words like "it's all right" or "this too shall pass." "Do you think I'll ever be able to speak about a given subject without comparing it to this current godforsaken time?"

"I don't know. I'm going through the same thing." He glanced up front where the other two had grown quiet, likely carried away by their own thoughts of this wayward time.

"Any suggestions, then?"

"We're to carry on the best to our abilities. That's the best we can offer—to ourselves and each other."

"Yes, good cheer is worthy of sharing." As if prodded, Elsa's thoughts jumped to springtime with the flora of this northern section of the Alps. She recalled a childhood book she had read repeatedly—dazzled by photographs of the beautiful Alpine flowers she'd never seen before. Blue monkshood, yellow arnica that had been used for herbal medicines throughout history, and daisy-like white edelweiss.

Erich's involvement in the mysterious group he'd hinted at came to mind. "Is this a good time to tell me more about the Edelweiss Pirates you mentioned?"

"Considering we have about an hour before we reach Salzburg, I guess it's as good a time as any to tell you about the outstanding group of people that I belong to—one that would guarantee my death if the Nazis were to find out."

"Despite your father's position in the party?"

"Maxwell Friedrich puts the success of the Reich first, even when it comes to family."

Erich hadn't lowered his voice to prevent the others from hearing. He'd met her eyes. "There is no need to be concerned about Adela and Werner. They know about my nefarious activities. My actions and involvement better be diabolical—that's how I like to think of my efforts." Erich hadn't blinked, flinched, or shown other traces of regret. "That is, my time spent better be harmful to the Nazis. I want to wipe them off the German map, off the face of the world."

The way Erich worded his sentence indicated he had more at stake than she had originally perceived and that he must trust her to share these risks that could lead to peril. There was always a chance that he had come up with a ruse to dupe her, Adela, and Werner and to bring them to their demise, but she couldn't see that happening. He had just narrowly escaped several checkpoints of interrogation and likely knew the details about her background, as well as Adela and Werner's, which could get him into a heap of trouble since he had concealed the truth from authorities upon leaving his home. Because Erich took risks to help others and continued forward without flinching, it was time for her to be truthful with him.

Warm from the adrenaline raging through her, she whipped off the blanket and straightened in her seat. "Including yourself, there's four of us in this car making a risky trip. We might have four different reasons motivating us, though I'm sure they interconnect. I'd like to know about you, your involvement with the Edelweiss Pirates, and about the loss of your three friends. But fair is fair. First, let me tell you about myself."

"You don't have to," he said so quickly that it jolted her, and she leaned away. "The less said, the better. Understand?"

"No, I don't understand. The past few years have become more complex. You don't know what my family or I have gone through just to keep alive."

"Elsa is not your real name—it's Edith Weber. You were born in Berlin and lived there until your Jewish family fled the country in 1939 on a ship bound for the United States via Cuba. Your parents, sister, and you ended up in Amsterdam."

Her mouth turned dry; the blood rushed from her head. Little stars exploded before her.

"Lean forward and rest your head on your lap until the dizziness eases."

How did Erich know life was swirling before her? All this time, with his knowledge of her and her family, he could have opted to betray and surrender her into eager Nazi arms.

Erich squeezed her hand. His warm touch expelled the last of the cold from her body.

"I've been in your exact shoes, but in reverse. I'm the son of a Nazi, surrounded by people who would not hesitate to kill me if they knew my actions—despite my father's prominent position in the Nazi Party. It's not a pretty picture."

"How long have you known about me?"

"A little while."

"When you stopped me on the stairs that day and asked about my mother?"

"Yes. I wanted to learn about you before my parents found out. As my mother alluded to, she knows what happens under her roof. Believe me, she'll go to extreme measures to find out." He frowned. "An odd hobby of hers."

"Like the truth of my name, Edith Weber, and how she took pleasure informing me that Edith was her name as well?"

"That was a coincidence. And not to take sides, but you did ask her."

"How exactly did you discover the truth about me? More importantly, why didn't you act upon this knowledge?"

"What do you mean?" He narrowed his eyes. "Feed you to the Nazis so they could earn yet another check mark on their score cards for who could kill the most Jews?"

Another round of chills washed over her. She again pulled the blanket closer around her.

"Edith. May I call you by that lovely name?"

She nodded, liking how her real name sounded on his lips.

"Edith, I'm not some hideous monster. I took the time to learn about you because you're a decent person, one I can tell has a good heart. I'd hoped my discoveries about you would help me to get you to safety." He gritted his teeth; she sensed he was trying to hold back a swear word. "Because it was only a short time until my dear father would find out the truth about you, and then any hope you'd entertained about seeing your mother and family again would be gone."

She sat up and waved away Erich's hand. "I'm fine. The dizziness has passed."

Adela had half-turned around in her seat, and Werner shifted his gaze from the road to the rearview mirror and back several times. What did it matter that they were listening? Yet, she was bothered about the usage of her name, unsure if it was a matter of intimacy or timing or something else. "Please, for reasons I'm unclear about, I'm now thinking that it's best to call me Elsa, not my birth name."

"That's absolutely fine." He chuckled. "Either name is pretty, but it's you that's prettier with your strength, intelligence, and kindness. I'm glad you're with us."

"Absolutely," Werner said.

Adela smiled. "I'm thankful that I've met you."

"I'm fond of the three of you as well." Elsa looked into Erich's green eyes and remembered when they had first met on the streets of Nijmegen and how willingly he'd come to her assistance. "However, with what you know about me, how do I know no one is going after my family right now?"

"That's a fair question. I have no indication that your family has been harmed by a direct connection to me. Actually, the information trail about them has gone cold. Only your history is known. That means that either they've taken different identities, are in hiding, or have escaped."

"Or have been sent to a camp." She couldn't say the kill word. Couldn't imagine her papa, mama, and sister out of her life permanently due to murderous hands.

"I'll tell you about the pirates now," Erich said. "The good and the bad."

Had he offered to share his background to get her mind off of her family's fate? Because he could trust her? Or had he accepted there was strength in uniting together with others? The more they knew about each other, the better chances they had of... "Wait." She held back a grimace.

Erich's eyes widened, and Adela lifted a brow.

"We're now on the level of full trust, correct?"

One by one, Erich, Adela, and Werner nodded.

"Excellent, because I'm still in the dark about something. Erich, before you tell me about the pirates, it's time I learn about what is awaiting us in Vienna? And why your mother made arrangements for me to disperse from the three of you once we arrived?"

"Allow me." Adela rested her chin on the back of her seat and looked squarely into Elsa's eyes. "As I've already told you, that is where I met and then lived with Daniel and Lara Ostrów. They escaped to Poland, begging me to take their youngest daughter, Miriam."

"Your *bebelus*." Elsa caught her error and shook her head. "Pardon. You didn't want me to ever utter that word again."

"No worries," Adela said softly. "It's a word I don't want to use because it breaks my heart over and over again."

Elsa leaned forward and patted her friend's shoulder. "Because of a horrific incident?"

"No." A lone tear meandered from Adela's right eye, and she

didn't brush it away. "Just the opposite. It's what Richard did for us that took Miriam far away from me."

Clearly Adela had done what was right even though it had broken her heart. Elsa's thoughts were confirmed when Werner, in a grandfatherly tone, reassured Adela that she'd chosen wisely for the both of them.

"So," Adela continued, "we're meeting Richard in Vienna because that is where he lives, and the snowstorm had indeed made it more difficult for him to come to us, and with the Herr's company descending on the house, it was for the best. We're not tracking down Miriam; rather he has a lead about my family and those I lived with in my *vista* in Bratislava."

"Stay strong and positive," Erich said. He turned toward Elsa. "My mother arranged an escape option because she's concerned about you. While her knowledge about you is limited, she realized that your goals and dreams may not match Adela's and mine. She wanted to give you a choice to opt out of a dangerous mission."

Elsa wasn't going to mince words. "A dangerous mission to find a missing Roma family?"

"Yes," both Adela and Erich said in unison.

"But, Erich, you and your brother are her sons—why wouldn't she go out of her way to protect the two of you?"

"Oh, she certainly has tried." Erich pulled at his stubbly chin. "Richard and I are two beasts she cannot tame." He snickered. "My Nazi father is a whole different matter. Mothers—wives!"

"And your two little brothers?"

"There you go—you just answered your own question. Wil and Fritz are young and easily influenced. She believes that under her watchful eyes—"

"And a fine bomb shelter," Werner said, his sarcasm unhidden.

"Yes, that too," Erich agreed. "The twins' odds of staying safer are better by her side, under her roof."

Elsa stopped short of saying that all mothers should think like Frau Friedrich. The Frau was a Nazi's wife. Her mother was Jewish with two Jewish daughters. The Frau had plenty of options, whereas her mother had none when it came to her daughters' safety. Her mother had had to put her and Krista into hiding, she saw that now.

"Have I answered your questions about Vienna?" Adela asked.

"Yes." The big mystery over Richard and what he was up to in Vienna remained unknown, but Elsa would find out soon enough. She'd have to resolve whether to continue on this mission or go with whatever the Frau had arranged for her in Vienna. "Now, Erich, about those pirates?"

Werner braked hard. "Ah, we've come to the Salzburg-Austria border checkpoint, and it doesn't look good." He glanced around the car with a look that Elsa had never seen cloud his eyes. Fear.

24

They might have been only a short drive from Vienna, but to Adela, it felt greater than the earth's circumference. They showed their identity papers expecting to be motioned through the checkpoint. Then Werner was ordered to surrender the car keys.

"*Schnell*! *Schnell*!" the tall guard commanded when Werner hesitated, his youthful looks betraying his fierce demeanor. After Werner handed over the keys, the guard ordered them out of the car. Questions were not tolerated. They had no other choice but to cooperate.

Harsh reality set in when both Erich and Werner were pulled away by two guards and led to a small building across the road. A different guard then motioned for Adela and Elsa to step the opposite direction.

"Where are you taking us?" Elsa screeched.

"Be quiet," the guard snapped. As ordered, none of them uttered a word. The guard then ordered them to enter a long and narrow building where they were instructed to sit at the table; he'd bring them a pitcher of water. They were to ask if they wanted the toilet, and a guard would accompany them to the latrine. Adela was thankful she didn't need to go and she hoped that her friend could endure as well, for who could trust these men?

True to his word, the guard fetched a tin pitcher and two glasses. He then turned a chair around and straddled it, staring at them with a look of expectation mingled with amusement. Chills pricked Adela's arms. Elsa's face was as chalk-white as the snow-covered ground, reminding Adela that her friend had been assaulted. Poor Elsa. This couldn't be easy for her.

"Do you know Father Wilhelm Schmidt or Walter Ferber?" he asked in German, though Adela detected a slight accent she couldn't quite place. This war reassigned one to places far from their home.

Both women shook their heads.

The guard leaned forward. "It's best if you verbally communicate with me. I wouldn't want to misunderstand you."

"*Nein*," they both replied.

"We do not know who Father Schmidt or Herr Ferber are," Adela added.

"Schmidt has denounced the Nazi Party—a lost cause if we ever find him. Ferber's a German journalist, a traitor to his Fatherland. Do you believe that after spending time in Dachau he, as a free man, now claims that over 1,000 Polish clergy have died from starvation?"

Fearing what Elsa might say, Adela jumped in. Her friend had a good, righteous heart, but her young age prompted her to speak boldly, despite potential dire consequences. In a bittersweet way, she hoped Elsa would never stop standing up for truth and justice. However, it was time for an untruth. "How horrible that anyone would claim such things went on in a German camp."

The officer's expression turned to stone. After a minute of silence had passed, the guard exhaled sharply. He motioned to the pitcher. "If you aren't going to drink, then I certainly will." He proceeded to pour himself a glass of murky water and gulped it down. "We've received information saying that these two men have been in close contact with each other and with a large vehicle as the one you're driving in, we thought to search it—that's happening as we talk.

We're also making phone calls to verify your identities." He looked at Elsa and smirked. "And you, Fräulein, your expressions betray you."

Elsa's mouth dropped open. "I didn't mean... I—"

"Quiet."

The door to the building crashed open. A guard they hadn't seen before crossed the room and asked to speak with their guard privately.

The door was shoved open again and in came Werner with blood trailing from his nose, then Erich with a battered left eye, followed by their armed guard.

Adela jumped to her feet.

Elsa cried out. "Erich! Werner!"

"We're fine." Erich held up both hands. "It's a misunderstanding."

Adela exchanged looks with Elsa. Fine, those two were not.

The guard accompanying Erich and Werner strode toward the table, pulled out two chairs, and ordered them to sit. His reddened cheeks showed an edge of guilt.

Without asking permission to speak, Erich addressed Adela and Elsa. "At first, they didn't believe that we're traveling to Vienna to see Richard. Not until I mentioned my parents did attitudes change."

The guards grumbled apologies, then offered them drink and food. Adela was relieved when her traveling companions passed on the invitation. Like her, they wanted to leave.

She peered at their captor, who had helped himself to more water. "Our vehicle? You mentioned that you're searching the car." She flashed a tight grin. "In case we were transporting Father Schmidt or Herr Ferber or both?" She held back that lack of space in the trunk due to the bottles of wine and stash of delicacies courtesy of Frau Friedrich would have made this impossible.

The guard slumped inward. "You are free to go," he said in a low, strained tone.

25

With its 17th and 18th-century Baroque architecture, Salzburg faded in the car's rearview mirror, along with the grandeur of the surrounding mountains as they began the drive through the lake towns of St. Gilgen and St. Wolfgang. Elsa had offered to drive to relieve the battered Werner and Erich, but both refused. In fact, after a heated discussion about who should drive, Erich had persuaded Werner to let him drive. "I may have one swollen eye but can still see clearly with the other. You, my friend, have a single nose, and it's broken."

Elsa pressed against the driver's seat. "It was good news that the guards could verify our identity papers, yes?"

Erich remained silent.

She was about to repeat her question, but Adela jumped in. "Did they reach your mother?"

"Yes. She gave the details they wanted."

Elsa strongly sensed that this was not the problem they were facing. She and Adela exchanged telling looks.

Werner shifted in his seat to roll down his window and tossed out the melting clump of snow he'd used to ice his nose. "Tell them, Erich. Best not to keep secrets."

"Right." Erich huffed. "My mother said that my father had phoned her to report that he believed he'd spotted us leaving the Nuremburg checkpoint. He pressed her to explain why we were driving her car, why it was the four of us traveling together, and, of course, where we were going. As you can imagine, my father can be quite good at obtaining information whenever he wants, from whomever he wants. My mother is no exception."

Elsa decided it was time to be candid. "A while back, I overheard your brother Richard and your father arguing."

Beside her, Adela visibly jumped. "Richard visited? Why didn't he..."

"Tell you he was home?" Elsa absorbed the disappointment emanating from her friend. Gently, she said, "From the sounds of Herr Friedrich's tone that night, Richard barely had time to gather the articles he came home for before he was forced to dart from the house."

Adela groaned. "When did this happen? Why didn't you tell me?"

"It was the first night after I moved into your room. I couldn't sleep, and not wanting to disturb you, I slipped out of bed and decided to stretch my legs. I didn't say a peep because I sensed it was wrong to roam the house." Like a guilty child, she looked away. "I'm sorry. I should have woken you."

"Stop," Erich said. "The past is past."

"Yes," Adela said so softly that Elsa had to strain to hear her. "I know Richard, know that if he could, he would have woken me, would have taken me back to Vienna with him that night."

"Yes, he would have, for sure," Erich said.

They were passing through St. Wolfgang, a town of old wooden houses, an ancient church, and a marketplace; if it was another place in time Elsa would have enjoyed exploring it. Instead, she pushed out the questions that had nagged her since that night. "I'm curious."

"When are you not?" Erich said in a distinctly playful and teasing manner.

Why did Richard talk to the Herr in a way that sounded as if the

Nazis had him on a political hit list? And why did it sound like Richard and his father were enemies?"

She had expected one or two quick replies, not the silence that filled the vehicle. Not the failure of Erich to make eye contact with her in the rearview mirror. Certainly not Adela's intense stare out her window. Fine. She had an inkling she'd find out sooner rather than later. But there was one item that was due for discussion. "Tell me, Erich, about this bunch of pirates you're associated with."

"You know you can't avoid answering her forever," Werner said.

"Whose side are you on?" Erich glared at him, an obvious attempt at humor.

Erich drove out of St. Wolfgang, further along the narrow mountain roads of the Salzkammergut region, and steered them toward Hallstatt. They passed fields of cows standing idly in snowy pastures, more lakes, and a group of daring folks crossing the land in snowshoes, as if a nod to better times.

"Let's see," Erich began. "If you wanted to pigeonhole Richard and me, you could say we've always been the rebellious types. Though we detested it, our parents—well, to be fair, Germany— mandated us to join the Hitlerjugend. Richard was 15 and I was ten at that time. Richard was conscripted into the army at 18, and ended up in Vienna in 1938."

"That's the year I met him," Adela said reflectively.

"Only 15-years-old, I lived at home, obliging my parents. I envied Richard and wanted to get away too, but that was also the year that Fritz and Wil were born, which made family matters more complex. Roles changed. We became distant. During the following year, the burning drive in me to escape home merged with a growing repugnance at the spread of Nazism. The only positive outcome of joining the Hitlerjugend was that I met and became good pals with Arno."

"He was one of your three friends killed in Cologne, right?" Elsa asked.

Erich bobbed his head. "That's right—I told you the night we met in the bomb shelter about Arno, Gunter, and Walter." He paused.

"They were three great friends whose lives were taken far too early—killed by the bombs dropped over Cologne."

"Did you and Arno meet the other two through the Edelweiss Pirates?"

"Yes. Arno was also from Monschau but moved to Cologne, where Gunter and Walter were from. Arno is the one who introduced me to the Pirates. I began working with them on the sly, helping them to sabotage the Nazis."

"Did your parents know what you were up to?"

"My mother might have had an inkling, but with two babies, she had her hands full, and conveniently could ignore what our father was up to."

"That's the way evil spreads," Adela said. "People are so wrapped up in day-to-day activities and survival that it becomes a habit to look the other way."

Erich cleared his throat. "When I turned 18, I feared conscription into the army. Not out of fear of death: I didn't want to help Germany win this wicked war. So, I had a good heart-to-heart with my mother. And by sidestepping the mention of my pirate activity, I had her persuade Vater to use his position in the Nazi Party to get me out of military service."

"Couldn't Richard have done the same to avoid the service?"

"Richard didn't have a chance," Adela said.

"That's absolutely correct," Erich said. "Richard and our father never had any respect or admiration for each other. If my brother ever asked for his help, he'd have to sacrifice a host of things that he wasn't about to surrender. Besides, he joined the army in the hope of discovering things that would help to achieve his goals."

"Did he?"

"Yes, he certainly did."

Elsa waited for more information about the mysterious Richard. When more details failed to materialize, she turned back to quiz him about the group of pirates. "What motivation do the members of the Edelweiss Pirates share?"

This time, there was no silences or hesitations from Erich. "Our refusal to recognize Nazi ideology and to do the party irreparable harm. We listened to forbidden BBC radio broadcasts, dropped leaflets full of anti-Nazi information in several towns, hid military deserters and escaped camp prisoners, and supplied several resistance groups with explosives and other means to fight. We didn't always have an easy go of it—several members were arrested and tortured by the Gestapo. A few of our best leaders have been hanged in public executions. Although punishment have stopped a few of us, the Pirates are going strong. Our goal is to keep fighting until we see an end to this war and the Nazi era."

"What's your role in this group? How can you afford to take a break to take us to Vienna?"

Erich glanced at Elsa before fixing his eyes again on the road. "Sometimes in life, no matter how busy we are, we have to help family and friends. There are other groups besides the Pirates fighting the same battles, like the White Rose group. Active in this group are a brother and sister I've met often—Hans and Sophie Scholl—as well as their friend, Christoph Probst. I fear they might be in great jeopardy as I speak, but I'm remaining hopeful."

"Your role?" Elsa prompted, with her admiration for Erich growing by the second. He was definitely not the good Nazi son she had originally assumed and feared. "I'm a recruiter. I also deliverer of basic goods—food, cash for bribes, writing paper—to members as needed."

"Using a few resources that your mother might have, uh, arranged for you?"

"As I've said before, you catch on fast."

Elsa smiled, and her growing curiosity about Werner prompted her to lean forward. "And you, Werner, my traveling friend? Are you German by birth?" She quickly apologized, saying he didn't have to respond if he didn't feel up to talking.

"No worries about my poor nose," Werner said quickly. "I'll be brief, though. Yes, I'm German, from an old German-Polish family in Hamburg. I came to need employment at a young age. Since I'm of the generation between the Great War and this present disaster and couldn't afford university studies, I answered the advertisement for work as a butler for the Friedrichs. During the interview in Herr Friedrich's office, one complete with a swastika banner draped over a photograph of Hitler, I thought it was wise to leave out the part about how my Jewish *opa* married my Christian *oma*."

"You never told me about the swastika part," Erich said.

"Let's just say that I learned years ago to keep mum about certain details. Besides, the truth that needs to be learned by many is to speak up about wrongdoings in society. I may have kept quiet about a stupid banner, but I've done my share of opening my mouth when certain folks wouldn't think that was the wisest of choices. And that's why I'm fleeing like the rest of you—I can't go back to the Friedrich house or chance an encounter with Herr Friedrich. After all these years, I know he's onto me."

"Fleeing?" Elsa echoed, not that she had any intentions of returning to Monschau and the Friedrichs either.

"In part, yes," Adela said. "We are escaping in the hope of a better life. For me, that means to find Richard so he can help me find my family."

And there it was. Most of the mysteries were now resolved. Missing were the pieces about Miriam, the child Adela was entrusted with. If it was meant for her to learn more, she'd find out. Elsa grasped her friend's hand and squeezed it. "Adela, I'm also glad I'm going to help you find your family."

Dear Mama,

What is it like to bring an innocent child into a world that can be so wonderful and horrible at the same time, knowing that you can't always watch out for them every second of their life? I ask because on this journey with my new friends, I'm learning about mothers and their love for their children, something I took for granted when I lived at home with you.

I want to tell you that in your wisdom, you've instructed me well about what to expect in this world, lessons I wish I never refuted. I'm hoping for tomorrow to exist, that this upside-down world can hold hands—at least, figuratively—and hatred can cease. Is that too much to ask for?

Love, love, and love,
Edith

"Wake up, Elsa. Come on, wake up, sleepyhead."

Elsa stirred awake, looked toward her right, and saw Adela, her forehead furrowed. "What's wrong? Why are you upset with me?"

Adela thumbed her chest. "Me? I'm fine, as reasonably as can be. You're the one thrashing about, calling out names. You must have been having a nightmare."

Elsa straightened and glanced at the front of the car. If Erich or Werner had overheard her utterances, they at least didn't embarrass her further by teasing her. She looked more closely. Werner had his head slanted against the passenger window, apparently enjoying a little nap. As for Erich, his attention was fixed on the road. "Whose names did I call out?"

"Mama, Krista," Adela said quietly to keep it between them.

"Krista's my sister."

"I gathered."

"Oh, dear. What did I say?"

"Nothing to be embarrassed about. Just that you missed them though from the groaning, I'm thinking it was more of a nightmare than a sweet dream."

Before Elsa's eyes, flashes of her sister boarding a tram and chugging kilometers away replaced the rolling hills and mountains they were driving past. Images of her mother, sobbing over her and her sister, followed the tram gaining speed away from her, replayed as if on a non-stop reel. She didn't know which was worse. A dream of loved ones she couldn't be with? The danger they were presently facing? A future that she couldn't imagine? Although this war hadn't ended, it was an inevitable conclusion that it had already changed the scope of the entire world's history and would likely shape its future. The only truth in her life was that the life she'd once known was no longer and could never be.

As a diversion, she pointed out the window. "Where are we now? And what is that ancient-looking building? A castle?"

"It is a castle," Adela answered. "According to Erich, we're in a town called Maria Enzersdorf. We have less than an hour's drive until we are in Vienna."

"I've been asleep that long?"

"About two hours," Erich said, jumping into their conversation.

"To answer your question," Adela continued, "though I need to learn more about Austria's history, I do know that the castle was built in the 1100s. Amazing, yes?"

"Definitely."

"Back home, we too had a castle."

"I imagine Bratislava has a rich history." A disturbing thought entered Elsa's mind. "Do you think it might be possible for buildings to outlast man?"

Adela gave a little nod before wiping her eyes. "Let's just hope that in our lifetime, this will be the last war we'll see."

"Well, Adela," Erich said. His tone was cheerful but twinged with gray pensiveness. "How does it feel to be back in Vienna?"

As if pressing her hand against the palm of an old acquaintance, Adela flattened her hand against the passenger window. She breathed in deeply. "I'm expecting to see a drastically changed Vienna. Richard may be there, but Miriam won't be. And with Bratislava just a little further east..." She paused, her pain obvious. "It's like I'm about to arrive at a house of ghosts."

26

With Austria sandwiched between Germany and Italy, it came as no shock to Adela that entering Vienna entailed crossing another checkpoint. After presenting their identity papers, they were waved on and permitted into the city.

"Is this good news that we breezed through the checkpoint or do you think this may be a setup and we should be wary?" Adela glanced about the car. All three of her traveling companions bobbed their heads in agreement but remained silent. Something didn't feel right. "What do you think?"

Werner, who had taken on the role of driver minutes before they'd arrived at the checkpoint, harrumphed. "Excellent question." After a painful pause, he added, "I'm trusting it will go as we would wish. What do you think, Erich?"

"I truly don't know. A short while ago, you mentioned arriving at a house full of ghosts. Well, I'm also haunted—I may be a Nazi's son, but I feel like I'm a sitting target. I'm definitely wary."

Werner continued toward the Margarenten, a once densely populated district of Vienna. Bordered by the Vienna River to the north, it was near the old town section of Vienna, but lacking its elegance of historic homes with balconies and courtyards and cobblestone streets, whatever was left of it. Richard had told her about the bombing in September 1942; she suspected worse destruction was in Vienna's near future. Truth be told, the sooner they departed Vienna, the better.

They pushed on in unusual silence. Adela studied her friends, wondering what would happen to them. Would these precious minutes be their last together? When Erich glanced at Elsa, Adela allowed herself a stray thought about those two possibly becoming a couple. Partners fighting against evil? Helping her escape the Nazis' clutches to find her family and others as well? Intimate lovers? People needed to latch onto love more than cling stubbornly to hatred. She could imagine Elsa and Erich falling for each other, despite their extremely different backgrounds, if they could survive this bloody war.

"And, Elsa," Erich said, "I imagine your ghosts also drop by for frequent visits as well."

"No. My ghosts have never left me." Elsa squeezed her eyes shut for a few seconds, then blinked them open. She pointed to her right temple and then patted her heart. "I hope you don't think me silly, but here's a confession. Since before we left your family's home, Erich, I've been composing letters in my mind to my mother in the hope of one day seeing her in person and telling her what I've written. Since we started our journey, I've written these letters—these apologies—in my mind."

"You're definitely not silly," Erich said. "But why do you say apologies?"

"Behavior upon my part that I'm not particularly proud of."

He gave her a sideways look. "Don't take this the wrong way, but since you aren't that old and have time to learn and improve yourself, don't you think you're a bit hard on yourself?"

Elsa shrugged. "Possibly, but I was brought up to know better when it comes to respecting my parents. I'll have to tell you more at another time."

"I'd like that. Since a good part of our journey lies ahead, whenever you're ready, so will be my supportive ear."

Adela resisted squirming. Although she was happy that her friend and Erich were getting along, her lonely heart thumped. "And you, Werner? Are ghosts visiting you?"

"Yes and no. I give them a good wallop on the noggin, and they back off for a while."

While Erich snorted and Elsa chuckled politely into her hand, Adela offered a big nod. "I like your style. I could use boxing pointers when you have the time."

Instead of responding, Werner veered off the road and came to an abrupt stop. "We're here." When no response came, he stared at Erich. "You did say this Kohligasse address, correct?"

Erich looked out at the three stories above a butcher shop. "Yes, but I wasn't expecting this place. A walk-up flat isn't quite my brother's style. Then again, let's just say our father wouldn't approve."

"Has he ever approved of your brother or his choices?" Werner asked.

From the corner of her eye, Adela noticed that Elsa had a distinct look of confusion stamped across her face. Her friend would find out the answers to her questions soon enough. She could only hope that she'd be receptive. Richard Friedrich did not need another person's scorn.

Erich wagged a finger. "You have me there, old pal."

"Let's get out of this vehicle before I get any older and can't climb those stairs!"

They tackled the three flights to the top level of the building with its plaster walls crumbling and the clang of ancient pipes echoing in the hallway. Two doors, situated across from each other, presented an uncertainty since neither was marked with a number or name. Erich and Werner exchanged looks and swore.

"It's the one on the left." Adela suppressed a smirk when both men and Elsa looked at her. "When Richard first moved into this flat, he told me it was the one on the left after climbing the stairs."

"I can see why Richard has often told me he's glad to have you in his corner." Erich knocked on the door. "If no one answers in a minute, we're out of here. This place gives me the creeps." Before he had finished speaking, the door to the flat opened wide enough for a pair of brown eyes to stare out of.

"Yes?" came a deep voice.

"Theodore sent us," Erich said. The code name was Richard's middle name.

The door opened wider. A blond, mustached man in his mid-thirties stole a glance at each of them. "Anyone else?"

"I'm Erich, Richard's brother. I'm with my friends, Elsa, Werner and Adela."

"Ah, Adela. I know that name. And, of course, yours. Please come in." After they had walked into a surprisingly large foyer, the man, dressed in black trousers and a tan sweater vest over a white shirt, shut and locked the door. "I'm Viktor. My sister, Catherine, is at work and won't arrive home until late this evening. Have a seat. Richard should be home soon. No one I know has been able to purchase coffee for a while, whether in a shop or on the black market, but may I offer you tea?"

Adela wished she could have a sip of the hard liquor her father stashed away for tough-times indulgence. How she longed to see her strong, always smiling father, to hear him singing the outrageous songs that he'd create off the top of his head, and to stroll beside him on the long walks he'd take to observe nature or visit an ill friend. She wished she could breathe in the aroma of her dear mother's cooking. Surprisingly, the swatting away of more birds from within the house and helping to calm her mother's panic were appealing thoughts. And her sweet sister? She wished to exchange girlish stories about husbands-to-be with Antonina, who, fate-willing, would be happily turning 30 this year. If she hadn't been captured and thrown into a death camp, or living obscurely in shame because she had been subjected to sterilization to decrease the Roma population and to make her undesirable to most men. Might she be one of the lucky ones to have survived this awful time of persecution, though separated from Adela by a continent or an ocean?

They accepted the offer of tea. Viktor gestured toward the end of the hallway that appeared to open into a parlor, then excused himself. The parlor was small but cozy, with two old settees situated across from each other. A library table adorned with framed photographs stood behind each of the small sofas. There were photos of Richard with his arm around Viktor, smiling happily for the camera, of Richard and Viktor sitting hip-to-hip on one of the parlor's settees. The two men, both wearing mock Nazi uniforms, faced each other so that the camera's eye could catch their exchange of wry grins.

Richard had told Adela about Viktor, their love for each other, and how they were as much against Nazism as the Nazi Party was opposed to their relationship. They were at risk alongside the Jews, Roma, and those with Nazi-deemed disabilities like blindness, deafness, and mental illnesses. She sensed Elsa peering at her and made eye contact with her friend. Elsa's mouth formed an "Oh." Adela nodded, relieved that Elsa smiled. Good. Now Elsa understood Richard and Viktor's relationship and why the Herr disapproved of his oldest son. The two men had to keep their relationship out of public view. Fortunately, Viktor's sister living with them helped to divert nosy questions from others.

Viktor entered the room, carrying a tray with a tarnished silver teapot and mismatched cups and saucers. "Sorry, but we're out of sugar and cream." A jangling sound came from the flat's entrance. "Now that's perfect timing—Richard's home."

Within seconds the spitting image of Erich, except taller, broader, and with a thick mustache and raven hair, strode into the room. He rushed directly to Adela and pulled her into an embrace. "Good God, I've missed you." He glanced at his brother. "I'm relieved to find you're fine and safe as well."

"That's better," Erich teased him and stood. Richard, still holding onto Adela, tugged him into his arms. "And this is our dear friend, Elsa," Erich added. "And of course, you remember Werner." Richard swept them into the group hug. When they pulled away from each other, Erich recounted their less than smooth journey from Monschau.

"To be expected," Richard said, in a hushed tone. "And that's why you and I are here, doing what we do best—not heeding the Nazi regime." He glanced at his watch. "You must be hungry. I can smell Viktor's famous chicken dish cooking."

Viktor smirked. "Famous? It's more like once-a-week chicken, if we're lucky."

"And the other days?" Elsa asked.

"Rabbit, a staple in many homes these days. Speaking of dinner, let me get the carrots warmed up—the few we've been allotted this week."

"During dinner, we'll talk more," Richard said. "Please, relax. However, I caution you, you must keep your voices to a mere murmur. We might trust our neighbors, but these days it's wise not to take chances."

Richard and Werner had a fast smoke outdoors on the flat's small balcony, which faced a copse of maples that, despite the loss of leaves, offered some privacy.

Fifteen minutes later, they all sat crammed around a white-painted table in the clean, cozy, and surprisingly comfortable kitchen. "We are lucky to have found this place," Richard said as he placed full dinner plates in front of them.

"Now that we've arrived in Vienna, I'm unsure of my place," Werner began after a forkful of chicken. "At this point, I'm considering myself as the former Friedrich butler. Although I should deliver the Frau's car back home, I need to keep out of the Herr's sight."

"As for the car, I can make arrangements with my mother for its return," Richard said. "Would you consider working with us? We need a messenger."

"If it's to defeat the Nazi Party, I might consider it. Tell me, if you're permitted to, what exactly do you do for work? Erich hasn't mentioned."

Richard leaned toward Werner; the others huddled closer as well. "Since I've served in the German army and have my connections, I work in a field office responding to telegrams or other messages that my Nazi commander tells me to."

Elsa gasped. Werner paled.

Richard lifted a hand. "It provides me with sustenance, cash, and extra time—that's how I discovered Adela roaming homeless back in '38. The bulk of my time is spent working with Heinrich Maier. He won't stop talking about soccer and is a Catholic priest dead against the Nazi Party. Let's just say that we're monitoring an alarming issue concerning Germany's creation of rockets. We've been receiving intelligence that rockets—flying bombs as they're referred to—are being built in northern France with long-range striking abilities."

"So, in theory, a rocket fired in France could strike Britain?" Werner asked.

"Yes, killing a legion of innocent people and destroying homes and businesses in its path on a level which the world has not yet seen. It's being developed under the cover of future space exploration, but that's not the main objective."

"See," Elsa said directly to Erich. "We were talking about space travel not too long ago, but not for the likes of harm."

"*Ja.*" Erich eyed his brother. "I wouldn't have imagined rockets and destruction coming from this."

Werner looked at Viktor. "And your work?"

"I'm an overnight lobby clerk at my father's hotel here in Vienna." Viktor jutted his chin at Richard. "During the day, I work with Richard and Heinrich—don't bother asking me if I sleep."

Werner gave a quick nod. "I might have just found myself a new career at the ripe old age of 55 then."

"Ha," Erich said. "I thought you were in your young forties."

Adela glanced about the table. "Richard, the two of us need to talk. Alone."

"We can talk right here." Richard reached across the table and grasped Adela's hands. "Erich and Viktor both know what I have to say."

Adela eyed Erich. "You already know? And you haven't breathed a word to me?" She didn't wait for a reply because she doubted it would be comprehensible or acceptable. Instead, she stood and rushed out from the kitchen, hoping to be left alone.

As she collapsed on a corner chair beside a heavily curtained window, she sensed Richard's presence. She twisted around to face him through tear-filled eyes. "How long have you known?"

"As for Miriam's family, a while back I'd learned that they made it into Poland, but I waited until this morning when I could confirm you were on the way here to verify my information."

"And?"

"It's not good." He pulled her into his arms and that's when she released the sobs that she couldn't contain a second longer, her body rocking back and forth. "After Germany occupied Poland, the Ostróws were rounded up with her brother and the other Jews in his village. They were supposed to be sent to one of the ghettos but never…"

"They escaped?" The question was foolish since he'd told her he didn't have good news, but she had to remain hopeful. Didn't she? Or was hope now the epitome of reckless optimism? She squeezed her eyes shut, waiting for his reply.

"They never made it—never had the opportunity."

The room turned sharply, and she swayed. Richard tightened his hold on her. "My darling, Vonni," he said tenderly. "They were gassed to death, trapped in a van. The vehicle was packed with others, sealed tight with no way out."

Hope, she ordered herself, despite her thoughts of seconds ago. Damn it. Be hopeful. "And Miriam? Have you tracked her down? I should never have agreed!"

"Yes, love. You had to agree with my mother." He gently shook her arm. "Please, Vonni. Open your eyes. Look at me."

"Why are you the only one who can say my true name as sweetly as if you're sprinkling rosebuds across the sky?"

"Because I'm your dearest friend and love you." He gave her a moment to absorb what he'd just shared. "Now, open your eyes and trust me with what else I have to say." She sniffled and blinked her eyes. "That's better. I'm so sorry. As Jews in Poland, Daniel and Lara and their daughter didn't have a chance of surviving."

"Tell me something good about Miriam. There must be one

speck of good news. Why should I have permitted your mother to find a home for my darling little girl? If I had to send her away from me, it should have been to England or Switzerland. Anywhere but Germany. With a mark on my head as a Roma, I'll never see her again, never be allowed to get close enough to offer a smile, a hug."

"Don't shortchange yourself. You did the best you could, given the circumstances. If it weren't for you, Miriam's chances of survival would have been slim. She's living a good life—has parental love, a home, food, and an education. You are, by far, one of the loveliest people I know. You dared to take countless risks that others would never consider."

Risks? When she first arrived with Richard to his parents' estate, she had faced living on the streets again with a young child since the Friedrichs wouldn't permit a child that wasn't their own to live with them. Richard had persuaded his mother to help hide them from his father, at least until another living arrangement could be made. Then, the Frau discovered she was Roma and not simply, as Adela had originally claimed, a reckless German girl who was a mother without the benefit of a husband. But Adela held her head up and worked her bones off without complaining. Frau Friedrich looked away. The big risk was hiding Miriam from the Herr in the cellar room. Never once during those early days of living at the Friedrichs' had she thought of herself as a risk taker, but yes, she could see it now.

"I couldn't have done this without your help, your love. You are a beautiful person." He opened his mouth, but she rushed on. "What about my family? Have you any news? Is that why Erich has brought me here to Vienna to see you? You better tell me excellent news because I can't bear one more heartbreaking word."

"I do have news, but it's neither good nor bad." He took a deep breath. "A few people from your family's *vista* escaped into the woods before the Nazis got to Bratislava. We believe they headed to the mountains, to the Low Tatras, to wait out the war away from the Nazis. We don't know if your parents and sister are part of this group, or whether these people can take you to your family, but it's worthwhile finding out, don't you think?"

"Of course. But how can I ever begin to look for them? I can't possibly trek through those mountains in winter."

"Yes, you can. I've collected clothing and supplies for you, my brother, and that friend of yours, if she wants to go. Viktor and I have also arranged to arm you with handguns, which I know Erich can use."

"I can use a gun as well. My father taught me how to defend myself as a Roma child whose fate was often in the hands of *gorgios*. But Elsa? I can't imagine her firing a weapon."

"You might be surprised when it comes to the rescue of a loved one, let alone herself. Erich told me Elsa's Jewish and despises the Nazis. So yes, I believe she'd trek through the mountains in wintertime. Have you seen the way my brother looks at her? It's obvious he's in love. He won't let harm come her way."

"But Richard, you know there's a great chance we'll encounter danger."

"Yes, just like I know you'll encounter danger by not disappearing into the Tatras. Listen, the three of you are strong, determined, young, and brave. You have what it takes and will make the trip just fine."

"But—"

"It's arranged. The longer you stay here, the greater your chances of being discovered. We're leaving in the middle of the night. I'll take you to Liptovský Mikuláš before I turn around to get back here to continue my work with Heinrich."

"Oh, I'm familiar with that town." She was startled and happy to hear the name of a place in her home country. "That's a long trip for you from Vienna. How can we possibly cross the border?"

Richard grinned, a confident expression she missed seeing on his lovely face. "My dear Vonni, I'm a certified Nazi, which comes in handy. My paperwork and well-rehearsed explanations will have you and your friends off to a running start. Do not worry. I have one request, though."

He thought of her as strong and brave; she saw herself as drained of energy and with dimming hope, one who perpetually peered over her shoulder to see what menace lurked behind. But the desire to unite with her family would propel her forward, whether across snow-covered fields or icy slopes that led to thick forests. No matter if they encountered bears annoyed with them for disturbing their winter sleep or gun-toting human enemies that hated her because she was Roma and Elsa because she was Jewish.

Footsteps squeaked on the bare wooden floor. Adela glanced over Richard's shoulder and saw Erich and Elsa. Her extended family. She stood and strode to her friends. "Are you prepared to march with me through the roughest terrain you've ever experienced?"

While Erich nodded, Elsa grasped her hands. "For you, yes."

Adela pulled Elsa and Erich into a hug, thanking them. She could do this. One day, sooner rather than later, she'd become Vonni again. Elsa would become Edith. It was time for this next part of their journey, one she prayed would bring both of them back to their families.

She faced Richard. "What's the request?"

27

Elsa stared wide-eyed at Richard, doubting she'd heard his reply to Adela correctly.

"I'll repeat it for you," Richard said as he turned around to face the others. "Once you leave Liptovský Mikuláš, follow the map I'll give you. It will take you to a mountain settlement. There, you'll find Soviet partisans fighting against Germany. You are not to stay there for more than one day and night. These partisans are hiding Jews who have fled from various Slovakian towns and have insight into the Roma from their native areas. They'll help you to where you'll go next. Here's the thing—there are two Jewish children who are now orphans and because of their young ages, they need to get out of there and into safety. The adults are willing to remain put and take a chance, but they've been hoping newcomers will come along and take this boy and girl with them. This is part of what I do to help the victims of the Nazis. Will you do this and help those in desperate need?"

One by one, they agreed. "My heart tells me it's the least we can do," Elsa said. Erich and Adela agreed.

"Excellent." Richard stood. "Let's get at least a few hours of sleep, considering we have a long drive ahead of us. You will then have a considerable hike to contend with."

Two in the morning rolled around fast, not that Elsa had slept a wink. After Catherine had phoned to say she was staying the night with her boyfriend, Elsa had shared Catherine's bedroom with Adela. Although Richard and Viktor had offered their bedroom to Erich and Werner, the latter two insisted on camping out in the parlor, making do with the small settees as beds. By half past two, Richard was driving his own vehicle with Erich beside him in the front passenger seat. Elsa and Adela were once again together, stretched out on the backseat. Werner remained behind with Viktor, who planned to introduce him to Heinrich Maier.

The weather cooperated, presenting them with clear skies but frigid temperatures. Elsa's thoughts strayed to the items that Richard had generously packed for their trek: woolen socks, thick hiking boots—he'd done a decent job estimating shoe sizes—snowshoes, skis, waterproof trousers, and heavy jackets. Plus, durable backpacks stuffed with canteens of water and foods suitable for hiking. Before they left, Erich snatched the bribe money from his mother's car. What they couldn't use they were free to pass on to those in need.

As they drove away from the building, Elsa smiled to herself. Richard and Viktor were nice men and she wished them well. She prayed no harm would come to them from the Nazis or anyone willing to sling prejudice at them for their preferred lifestyle. They deserved happiness like any other person.

The silence in the car lasted only until the outskirts of Liptovský Mikuláš. This time, it wasn't a checkpoint that stopped them but three black vehicles blocking the road.

Erich groaned and Richard swore.

"What is it?" Elsa asked.

"Should we get our identity papers out?" said Adela.

"It's our father." Richard pulled off on the shoulder. He glanced around the car, then at the five uniformed SS men with guns aimed at them, and at Herr Friedrich approaching their vehicle at a speedy clip. He had a gun trained on Richard. "Do not ask questions or attempt to reason. I will speak if necessary." He glanced at his brother, who nodded. "As well as Erich."

The tallest of the SS officers, wearing a black leather greatcoat, approached the car. Without a doubt, all of the men were high-ranking officers. Elsa's mind went blank, but she ordered herself not to show any fear. She squeezed Adela's hand quickly and exchanged one last look. One way or the other, we'll be fine, she silently comforted her friend.

"*Aus! Macht schnell!*"

No one waited for another command to get out of the car. As if they could only dream of invincibility in a group formation, Elsa, Adela, Erich, and Richard bunched together, hands lifted in surrender.

Maxwell Friedrich toggled his weapon's aim between Richard and Erich. "My two worthless sons, we meet again." He darted his steely gaze between Elsa and Adela. "Jew and Roma—it's time for you to disappear. Forever." He ordered all of them to walk ahead into the woods. Richard led the way, plowing through the knee-deep snow. Erich followed, then came Adela and Elsa. The power of the gun the Herr held at the ready was as tangible as the cold truth that he'd tracked them down, prepared to kill his sons and friends. Elsa wanted to turn around to see if the other five men were following but didn't dare face any of the unforgivable sorry excuses for human beings. With no wind and the sound of only one set of footsteps crunching behind her, she sensed that just the Herr marched with them while the others remained by the vehicles. Well, at least they'd get their jollies by hearing the shots that were about to be fired.

"Edith," Erich suddenly shouted, breaking the silence. His use of her real name, sounding like a symphony on his lips, filled her with warmth and chased away the lingering fears of what they were about to face. "I love you. And unlike what I told you about my reluctance to marry when we first met, I want you as my wedded bride."

Despite the Herr snickering, it was time for Elsa to become Edith again, if for just mere seconds. She swallowed hard, not from fear of Erich's father or what he may do with his son's sentiments for her, but from the joy of knowing she was loved and treasured by Erich. She loved him too and facing her death, she had to tell him.

She gazed at Erich, a German man from a Nazi family who had taught her the biggest life lesson—the power of love. That love can indeed occur despite hatred, and that love can come from the least likely person. In this case, an enemy's son. "I love you too, Erich." Her words were strong and loud, and she was confident that not only Erich would hear them but his father as well. She pushed back tears of joy mingled with sorrow. "We'll always be together, if not now then in eternity."

"Vonni," Richard called. "You're the dearest, most beautiful friend I've ever had."

"And you are my world, Richard," Vonni replied. "You alone saved me from the horrors I faced on the streets of Vienna. You gave me hope and a home for Miriam."

"Shut up," the senior Friedrich shouted. He ordered them to keep walking toward a pine-lined copse up ahead. The tree covering was thick enough to camouflage what would soon be their dead bodies, but the spot was close enough to the road to ensure the echo of gunshots would be heard. He ordered them to halt. "With your hands remaining up, turn around and face me."

One by one, they turned toward this sinister man, who was far from a loving father. But what was this? His gun was chucked on the snow-covered ground.

"I did not track you from Germany to kill you."

"Vater," Richard said, "nor do I suspect you came here to tell of your esteem for us."

Friedrich pursed his lips. "You're wrong, my son. But this time, I'm glad you are."

Edith combed Richard's face for an expression to better understand this curious exchange, but none was found. Standing the closest to Friedrich, she jumped when Erich wrapped an arm around her. His warmth flowed immediately to her chilled bones.

"I don't approve of your choice of companions, Richard." Richard opened his mouth, but Friedrich held up a hand to silence him. "Hear me out, son—time is ticking. Those five SS men have my orders to come searching for us if they don't hear gunfire within 20 minutes."

"Gunfire?" Erich said, pulling Elsa tighter. "But you just—"

"Quiet!" Friedrich returned his attention to his oldest son. "I've thought about our conversation the last time you were home. And I talked with your mother." He paused, observing his son from head to toe. "You are my son. While I do not understand your desire for men, I've concluded that it is your business, your life. I will not surrender you to my fellow Nazis and have your life ended at their hands. Nor my own hands."

Friedrich stepped up to Erich, who did not flinch. Edith started to squirm, but the older man shook his head. "Don't. I will not hurt you, either." He glanced at Vonni tucked within Richard's hold. "Nor you."

He stooped to retrieve his gun but pointed it into the air. "Listen carefully. As a member of the Nazi Party, my only regret is how I've treated my sons. However, my support and loyalty will remain with Germany. I am going to fire this gun four times into the air, once for each of you. Then I will go back to my men. I will tell them that for now we will leave the vehicle behind and take off. Give us a half hour before you go out to your car for the supplies that I assume you have. I give you my word that there are no other SS or soldiers waiting to ambush you. Get your gear and march deep into the Tatras. You will be assumed dead so no one will be looking for you." He stared firmly into Richard's eyes. "That means that you too will have to journey with your brother and friends and cannot return to Vienna. I've already taken measures to assure that no harm will come to your lover and that a message will be delivered to him at the hotel where he works, telling him in the briefest of terms that you are fine."

While Maxwell Friedrich did not address the resistance

movement Richard was involved in, it was obvious to Edith that his knowledge spanned more than either of his sons had been aware.

Richard pulled his father into an embrace. "Thank you."

Erich gave his father a fast hug; Edith and Vonni nodded.

Friedrich stepped a distance away from them and pulled the trigger. A loud boom filled the air. Three more gunshots followed. The flutter of wings, likely from a black grouse, boomeranged between the trees. By now, the noise of presumed death would have reached Friedrich's cohorts.

"Do not come back home. Ever," Friedrich murmured as if concerned his words could carry to the other Nazis' ears. "Know that I do not hate you. Not one of you."

It wasn't the I-love-you words Edith believed his sons had yearned to hear or the sudden respect for Jews, Roma, and homosexuals that the Reich opposed, but it would have to suffice. Without another word exchanged, she, Erich, Richard, and Vonni watched as Friedrich marched out of the woods. His head was lifted in victory as he trudged through the snow back to his men.

As instructed, they waited half an hour before retrieving the camping supplies from Richard's car. Except for Vonni, they all had experience with snowshoeing through dense woods. They promised to help her as they began the next part of their trip to the refugee settlement. It was at least a seven-hour trek, but that was on a sunny and warm day. Still, they agreed that together they'd make it, not only for their own sakes but to offer their help to innocent strangers who had become refugees. God willing, they'd either find Vonni's family or receive some positive news.

At first, they chatted about the eagles and falcons that filled the sky, the roaming chamois, and the open clearings that provided scenic views of distant mountains. These sights helped to pass the time and took their minds off the cold temperature and concerns about what awaited them. Fortunately, they never saw one brown bear, and concluded they hadn't roused them from hibernation. Fueled by renewed hope of a good future, they were determined to reach their destination by dusk.

Dear Mama,

This is just a quick note because the next time I address you I vow it will be face-to-face. I will not stop until we are together again. The biggest lesson I've learned since we parted is how fragile and precious love, family, and friendship are and that they should never be taken for granted.

I'm on my way home! We might have to wait out the war hidden in the woods, but I promise soon enough, we'll see each other. And I'll be your loving Edith once again, never, ever doubtful Elsa.

I cannot wait to tell you how much I've come to see you as my hero. If you hadn't braved putting me into hiding, I would not be the person I am today, let alone alive. You've graced my life with love and hope, and for this very reason, I say with confidence that I will see you soon.

Love always,

Edith

28

December 11, 1945. As if her hand could float, Edith paused with her index finger hovering over the phone. She'd been set to call her parents for the first time since she and Erich had moved into Plantage, the same neighborhood where her family had first settled upon arriving in Amsterdam. Despite the determination to contact her parents, she'd picked up the phone a few times only to dial the number and then quickly hang up before the phone could ring on the other end. She'd verified her parents' address and phone number, so it wasn't a question of potentially ringing a stranger. Now, beside the phone desk in the small but lovely apartment she and Erich rented, she nearly slammed the receiver down. "I can't do this."

"Yes, you can, my love." Erich leaned over and kissed her on the cheek. "You can accomplish whatever you set your fine mind to."

She smiled and dialed her parents' phone number, this time allowing the call to go through. On the third ring, it was picked up. "Mama!"

What she didn't expect to greet her was silence. She tried again. "It's me—Edith."

"Yes, of course I know who this is. Darling daughter, I can't forget your voice." Her mother's voice quaked. Edith then heard her mother shout out her father's name. Good God. They were both alive. They had survived the war! Her father had come back to her mother!

"Don't cry, Mama." Edith sniffled.

"Where are you? Are you well? Tell me." Her mother sucked in a big breath. "Pardon my questions."

Her mother told her father who was on the phone and suddenly he was speaking into her ear. "I've missed you, Edith. Both your mama and I have. Where are you?"

"In Plantage."

"In the Netherlands?" both her parents said in unison and chuckled. Then her mother got back onto the phone. "Tell me the address, and we'll walk right over."

The parlor swirled around Edith. Erich gripped her arm and held her firmly as she continued. "Is Krista there too?"

"She'll arrive home tomorrow. We'll be together to celebrate the end of this hideous war and yet another birthday, belated and all, for you."

"I'd like that, but Mama, there's news you must know." Edith braced herself, combing her mind for what she'd mentally rehearsed since she and Erich had moved into the apartment a month ago.

"Tell me. Sweetheart, there's not one word you could say that would make us judge you. You know that, don't you?"

"Mama, I'm married." She gulped, hoping her mother didn't connect the family name she was about to utter. "His surname—my married name—is Friedrich."

"Does this man have a first name?" her father asked, evidently pressing his ear to the phone.

"Of course." Edith winked at her husband. "His name is Erich, though I often call him "Wonderful" for short. When we returned to Amsterdam, a long story in itself, we wanted to live together. But neither of us wanted to do so without the benefit of a civil wedding ceremony. As you know, we first needed a legitimate address. But Mama"—how she loved saying that word directly to her mother— "we plan to have a secular wedding because of Erich's..."

Her mother talked over her, saying that the reason didn't matter as long as they loved each other and vowed to cherish each other.

Edith inhaled deeply and continued. "Mama, we've set the date for New Year's Eve, five years from now, in 1950."

"Five years? Why so long?"

"I promised myself to study at university to become a history teacher. I want to make sure students don't forget what has occurred during this war. And Erich wants to establish a career as well." There was another reason why she and Erich had decided to wait, one that would entail a bit of research and lots of communication. "But Mama, that's only—"

"Yes, five years. I know." Edith heard her mother's sharp intake of breath and tried to prepare herself for the typical question only a mother could ask, given the circumstances. "Edith, honey. Do you and my new son-in-law have children or are you expecting now?"

Although her parents couldn't see her over the phone line, Edith blushed. Erich rubbed her back tenderly. "Not yet. Listen, we have plenty to share with you. And, I have lots of apologies for you and Papa."

"Apologies? Why?"

"I've grown up these past few years. Trust me, I now see why you and Papa did what you had to do to save me, to save Krista."

"Oh, my sweet child, you have indeed become the woman I've always hoped you'd become. And I want to tell you that I've done what only a mother can do for her children. Believe me, I've felt my own share of guilt for doing so. Here's the thing. You survived this war, this hardship, not just because of fate but because you're a resilient woman. You're strong and gutsy, and better yet, you're ready to proceed through the next glorious years of your life with..."

"Mama! Are you crying?"

Herta sniffled. "My daughter, I'm crying joyous tears. Why? Because I didn't give you away because I wanted you out of my life but to give you life and you realize that. Because you're moving on with your life, with a new husband, a career in the making to help others, and you've come home to us. Let's end this phone conversation now."

Edith blinked at the phone in her hands. "Pardon? Have I upset you?"

"No, no. I don't want to wait another second longer to pull you into my arms for a great big hug, and Erich as well." She heard her mother groan into the receiver.

"What's wrong?"

"Is it too soon, this meeting, this reconciliation? Do you need more time, more privacy?"

"I've been waiting for this moment since I last saw you, which now is a long, long time ago. I've mentally composed letters to you and can't wait to share what I've written with you, face-to-face. It's not too late for us, is it?"

"Too late for love and family and to reunite? Of course not."

And it wasn't. Herta Weber was always right because she had the best intentions when it came to her family, a lesson Edith was determined to master for Erich as well as their future children.

On a cold but clear New Year's Eve, Vonni rushed down the banquet hall toward where Edith and Erich waited to greet their guests. A large, loving smile brightened Vonni's face and she pulled them into a hug. Although they now lived only three blocks away from each other, and were constantly visiting, the meeting was warm and heartfelt. "I wouldn't have forgiven myself if I didn't make it back home in time to attend this wedding."

"Oh, yes you would have." Edith grasped Vonni's hand. "It may be five years since the war ended, but your work with displaced persons, helping them find loved ones and homes, is beyond indispensable."

Vonni nodded quickly but glanced over her shoulder toward the hall where Edith's family and a few guests were seated. Edith sensed it wasn't a sudden bout of awkwardness overcoming her dear friend but rather memories of her own family. Vonni had told her in confidence that it was easier to cope with this heartache of hers by visiting with her beloved lost ones whenever the need arose rather than fight the sorrow. Edith thought her friend showed strength, considering Vonni had recently learned the truth about her parents and most of her *vista* who perished in the Zigeunerfamilienlager section of Auschwitz II-Birkenau.

Fortunately, they had been able to track down her sister Antonina and her then-boyfriend-now-husband Stephan. Just as Vonni had once imagined, Antonina and Stephan had eloped and left for the Alps the day their father disappeared. Erich, Edith, and Vonni had visited Antonina and her husband. The newlyweds proved that love at first sight existed outside of storybooks and adopted the Jewish boy and girl they'd rescued in the Tatra refugee settlement. They couldn't travel to Amsterdam for the wedding, though, due to Antonina's late stage of pregnancy, but Edith and Erich understood and wished them the best of life in their mountain village.

Erich placed a hand on Vonni's arm. "Are you okay?"

Vonni stood tall and found her temporarily lost smile. "Look at you, Edith, dressed in that gorgeous, romantic white gown of lace and tulle—you're the most beautiful bride I've ever seen." Vonni then peered into Erich's eyes. "And you, handsome forever you are. I'm so happy for you both. Now tell me, friends, how did your parents take the news about Erich's family?"

"So-so." Erich wiggled his right hand. "To say they had an adjustment to make is not to say enough."

Edith intertwined her arm with her husband's. "My parents love their son-in-law for who he is—a strong, intelligent man who never sided with the Nazi Party."

"Wonderful," Vonni said. She glanced at Edith's sister approaching. "I'm going to slip into the hall. I am looking forward to seeing you two march in!"

"Wait," Erich said. "You hadn't answered my question. Are you okay?"

Vonni smiled. "I'm more than okay. I just don't want to take attention away from you two on your wedding day."

Edith hooked her elbow. "You're not going anywhere with that answer. Tell us your news."

"Miriam," Vonni said, the one word Edith wouldn't have expected her to say. "I located where she lives and contacted her adoptive parents, reassuring them that I just want to visit. They've given me their blessings to visit whenever I want. I'm going there next week."

Edith pulled her friend into a hug. "I'm so thrilled for you."

"Thank you." She looked into Edith and Erich's eyes. "Before I start crying my head off, I'm going to find a seat and wait to see you two walk down the aisle."

Before Edith or Erich could say a word, she disappeared into the grand hall where the wedding was to take place.

At least this time, Edith thought, Vonni—and the rest of them—were not disappearing to keep away from harm. It was time to live and to love.

Edith eyed her 21-year-old sister Krista making her way across the room, a smile stretching her lips wide, her eyes bright with excitement. She was now a grown woman and even more beautiful than when she was younger. Edith's dream for the past five years was finally about to come true. "Have they arrived?"

"All seven of them—fresh off the ship."

"And Mama and Papa have no suspicions?"

"From what I can tell, not one. What an accomplishment, sister! They're freshening up but will do as you've requested, walk into the hall first, before you and Erich."

"Perfect." It was just then that Zofia and Eban stepped out from the restrooms and hurried to Edith's side. The lovely mother and son had made the trip on the *St. Louis* as pleasant as possible, considering the tragic developments. Huge smiles added to their sparkling eyes.

"My goodness, Edith and Krista," Zofia said, in perfect non-accented English. After studying the language for years, they'd agreed to speak in it exclusively. Despite a little gray in her hair, she looked as beautiful as Edith remembered. "Look at how you've grown, and now you're a bride." She beamed at Erich. "And this is Erich, your handsome partner for life?"

Erich grasped Zofia's hand and tugged her inward for a kiss on her cheeks, then shook Eban's hand. "It's an honor to meet you both. Thank you for coming to celebrate our wedding with us."

"I cannot imagine not witnessing and celebrating this lovely occasion, and I can't wait to see your parents again."

"I'm so thrilled you traveled this great distance just to be with us and to surprise my parents. This, by far, is the best wedding gift ever." Edith smiled at Eban. "And soon I can call you Dr. Badower?"

"Just Eban. Always Eban."

Edith craned her neck. "Where's your fiancée?"

"She'll join us momentarily."

Zofia beamed proudly at her son. A man with thick white hair, dashing handsome features, and a trace of a limp hurried from the washroom up to Zofia's side—Jabez! He heartily seized their hands and shook them as he introduced himself.

Zofia smiled at Edith and Krista, then glanced at a woman, a man, and a little girl about four years of age: Aanya, her husband Artur, and their daughter Kasia. Zofia signed and said just loud enough for Edith to understand. "Edith and Erich, this is my dearest friend, Aanya, one I cannot imagine living without." Zofia then introduced Artur and Kasia.

Edith, using Erich's contacts, had located Zofia in New York. After conversing on the phone several times with her, she knew that though Aanya was deaf, she expertly signed as well as read lips. She faced Aanya. "I'm so pleased that you, your husband, and your precious daughter made this huge journey to be with us."

"I wouldn't have missed it for anything," Aanya verbally replied. "What a spectacular way to welcome in the new year, yes?"

"Definitely," Edith and Erich said together, and chuckled.

Zofia grasped Edith's hand. "We'll enter the hall now so we can watch Herta's face when the bride and groom walk into the room." She winked and grinned. "And us too!"

For a second, Edith couldn't tell what excited her more—her

wedding or that these lovely people had traveled across the Atlantic Ocean for the first time since they had left Europe to share this special time and to see her parents again. Just then, a young woman ran up to Eban. Ah. Audrey, another bride-to-be!

"Go on in," Edith mouthed. "I want to hear my mother's squeals of delight." Seconds later, shouts of joy filled the hall as the special guests joined her parents, their lovely friend Julia and her three daughters, Julia's in-laws, Mila and Liam, Richard and Viktor, and a few friends and neighbors of Edith and Eric's. This was a memory in the making.

"They're so jubilant." Erich pulled Edith into an embrace. "You successfully pulled this off. I am so proud of you, sweetheart. Are you happy?"

"Beyond happy, my handsome husband, but I couldn't have done it without you." She grew serious. "I'm just sorry that your parents and younger brothers can't be here with us."

His parents and Wil and Fritz—now 12—had fled Germany in April 1945, two weeks before Hitler had killed himself. They'd never contacted Erich or Richard, who continued to live in Vienna with Viktor. The older sons hadn't a clue as to where his parents and younger brothers were living. Although Erich had often murmured to Edith "just as well," she wondered if Erich would one day try to find his parents and younger brothers or vice versa. Time would tell. Her husband was a forgiving man and believed in second chances, as proved possible by both of his parents.

"You are my priority, sweetheart. You are what I'm living for." He kissed his bride. "You are my family now. Ready to marry me?" He smiled. "Again?"

"I most definitely am, especially on this symbolic day."

Erich lifted a brow. "What have you kept from me?"

"Have you forgotten? Aside from New Year's Eve giving us hope for a good year to come, we'd met on New Year's Day in 1943 when I had chosen to leave the safe house. The holiday always reminds me of daring to live. What a perfect time to get married." She kissed him. "Again."

"I love how you think, love you."

"And I love you and will love you forever." Edith nodded to her sister, her bridesmaid, who began her solo march into the hall. Arm in arm, she and Erich walked down the aisle toward the rest of their lives together.

ABOUT THE AUTHOR

Elaine Stock writes Historical Fiction, exploring the role of women who are courageous and gutsy (courageous with added spirit and determination). She enjoys creating stories showing how all faiths, races, and belief systems are interconnected and need each other.

Elaine's grandparents, on both sides of her family, narrowly escaped World War II by immigrating from Poland and Austria to the US. Fascinated by the strong will of people to overcome the horrors from this era, she wrote *We Shall Not Shatter*, Book 1 of the Resilient Women of WWII Trilogy, inspired by her deaf great aunt who was left behind as a teenager in Brzeziny, Poland and perished in the Holocaust. The novel has earned the Historical Fiction Company 5-star and "Highly Recommended" Review, won the Finalist Award in the Historical WWI-WWII category of the Historical Fiction Company Contest, and took the 2022 Silver Medal in the Coffee Pot Book Club Book of the Year Award. Book 2, *Our Daughters' Last Hope* has also won Historical Fiction Company 5-star and "Highly Recommended" Review. Both books have won awards for their audiobook editions.

Elaine is a member of Women's Fiction Writers Association and The Historical Novel Society. Born in Brooklyn, New York, she has been living in upstate, rural New York with her husband for more years than her stint as a city gal. She enjoys long walks down country roads, visiting New England towns, and of course, a good book.

Website: https://elainestock.com

Dear Reader,

If you have enjoyed reading my book,
please do leave a review on Amazon or Goodreads. A few kind words would be enough. This would be greatly appreciated.

Alternatively, if you have read my book as Kindle eBook you could leave a rating.
That is just one simple click, indicating how many stars of five you think this book deserves.
This will only cost you a split second.
Thank you very much in advance!

Elaine.

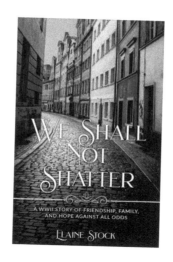

We Shall Not Shatter is Book 1 of the Trilogy **Resilient Women of WWII.**

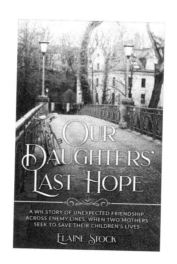

Our Daughters' Last Hope is Book 2 of the Trilogy **Resilient Women of WWII.**

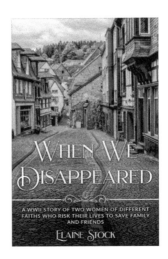

When We Disappeared is Book 3 of the Trilogy **Resilient Women of WWII.**

READERS GROUPS DISCUSSION GUIDE

1. In the prologue to *When We Disappeared*, Krista advises Edith/Elsa to deal with fears as if handling a school bully: not to give the bully attention because it will provoke the bully to cause additional trouble. How do you cope with fear?

2. Acting to save her life, Elsa was obliged to lie several times about her identity. Have you encountered a battle between upholding your morals and engaging in an activity you would rather not in order to protect yourself?

3. Elsa comes to redefine "home" beyond a specific location or a physical structure. How do you define home?

4. Elsa is Jewish, Vonni/Adela is Roma. Both have experienced comparable and differing prejudices. Have you or a loved one ever encountered prejudice? How have you dealt with it?

5. On the evening of *Kristallnacht* erupts in Vienna, not only does Adela face taking Lara's baby, but also compares this dilemma to her

own personal situation in which, as the youngest member of her own family, she too might be the only one that survives the war. What do you think it might feel like to be in Adela's situation?

6. Upon first becoming roommates with Adela, Elsa ponders family—what family could have been and what it should have been. Are you haunted by changing concepts of family, or perhaps friendships?

7. Before Elsa departed to Austria with Adela, Erich, and Werner, she'd come to realize that as each new day passed, she had lessons about life to learn. Looking back over the years, and thinking about the future, do you see this as true? Are you open to new life lessons?

8. The definition of "turning point" is a point at which a pivotal change in a situation occurs. In a story, this can be both plot-wise and character-wise. What would you mark as the plot turning point of *When We Disappeared*? What is the turning point, character-wise, for Elsa?

9. Elsa mentally composes letters to her mother. Have you ever done so yourself to someone of great importance who for one reason or another was absent from you? Do you think this this type of mental correspondence can offer help to hurting or lonely people? How does this compare to writing in a journal?

10. En route to Vienna, Elsa, Adela, Werner and Erich discuss pogroms throughout history. Do you believe that the persecution of groups of people—due to their differences in faith, ethnicity, race, lifestyle—can be stopped once and for all?

11. People aren't necessarily who they first appear. "Bad" people can have good qualities, and certainly, "good" people can exhibit unpleasant traits. People can surprise and shock us. Which character in *When We Disappeared* has surprised you the most? Who in real life has done the same?

12. Bonus Question: What are the various ways in which one can disappear in real life?

ACKNOWLEDGMENTS

Perhaps the best place to begin this page of gratitude and recognition of the last book of a trilogy is to bring it back to the beginning: thank you, Liesbeth Heenk of Amsterdam Publishers for believing in these three stories making up the Resilient Women of WWII trilogy. Although fictionalized tales of the very real tragedy of the Holocaust, you saw the power and reach of Zofia and Aanya, Herta and Julia, and Edith and Vonni. Most of all, you saw a potential in me and my writing that I hadn't been aware of; one I still work diligently to not disappoint as a storyteller.

A great big thank you to my editor Malin Lönnberg for your amazing editorial skills, sharp catches, and brilliant suggestions.

While I'm beyond elated that Books 1 and 2 of this trilogy have won awards, I'm most thrilled that so many readers have enjoyed these books. To me, reader satisfaction is the true reward! Heartfelt thanks to each of one of you!

To Megan Whitson Lee—whatever will I do without you? I wish you the very best in all of your publications. I look forward to more winning titles from London Clarke! At least I still have your friendship to carry around in my heart.

Heartfelt thanks and appreciation to beta reader, Sue Roberts. Your generous review of this story, plus your encouragement throughout this trilogy, goes beyond outstanding.

Thank you to Shirley Chapel—as promised, I've named a character after you! Though she is a minor character, you're certainly a wonderful friend and I'm grateful for all of your encouragement.

A big thank you to my sister-in-law Nancy for sharing with me your knowledge of dogs.

Once again, thank you, Wally, for all you do for me. Understatement of the century!

AMSTERDAM PUBLISHERS
HOLOCAUST LIBRARY

The series **Holocaust Survivor Memoirs World War II** consists of the following autobiographies of survivors:

Outcry. Holocaust Memoirs, by Manny Steinberg

Hank Brodt Holocaust Memoirs. A Candle and a Promise, by Deborah Donnelly

The Dead Years. Holocaust Memoirs, by Joseph Schupack

Rescued from the Ashes. The Diary of Leokadia Schmidt, Survivor of the Warsaw Ghetto, by Leokadia Schmidt

My Lvov. Holocaust Memoir of a twelve-year-old Girl, by Janina Hescheles

Remembering Ravensbrück. From Holocaust to Healing, by Natalie Hess

Wolf. A Story of Hate, by Zeev Scheinwald with Ella Scheinwald

Save my Children. An Astonishing Tale of Survival and its Unlikely Hero, by Leon Kleiner with Edwin Stepp

Holocaust Memoirs of a Bergen-Belsen Survivor & Classmate of Anne Frank, by Nanette Blitz Konig

Defiant German - Defiant Jew. A Holocaust Memoir from inside the Third Reich, by Walter Leopold with Les Leopold

In a Land of Forest and Darkness. The Holocaust Story of two Jewish Partisans, by Sara Lustigman Omelinski

Holocaust Memories. Annihilation and Survival in Slovakia, by Paul Davidovits

From Auschwitz with Love. The Inspiring Memoir of Two Sisters' Survival, Devotion and Triumph Told by Manci Grunberger Beran & Ruth Grunberger Mermelstein, by Daniel Seymour

Remetz. Resistance Fighter and Survivor of the Warsaw Ghetto, by Jan Yohay Remetz

My March Through Hell. A Young Girl's Terrifying Journey to Survival, by Halina Kleiner with Edwin Stepp

Roman's Journey, by Roman Halter

Memoirs by Elmar Rivosh, Sculptor (1906-1967). Riga Ghetto and Beyond, by Elmar Rivosh

---

The series **Holocaust Survivor True Stories WWII** consists of the following biographies:

Among the Reeds. The true story of how a family survived the Holocaust, by Tammy Bottner

A Holocaust Memoir of Love & Resilience. Mama's Survival from Lithuania to America, by Ettie Zilber

Living among the Dead. My Grandmother's Holocaust Survival Story of Love and Strength, by Adena Bernstein Astrowsky

Heart Songs. A Holocaust Memoir, by Barbara Gilford

Shoes of the Shoah. The Tomorrow of Yesterday, by Dorothy Pierce

Hidden in Berlin. A Holocaust Memoir, by Evelyn Joseph Grossman

Separated Together. The Incredible True WWII Story of Soulmates Stranded an Ocean Apart, by Kenneth P. Price, Ph.D.

The Man Across the River. The incredible story of one man's will to survive the Holocaust, by Zvi Wiesenfeld

If Anyone Calls, Tell Them I Died. A Memoir, by Emanuel (Manu) Rosen

The House on Thrömerstrasse. A Story of Rebirth and Renewal in the Wake of the Holocaust, by Ron Vincent

Dancing with my Father. His hidden past. Her quest for truth. How Nazi Vienna shaped a family's identity, by Jo Sorochinsky

The Story Keeper. Weaving the Threads of Time and Memory - A Memoir, by Fred Feldman

Krisia's Silence. The Girl who was not on Schindler's List, by Ronny Hein

Defying Death on the Danube. A Holocaust Survival Story, by Debbie J. Callahan with Henry Stern

A Doorway to Heroism. A decorated German-Jewish Soldier who became an American Hero, by Rabbi W. Jack Romberg

The Shoemaker's Son. The Life of a Holocaust Resister, by Laura Beth Bakst

The Redhead of Auschwitz. A True Story, by Nechama Birnbaum

Land of Many Bridges. My Father's Story, by Bela Ruth Samuel Tenenholtz

Creating Beauty from the Abyss. The Amazing Story of Sam Herciger, Auschwitz Survivor and Artist, by Lesley Ann Richardson

On Sunny Days We Sang. A Holocaust Story of Survival and Resilience, by Jeannette Grunhaus de Gelman

Painful Joy. A Holocaust Family Memoir, by Max J. Friedman

I Give You My Heart. A True Story of Courage and Survival, by Wendy Holden

In the Time of Madmen, by Mark A. Prelas

Monsters and Miracles. Horror, Heroes and the Holocaust, by Ira Wesley Kitmacher

Flower of Vlora. Growing up Jewish in Communist Albania, by Anna Kohen

Aftermath: Coming of Age on Three Continents. A Memoir, by Annette Libeskind Berkovits

Not a real Enemy. The True Story of a Hungarian Jewish Man's Fight for Freedom, by Robert Wolf

Zaidy's War. Four Armies, Three Continents, Two Brothers. One Man's Impossible Story of Endurance, by Martin Bodek

The Glassmaker's Son. Looking for the World my Father left behind in Nazi Germany, by Peter Kupfer

The Apprentice of Buchenwald. The True Story of the Teenage Boy Who Sabotaged Hitler's War Machine, by Oren Schneider

Good for a Single Journey, by Helen Joyce

Burying the Ghosts, by Sonia Case

American Wolf. From Nazi Refugee to American Spy. A True Story, by Audrey Birnbaum

Bipolar Refugee. A Saga of Survival and Resilience, by Peter Wiesner

---

The series **Jewish Children in the Holocaust** consists of the following autobiographies of Jewish children hidden during WWII in the Netherlands:

Searching for Home. The Impact of WWII on a Hidden Child, by Joseph Gosler

See You Tonight and Promise to be a Good Boy! War memories, by Salo Muller

Sounds from Silence. Reflections of a Child Holocaust Survivor, Psychiatrist and Teacher, by Robert Krell

Sabine's Odyssey. A Hidden Child and her Dutch Rescuers, by Agnes Schipper

The Journey of a Hidden Child, by Harry Pila and Robin Black

The series **New Jewish Fiction** consists of the following novels, written by Jewish authors. All novels are set in the time during or after the Holocaust.

The Corset Maker. A Novel, by Annette Libeskind Berkovits

Escaping the Whale. The Holocaust is over. But is it ever over for the next generation? by Ruth Rotkowitz

When the Music Stopped. Willy Rosen's Holocaust, by Casey Hayes

Hands of Gold. One Man's Quest to Find the Silver Lining in Misfortune, by Roni Robbins

The Girl Who Counted Numbers. A Novel, by Roslyn Bernstein

There was a garden in Nuremberg. A Novel, by Navina Michal Clemerson

The Butterfly and the Axe, by Omer Bartov

To Live Another Day. A Novel, Elizabeth Rosenberg

A Worthy Life. Based on a True Story, by Dahlia Moore

The series **Holocaust Heritage** consists of the following memoirs by 2G:

The Cello Still Sings. A Generational Story of the Holocaust and of the Transformative Power of Music, by Janet Horvath

The Fire and the Bonfire. A Journey into Memory, by Ardyn Halter

The Silk Factory: Finding Threads of My Family's True Holocaust Story, by Michael Hickins

---

The series **Holocaust Books for Young Adults** consists of the following novels, based on true stories:

The Boy behind the Door. How Salomon Kool Escaped the Nazis. Inspired by a True Story, by David Tabatsky

Running for Shelter. A True Story, by Suzette Sheft

The Precious Few. An Inspirational Saga of Courage based on True Stories, by David Twain with Art Twain

---

The series **WW2 Historical Fiction** consists of the following novels, some of which are based on true stories:

Mendelevski's Box. A Heartwarming and Heartbreaking Jewish Survivor's Story, by Roger Swindells

A Quiet Genocide. The Untold Holocaust of Disabled Children WW2 Germany, by Glenn Bryant

The Knife-Edge Path, by Patrick T. Leahy

Brave Face. The Inspiring WWII Memoir of a Dutch/German Child, by I. Caroline Crocker and Meta A. Evenbly

When We Had Wings. The Gripping Story of an Orphan in Janusz Korczak's Orphanage. A Historical Novel, by Tami Shem-Tov

Jacob's Courage: A Holocaust Love Story, by Charles S. Weinblatt

Want to be an AP book reviewer?

Reviews are very important in a world dominated by the social media and social proof. Please drop us a line if you want to join the *AP review team* and show us at least one review already posted on Amazon for one of our books. info@amsterdampublishers.com